IMPLEMENTING
B2B COMMERCE
WITH .NET

IMPLEMENTING B2B COMMERCE WITH .NET

A GUIDE FOR PROGRAMMERS AND TECHNICAL MANAGERS

LYN ROBISON

✦▾ Addison-Wesley

Boston   San Francisco   New York   Toronto   Montreal
London   Munich   Paris   Madrid   Capetown
Sydney   Tokyo   Singapore   Mexico City

The publisher offers discounts on this book when ordered in quantity for special sales. For more information, please contact

Pearson Education Corporate Sales Division
One Lake Street
Upper Saddle River, NJ 07458
(800) 382-3419
corpsales@pearsontechgroup.com

Visit AW on the Web: www.awl.com/cseng/

Library of Congress Control Number: 2001 134011

ISBN: 0-201-71932-0
Text printed on recycled paper
1 2 3 4 5 6 7 8 9 10–MA–05 04 03 02 01
First printing, December 2001

To Capri, Mitchell, Jeffrey, and Patrick

About the Author

L yn Robison has been involved with B2B projects since 1998. He has worked as a developer and technical lead in various B2B development projects. He has also trained over 300 developers in weeklong B2B training classes.

In 1998, Lyn authored his first book entitled *Teach Yourself Database Programming with Visual C++ 6 in 21 Days* (Sams Publishing).

Contents

Foreword

In a few short years, B2B has grown from an acronym nobody knows into one that's as familiar as HTTP, HTML, and others. Consumer Web sites receive the public's adulation and attention, but B2B sites have the potential to impact the way the world goes about its business more than all the *Amazon.com*s and *eBay*s of the world put together.

Building a B2B Web site isn't easy. If anyone tells you otherwise, he's never built one. Building B2B sites that utilize the Microsoft .NET Framework is especially dicey because the platform is so new that few people possess real expertise in it. That's unfortunate, because .NET has no peer when it comes to providing the services and infrastructure that enable Web applications to thrive. Web forms and Web services, both of which are woven into the fabric of the Framework, are no less revolutionary today than Java and ASP were in the 1990s and GUIs were in the decade before that. At Wintellect, our customers are telling us that they get products to market up to 50 percent faster when they deploy on ASP.NET, which is the component of the .NET Framework that serves Web programmers. For B2B developers, I'd guess that even 50 percent is conservative. Given the Framework's rich support for SOAP and XML and the typical B2B application's need for both, enormous productivity gains can be had if knowledge of the .NET Framework is coupled with the know-how to architect and implement B2B apps.

Implementing B2B Commerce with .NET: A Guide for Programmers and Technical Managers is a road map for developers trying to find their way through the thicket that is B2B development. I can't think of anyone better than Lyn Robison to show the way. He's been building real sites for real clients for a long time. He's one of the relative handful of developer authors who understands the intricacies of Microsoft .NET. And he's one of the few people I know who appreciates that people skills are as important as technical skills in designing, building, and rolling out a B2B site. The knowledge he dispenses in this book attacks the problem from all angles, explaining not only the hows of B2B, but the whys and the what-to-look-out-fors as well. I'm confident that *Implementing B2B Commerce with .NET* will pay for itself many times over. That, after all, is what great computer books are all about.

Jeff Prosise
Cofounder, Wintellect

Preface

AUDIENCE AND GOALS FOR THIS BOOK

There are several business-to-business (B2B) Internet commerce books on the market. Many of these books are intended for business executives, and they explain *why* Internet commerce is valuable. In contrast, this book is intended for developers and technical managers, and it explains B2B Internet commerce in terms of *what* to build and *how* to build it.

This book covers issues that are important in extranet/B2B development, including issues of development, management, and what to build. Therefore this book is organized into three parts: Part 1 covers development issues, Part 2 management issues, and Part 3 what-to-build issues.

Part 1 is for developers, Part 2 is for managers, and Part 3 is applicable to both groups. Developers should concentrate on Parts 1 and 3 but may want to look over Part 2.

Managers can skim over Part 1 but should concentrate on Parts 2 and 3. They should read Part 3 first to gain a context on what needs to be built and then read Part 2 for information on the people and project issues involved in building software systems such as these.

EXPECTATIONS FOR THIS BOOK

This is a "do-it-yourself" book for people who need to build B2B applications. Developers cannot compile and run the source code examples in this book without an understanding of and a willingness to use basic debugging techniques. While the code in the book is correct, the reader must know how to deal with differences in machine configurations and software versions and how to track down solutions to their own mistakes to make the code work for them.

This book does not provide a complete, finished B2B application. The source code examples illustrate elementary coding techniques for implementing typical B2B design patterns. This book tells you what the hard parts are and offers guidance for writing the code, which readers must complete on their own.

PREREQUISITES

B2B development requires the melding of technology from several different branches of computer science. Therefore, to understand the code samples in Part 1, the reader must have a working knowledge of the following B2B-enabling technologies:

- Object-oriented programming languages

- Databases and relational database servers

- Web servers, browsers, and N-tier development

- Networking and security

- Server-side component technologies

The source code examples in this book will be useful to programmers who read the book *after* they have obtained a solid understanding of these B2B-enabling technologies on the Microsoft platform. If you are a developer and would like to assess your own knowledge, refer to the last several pages of Chapter 10 for a list of B2B technical skills. If many of the terms in the list are unfamiliar to you, you may have difficulty with the source code examples in Part 1.

Note: If you are a developer who is unfamiliar with object-oriented (OO) languages such as C++, Java, or C#, you may have trouble understanding the source code examples in this book. This book assumes that developers who work through the code samples are already proficient with such OO concepts as static methods, virtual methods, abstract base classes, and so forth. You will want to familiarize yourself with true OO concepts before tackling the source code examples.

PART 1: CODING FOR B2B APPLICATIONS

The chapters in Part 1 deal with the *technical* portion of *how* to write B2B applications. Part 1 contains B2B coding examples that are implemented using the Microsoft .NET Framework. This part is particularly relevant for developers.

As of this writing, .NET is very new, so I assume that many readers may not yet be proficient in it. Therefore I progressively disclose .NET development topics so readers have the opportunity to become proficient in the .NET Framework as they proceed through Part 1. Readers should also plan to use additional sources to develop a thorough proficiency in the .NET Framework.

In a progressive sequence I explain the particular segments of the .NET Framework that are relevant to B2B programming. Readers who are new to the .NET Framework may find it helpful to use this book as a syllabus or sequence of topics to learn about it.

If you are a developer and would like to work through the code examples in this book yourself, you will need the following Microsoft software:

- Windows 2000 Server or Advanced Server, or Windows XP

- SQL Server 2000 or later

- Internet Information Server (IIS)

- Visual Studio .NET

With Visual Studio .NET, you must install the following items:

- C# Compiler

- C++ Compiler

- Web Development Server Component

- .NET Framework SDK

- .NET Framework SDK samples

PART 2: PEOPLE, POLITICS, AND B2B PROJECTS

To be successful in B2B development, you must handle appropriately the strategic issues that go beyond tools and technologies. Part 2 explains the *people* portion of the *how* to write B2B applications. This part is particularly relevant for managers.

To build B2B applications successfully, you must form a team of the right people with the right skills. Chapter 10 discusses the development team and the necessary skills.

Once you have the tools and the team, you will need a methodology for your projects, an organized process for designing your B2B applications, and a repeatable and reliable project methodology for building them. There are several possible procedures, but many are not appropriate for a B2B project. Chapter 11 presents one methodology with which the author has seen repeated B2B successes. In addition to the tools, the people, and the methodology, you need to know *what* to build.

PART 3: VISION DOCUMENTS FOR TYPICAL B2B APPLICATIONS

When it comes to B2B Internet commerce, you can find lots of advice on *why* you should do it, but (outside of this book) you will find very little advice on *what* you should build. Part 3 is relevant to both developers and managers. Managers should perhaps read the chapters in Part 3 first and then go back and read Part 2. Finally, they can skim Part 1 to get a context on what B2B developers are up against.

The general concepts of B2B applications are apparent. However, the devil is truly in the details of B2B implementations. Fundamental questions such as "What should the application do?" can be difficult to answer because of the general lack of information and advice.

This book helps you with the question of what B2B applications should do by providing the Vision documents for typical B2B applications. These chapters should provide a good point of departure for you as you begin to spec out your own applications.

INFORMATION THAT IS *NOT* IN THIS BOOK

This book is not a tutorial on OO, RDMBS, or Web technology. Knowledge of diverse technologies is a prerequisite for building B2B Web sites and applications. These technologies include object-oriented programming, database servers, Web technologies, and network security. These topics are so broad, however, that tutorials for each require a book of their own and thus are not included in this book.

This book does not provide B2C commerce information. Internet transactions between businesses are generally not conducted with credit cards. This book does not explain how to build a Web site that performs credit card processing because it is not highly relevant to B2B commerce. This book does not deal with other business-to-consumer (B2C) commerce development issues either.

This book does not tell you how to build B2B marketplaces. B2B marketplaces are intended chiefly to automate transactions. As the Introduction explains, B2B commerce involves far more than the automation of transactions. Instead of talking about marketplaces, this book focuses on extranet-based B2B commerce. In extranet-based B2B commerce, every company has its own extranet and uses that extranet to host B2B applications, which enables each company to move its business to the Web.

This book does not provide a complete sample B2B application. The soup-to-nuts source code for a complete B2B application would be lengthy, and it would also contain a lot of repeated concepts. Therefore, to convey valuable information in a concise way, the book includes only the fundamental parts of the source code for B2B implementations.

Finally, this is not a paint-by-numbers book. It does not provide everything you need to implement B2B commerce. This book covers only the little-known aspects of B2B commerce development, topics not covered in detail elsewhere.

SOURCE CODE FOR THIS BOOK

The source code for this book is available for download on the author's Web site at *www.howtob2b.com.*

Acknowledgments

Many people have provided me with valuable help and advice on this book, and I owe them my thanks.

The following offered technical and editorial advice or helped in other ways to advance the progress of my manuscript: Yvette Bohanan, Sarita Dua, Arun Garg, Colin Goble, Anita Gutierrez, Ben Hickman, Jimmy Hutson, Akhlaq Khan, Gary Liao, Sean Murphy, Gary Raetz, Ed Rarick, Stuart Rehbein, Jeffrey Richter, Doug Root, Sharon Russell, Nick Stier, Bob Uva, Bob Vandehey, and Gary Whitney.

Steve Paquin and Venkatesh Ramachandran deserve special recognition for the pioneering code they wrote using the Beta 1 version of .NET Framework SDK, and they deserve special thanks for allowing me to use derivatives of their code in this book.

My wife, Capri, and our three sons, Mitchell, Jeffrey, and Patrick, made many sacrifices while I wrote this book. They provided me with the love and encouragement I needed to persevere. Capri's help with the illustrations and editing and her willingness to be a virtual single parent for months on end were instrumental in my completing the manuscript.

Introduction

SELF-SERVICE, AN UNEXPECTED REVOLUTION

In December 1945 (long before I was born), my father purchased the Payless drugstore in St. Helens, Oregon. This store, like almost every other drugstore in Oregon at the time, was not self-service, which meant that customers were not able to pick the products off the shelves. Instead, customers had to tell the clerk behind the counter which products they wanted, and the clerk would collect the items from the shelves and bring them to the cash register.

The first thing my dad did was to make the store self-service, one of the first self-service drugstores in Oregon. In his store, customers could take what they wanted themselves without having to ask a clerk. Customers could then examine and choose the merchandise at their leisure, and the clerk was no longer a bottleneck in their shopping process. It turned out that customers liked their newfound freedom to serve themselves.

Before switching to self-service, the revenue from the store was about $60 per day. Within one week of converting the store to self-service, the store's sales volume soared to $600 per day. The store was so busy that people would come and look in the windows just to see all the activity. Eventually, the store's sales volume stabilized at $250 per day, a fourfold increase.

In my father's drugstore, self-service was a revolution. Today, Internet commerce provides another opportunity for a self-service revolution. Internet commerce can grant customers access to a company's products, services, and information without a company representative becoming a bottleneck in the process.

TO B2B OR NOT TO BE?

When people think of *Internet commerce*, they typically think of retail business-to-consumer commerce. There are several high-profile business-to-consumer sites on the Web, such as Amazon.com. However, business-to-consumer Internet commerce ultimately will not be the most significant area of Internet commerce.

It is important to realize that business-to-business (B2B) commerce is potentially much bigger than business-to-consumer (B2C) commerce. If you think intuitively about the brick-and-mortar world, you will realize that more commerce is conducted between businesses than is conducted between business and consumers. B2B Internet commerce is potentially big, but what is it?

Most people connect B2B Internet commerce to Electronic Data Interchange (EDI). Typical EDI applications deal with fixed-scope transactions of buying, selling, and paying. However, businesses can take B2B far beyond the particular transactions defined by EDI. Businesses can use B2B Internet commerce to do much more than process transactions.

When people think of B2B, they might think of online exchanges or marketplaces, where companies buy and sell commodities online. In reality, bringing buyers and sellers together and automating their transactions is only a small fraction of the potential of B2B Internet commerce.

B2B Internet commerce has the potential to improve a company's relationship with its customers, partners, suppliers, and resellers dramatically. B2B applications can automate every facet of the process of doing business. They can shrink cycle time, reduce manual effort, and link various companies and their business processes in ways that are highly profitable and not possible otherwise.

So, contrary to popular belief, performing B2B Internet commerce does not mean creating an online marketplace and automating transactions between businesses. It is much more than that. It is about moving complex, multifaceted business relationships to the Internet.

Moving business relationships to the Web requires the secure flow of sensitive information between specific individuals over the Internet. An extranet that hosts Web-based B2B applications is what enables this secure flow of information. So each company that wishes to engage in B2B commerce will eventually need its own extranet site on which to host its B2B applications. This book explains how to build an extranet and use it for B2B commerce applications.

This secure flow of targeted information and the collaboration capabilities that come with it make extranets and B2B apps valuable in the following areas:

• Publishing catalogs of complex and customized products that contain special prices for particular resellers and customers and that enable the sale of these complex products in online selling-chain management applications

- Managing the complex communications, documentation, and reporting tasks in large construction projects

- Securely publishing and gathering data during clinical trials in the pharmaceutical industry

- Providing collaboration between broker/dealers and their registered representatives in the financial services industry

- Giving privileged access to resume and job databases for subscribers in the professional recruiting industry

- Optimizing production and inventory levels in supply-chain management applications in the manufacturing industry

You can see that these applications do not merely consist of automating transactions between buyers and sellers of commodities. Certainly, each of these applications could involve online transactions where significant amounts of money are exchanged for products and services, but online transactions are only a small fraction of the B2B world. The other parts involve serving up secure content and enabling private collaboration between particular individuals and departments. In summary, moving business relationships to the Web involves three things: commerce, content, and collaboration.

In the real world, relationships between businesses are complex. This means that B2B applications are often complex, too, but it is still feasible to implement B2B apps in a way that reduces their inherent complexity and risk.

Given the proper development infrastructure, companies can start small with a 90-day project to build a B2B application that has immediate payback. Ninety-day projects succeed or fail in a short period of time with relatively little money spent. Projects like these enable the B2B champions in a business to earn their wings and their credibility. After one successful implementation, they can tackle other, more ambitious B2B projects.

Even when the project is restricted to 90 days, implementing that first B2B application can be a daunting project. There are several business tasks that must be completed, such as defining the business processes to the point of automation and gathering content for the applications. There are also several technical challenges that must be overcome. For example, the computing platform, the security, and the entire application infrastructure must be built or bought.

HOW THIS BOOK WILL HELP

This book was written to help you with the technical as well as the strategic challenges you will encounter when building an extranet and B2B applications. Some of the challenges you will encounter in B2B development are technical. This book includes source code examples and coding advice that will help you over those technical hurdles. These technical hurdles involve how to write the code that implements extranet-based commerce, content, and collaboration.

Commerce

As I said in the Preface, transactions between businesses are generally not conducted using credit cards but by exchanging documents such as purchase orders and invoices. This book introduces XML Web services and BizTalk Server to transfer business documents, such as purchase orders and invoices between businesses securely.

Content

Providing privileged users with secure access to content on a Web site is fundamental to B2B commerce. Business commerce depends on individuals and departments being able to convey targeted and secure information among themselves. This book explains how to build an extranet site where people can log in and see information that is for their eyes only.

Collaboration

Before companies can consummate business transactions, they typically collaborate for a period of time on issues that are relevant to their relationship. This collaboration needs to occur in a private setting, where the parties can have confidence that their communications are guarded and secure. This book explains the technical foundation of an extranet that is needed for secure collaboration.

Strategic Issues of B2B Development

Other challenges you will encounter in B2B development involve people, politics, and project management. I have tried to provide helpful advice, born of experience, in those areas, too.

CODING FOR B2B APPLICATIONS

When it comes to business-to-business Internet commerce, this book explains *what* to build and *how* to build it. Part 1 covers the *technology* portion of *how* to build B2B applications. It is based on two technologies: the Microsoft .NET Framework and the Webridge Extranet Framework.

The Microsoft .NET platform is the successor to Windows Distributed Internet Architecture (DNA), and it provides a more capable platform for building B2B applications than Windows DNA. It also provides much of the infrastructure or "plumbing" that is required in average B2B applications. (As you may know, "plumbing" code is code that is necessary but does not directly implement the features of the application.)

Using the .NET Framework, developers do not have to build as much plumbing for their applications as they would have to if they were using Windows DNA. With the .NET Framework, developers can concentrate more on implementing features and less on infrastructure. Chapters 1 through 6 provide explanations and code samples of B2B development using the .NET Framework, XML Web services, and the BizTalk .NET Enterprise server.

Even though .NET is a more B2B-capable platform than Windows DNA, certain types of sophisticated B2B applications have requirements that go beyond the off-the-shelf capabilities of the .NET Framework. Building certain advanced B2B applications using the .NET Framework alone could require developers to write significant amounts of plumbing code to handle application functionality that the .NET Framework does not provide. (To get an idea of just how complex real-world B2B applications can be, take a look in Part 3 at the chapters on *what* to build.)

For particularly complex B2B applications, using the .NET Framework in conjunction with Webridge Extranet eliminates much of the plumbing that developers would have to do if they were using .NET alone. Webridge Extranet works in concert with and enhances .NET for complex B2B development work.

CHAPTER 1

Web-Based Applications

The first step to building an extranet site successfully is understanding what you are up against—the essence of what it is that you are building. Of course, the project specifications should provide that information, but there are fundamental B2B concepts that are more basic than those typically spelled out in project specifications. An understanding of these fundamental concepts is crucial to your success in any B2B project.

This chapter clarifies, in a fundamental sense, what you are building when you build an extranet site, called a *B2B Web site* in this book, for hosting B2B applications.

The key points for this chapter are the following:

- Web sites come in three flavors: static sites, dynamic sites, and sites that are business applications.

- B2B Web sites are actually N-tier, Web-based business applications.

- The middle-tier of B2B applications is the best place for the logic of the application.

- B2B applications need business objects on their middle tier and must support diverse clients.

- The .NET Framework provides an excellent platform for building business objects and Web-based applications.

- The .NET Framework Class Library is a copious set of objects that you can use as a foundation on which to build your own business objects.

No doubt this chapter contains information that you already know. Nevertheless, this information bears repeating and clarifying because it is so fundamental to B2B development.

Note: If you have not read the Preface and Introduction yet, please do so before proceeding. The Preface explains what you can expect from this book. The Introduction enables you get in sync with the book on the context and scope of B2B Internet commerce as explained in these pages.

1.1 WEB SITES THAT ARE FILES

Back when the Web was young and life was simple, a Web site consisted of a collection of files. These files were text files containing HTML code and perhaps included references to the image files that were to be displayed on the page. A Web site that consists of a collection of text files and image files is called a "static" site.

As you know, when you want to browse a static site, you point your browser at the name of an HTML file on the Web site server machine. The default or main page of a static site is called the "home" page.

You point your browser to an HTML file using a uniform resource locator (URL), which is a standard way of referring to servers, programs, and pages on the World Wide Web. This is the structure of a URL:

```
protocol://SiteAddress/Directory/Filename
```

The typical protocol for browsing Web pages is HTTP. The site address can be a numeric TCP/IP address or a fully qualified domain name, as follows:

```
MachineName.DomainName.DomainType.CountryCode
```

Although "www" is the most common machine name for Web servers, this is merely a convention. The machine name could be anything, such as "mail," "marketing," or "lyn."

The directory portion of the URL specifies the directory, with the subdirectories separated by forward slashes (/), on the Web server. The last portion of the URL specifies the name of the file.

The following URL specifies the HTTP protocol, a machine named "www," on the "howtob2b.com" domain, the "webridge" directory, the "samples" subdirectory, and the "index.htm" file:

```
http://www.howtob2b.com/webridge/samples/index.htm
```

The browser sends the URL as a character string to the Web server. The Web server reads the file and sends the contents of the file as a string of HTML back to the browser. This is illustrated in Figure 1-1. The browser then requests the images that are referenced in the HTML page, and the server sends them to the browser.

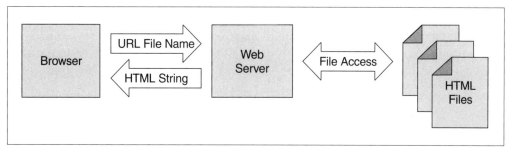

FIGURE 1-1 *Web Sites That Are Files*

The technology required for setting up a static Web site is pretty straightforward. With modern Web site development tools, setting up a Web server to serve up static HTML pages is not difficult. Designing effective Web pages, however, is not easy.

Creating effective Web pages is both an art and a science. The art part involves making the pages aesthetically pleasing. The pages need to communicate clearly their information as well as their navigation mechanisms. The pages also need to be consistent throughout the site.

It is important not to go overboard on the creative design of the pages. The pages should not try to convey too much information, and the page format should be representational and concrete, not abstract. It is easy to get too elaborate with the artwork and produce pages that look great to the members of the project team but are confusing to users.

The science part involves producing pages that the server can generate quickly and browsers can load without a long delay. It is tempting to saturate the pages with too much information or too many graphics, but these pages can take a long time to download to the browser. One likes to think that users won't mind waiting a few more seconds because the pages look so cool or are so packed with information, but that is a fallacy. Users *always* want fast pages.

Another area of difficulty is the design of the overall site, often called the site's information architecture or navigation model, which deals with how the pages relate to each other and how people who browse the site can navigate through the pages. Creating an effective information architecture for a Web site is not as easy as you might think.

The functionality of a static Web site can be likened to an electronic brochure. The primary function is that of transmitting information. A static Web site is not built to collect or process information (other than hit counts or usage information) but to publish information.

Static sites are intended to publish information that is static. The content of a static site typically does not change or get updated more than once per day. Yes, there are exceptions to this rule of thumb. However, in general, if an organization needs to publish information that changes more frequently than once per day, the organization typically does not use a static Web site. This is because a collection of static HTML files is difficult to keep current when the information changes very frequently.

1.2 WEB SITES THAT ARE PROGRAMS

In Web sites where the information changes frequently, perhaps several times a day, it is often more practical to keep the information in a database instead of in static HTML files. Information in a database can be updated more easily than information that is buried inside a collection of HTML text files. With the information in a database, it is possible to write a program that reads the information from the database and combines it with HTML on the fly, as browsers request it.

In other words, a program creates the HTML that the Web server sends to the browser. The HTML doesn't come from a text file on the Web server's hard disk but from a program that combines HTML markup with the information that the program reads from a database each time a browser requests it. A Web site that uses programs to produce the HTML on the fly is called a "dynamic" site (Figure 1-2).

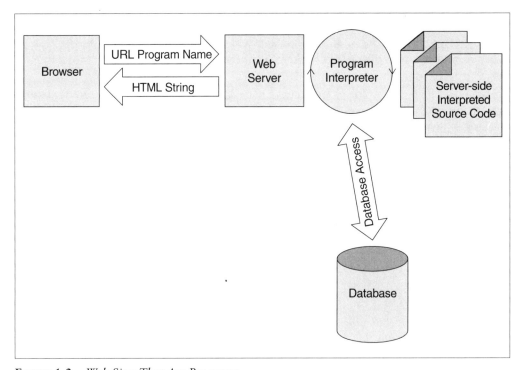

FIGURE 1-2 *Web Sites That Are Programs*

Building a dynamic site is more complicated than building a static site. You have the same page design and site design challenges that you face when building a static site, but in addition, you must create a database to hold the information. You also need to make it easy for content managers to update the information in the database. Additionally, you have to write the programs that read the information from the database and combine it with HTML.

Programs that read the information from the database and combine it with HTML are typically written using a relatively simple programming or "scripting" language. These script programs are interpreted and run by the Web server and run on the Web server machine.

These programs execute when a browser submits the program name in a URL. In other words, the browser does not specify the name of an HTML file but the name of a program in the URL. The program outputs HTML, which is downloaded and rendered in the browser. This URL specifies a program called "samples.asp."

```
http://www.howtob2b.com/microsoft/samples.asp
```

The "asp" extension indicates this is an Active Server Page (ASP) that probably contains some combination of HTML markup and server-side script code. The script code could read data from a database and combine it with the HTML markup. The program resides in the "microsoft" directory of a machine named "www" on the "howtob2b.com" domain.

Using server-side programs to output dynamic HTML enhances the functionality of the Web site without sacrificing compatibility with Web browsers. The site can produce Web pages that contain up-to-the-second information, and the information for the site is managed by a database to simplify the updates to the data.

Database-backed dynamic sites are very good at publishing information that changes frequently. However, a database-backed Web site does not provide the complete foundation that B2B applications need.

1.3 WEB SITES THAT ARE APPLICATIONS

A B2B Web site needs to do more than merely publish information and, therefore, must consist of more than just dynamic HTML pages. A B2B Web site is, in fact, a business application that uses a Web browser as its primary user interface. Therefore the term *B2B application* is more descriptive than the term *B2B Web site*.

A B2B application must be able to perform the tasks that business software typically performs, such as the following:

- Accept input from users (using browsers)
- Share data with enterprise applications and enterprise databases

- Perform business processes in conjunction with enterprise applications

- Process data and transactions from other companies' B2B applications

- Implement complex logic, business rules, and business processes

Tasks like these require code, written by the application developer, that performs these functions. The question is, where do you implement the code?

1.3.1 DON'T MAKE YOUR CLIENTS FAT

In the not-so-long-ago days of client/server applications, lots of code could be built into the client application. However, a fat client application will not fit the requirements of many B2B applications. The fat clients of the client/server days may not be appropriate for B2B applications for a variety of reasons:

- It is difficult to keep the fat client application updated and current on the client machines.

- It may not be possible for client machines to meet the hardware, software, and operating system requirements.

- The time and money that a company has to expend for development, documentation, and support work on fat client applications might make them unfeasible.

Given that you cannot always count on being able to use a fat client app, you cannot code the application's logic into the client.

1.3.2 DON'T USE YOUR BACKEND FOR LOGIC

With a dynamic, database-backed Web site, you might consider trying to implement this code inside the database. Relational databases are built primarily to store and manipulate data, not to implement entire applications. Therefore writing the code for all of the logic for an application in a relational database would be cumbersome at best.

1.3.3 THE SWEET SPOT IS IN THE MIDDLE

Given the difficulty of putting the application code in the client and in the database, you might consider implementing the code somewhere in the middle: between the client app, which is often a Web browser, and the database.

As mentioned earlier in this chapter, some popular Web servers include an interpreter that can run programs written in a scripting language. This interpreter can be used to execute server-side programs, which run on the Web server, between the browser and the database.

In actual practice, the middle tier provides a sweet spot for implementing the code for Web-based applications. In B2B applications, the Web server provides a nice platform for the middle tier. However, the middle tier of a B2B application needs something more than the Web server's script interpreter.

B2B application logic requires a powerful programming language. B2B applications usually involve complex logic and require complex code to implement that logic. Script languages do not provide sufficient programming flexibility or power to implement the logic for an entire B2B application. Fortunately, it is possible to move beyond these Web-server script languages to use server-side objects, which you can create yourself. These server-side objects are often referred to as business objects.

Microsoft's .NET Framework provides business objects on the middle tier. The .NET Framework is Microsoft's most recent platform for application development and enables developers to use powerful programming languages to build their own business objects. With the .NET Framework, you can use languages such as C/C++, C#, and VB to build your own business objects that can implement the complex logic of your application.

This ability to use powerful programming languages to build business objects enables you to write robust application code that runs on the middle tier of your B2B application. With the .NET Framework, you can use the power of advanced language constructs, as well as encapsulation, inheritance, and polymorphism, to handle the complexity of B2B application logic. You can also achieve the right balance of ease of development, execution speed, and code complexity for your development effort.

B2B applications have more clients than just browsers. Web servers are, of course, built to handle requests from Web browsers. If browsers were the only clients of B2B applications, the Web server could handle everything. However, B2B applications must do more than merely respond to browsers.

B2B applications need to integrate with other applications and data within the enterprise. In addition, B2B applications may need to process data and transactions from other companies' B2B applications across the Internet. This need to communicate and integrate with multiple types of clients means that a Web server alone can't do the job. B2B applications must have remote procedure call (RPC) and interprocess communications (IPC) facilities to handle fat client and server-to-server communications.

Therefore B2B applications require a server that goes beyond the capabilities of a Web server alone. The Microsoft .NET Framework, with ASP.NET and XML Web services, makes an excellent platform for building applications that can serve diverse clients. We will examine ASP.NET and XML Web services more later. The structure of a Web site that is a B2B application is shown in Figure 1-3. Some

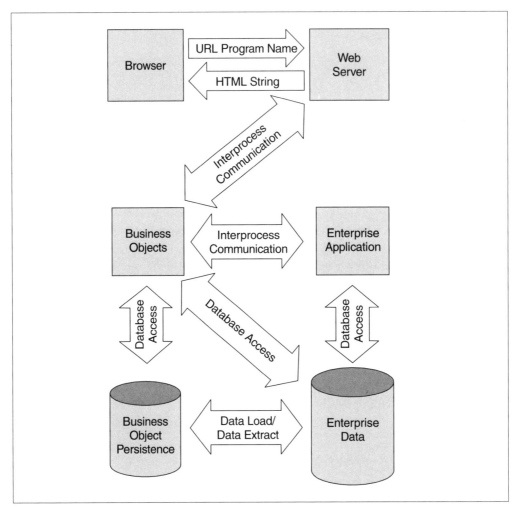

FIGURE 1-3 *A Web Site That Is a B2B Application*

concepts illustrated in Figure 1-3 may intrigue you. Later chapters explore these topics and illuminate details on how to build Web sites that are B2B applications.

1.4 BUILDING APPLICATIONS USING THE .NET FRAMEWORK

As I said in the Introduction, the .NET platform is the successor to Microsoft's Windows DNA platform. The .NET platform consists of the Common Language Runtime, the .NET Framework Class Library, and the .NET Enterprise Servers.

Incidentally, .NET also encompasses Microsoft's *vision* of how software will evolve in the future and Microsoft's impending *application-hosting* business. However, this book deals only with the developer-related topics of the Common Language Runtime, the .NET Framework Class Library, and the .NET Enterprise Servers.

The Common Language Runtime (CLR) is the runtime for the .NET *managed* programming languages. Having a common runtime means that programs written in one managed programming language can use objects created in any of the other managed programming languages. In other words, .NET objects are language-independent and are accessible across all of the .NET programming languages.

The .NET Enterprise Servers include Exchange Server and SQL Server, which were previously part of the BackOffice server suite. Also included in the .NET Enterprise Servers are BizTalk Server and SharePoint Portal Server.

For developers, the .NET Framework Class Library is probably the most significant element of the .NET platform. The .NET Framework Class Library consists of a large set of software objects that developers can use to create several types of applications and services, including the following:

- Console applications

- Windows XP, 2000, and NT services

- Windows GUI applications

- XML Web services (using Microsoft ASP.NET)

- Web Form applications (using Microsoft ASP.NET)

In addition to applications and services, developers can create their own business objects that are based on classes in the .NET Framework Class Library or classes derived from them.

Developers can use any of the .NET programming languages with the .NET Framework Class Library. Microsoft provides several .NET language compilers.

- C#, which was designed specifically for the .NET CLR

- C++ with managed extensions, which eases migration from C/C++ to .NET

- Visual Basic, which accommodates VB programmers

- Jscript, which makes .NET available in scripting environments

- Intermediate Language, which is .NET Assembly language

All of the code samples in this book are written in C# (except, of course, SQL Server–stored procedures, which are written in SQL).

Web applications using .NET, are built using a portion of the .NET Framework called ASP.NET. You might be anxious to dive into some ASP.NET code, but starting with ASP.NET in your exploration of the .NET Framework would involve learning several new concepts simultaneously. It is more productive to approach new concepts in .NET one or two at a time. The best place to do this is the .NET Framework Class Library.

1.4.1 THE .NET FRAMEWORK CLASS LIBRARY

Because it is more productive to tackle one or two concepts at a time when learning .NET, let's put aside the Web-based application stuff for a moment and concentrate on the tools you need to build business objects. This is done by deriving your own classes from the Framework classes or by implementing some of Framework's interfaces with your own code. A good way to begin exploring the .NET Framework Class Library is to build a simple console application using C#.

BUILDING A CONSOLE APPLICATION IN C#
This example illustrates how to use some of the .NET Framework classes, which are in the System, System.Net, and System.IO namespaces. I borrowed this particular example from Jeffrey Richter's excellent *Programming the .NET Framework with C#* training course (*http://www.wintellect.com/*).

For this example, it is not necessary to run Visual Studio .NET. The source code file can be created with Notepad or some other text editor and compiled with the C# command-line compiler, *CSC.EXE* (which stands for C Sharp Compiler).

To compile and run the code from this example, you will need to have installed the Microsoft .NET Framework SDK. You can install the Framework SDK as part of the Visual Studio .NET installation process. (You will need Visual Studio .NET for examples in subsequent chapters, so you may want to install both Visual Studio .NET and the .NET Framework SDK at this time.)

Your PATH environment variable needs to point to the directory that holds the *CSC.EXE* file. The PATH environment variable also needs to point to the Microsoft.NET\ FrameworkSDK\Bin directory on the drive on which the SDK is installed.

On Windows NT 4.0, Windows 2000, and Windows XP, the setup process for the SDK should have configured these environment variables for you. For Windows 98 and Windows ME, there is a batch file in the Microsoft.NET\FrameworkSDK\Bin directory that you can use to set these environment variables. In the .NET SDK, the batch file that sets the environment variables is named *corvars.bat*.

A Very Brief Introduction to C#   An application has one or more C# source code files whose files have a *.cs* extension. The order of compilation of the source code files doesn't matter, so there are no forward-reference issues. Source files are compiled directly to executable *(EXE/DLL)* files without *OBJ* files or linking. You gain access to other types (a.k.a. *classes*) by referencing their assembly *(DLL* or *EXE)* using the /reference:assemblyname compiler switch, so there is no need for header files and library files.

C# is a case-sensitive language, so *myVar* is different from *myvar*. Each executable defines at least one type (a.k.a. *class*). One type in the executable must have a static Main method. Main is the application's entry point and must be a static method and may return an Int32 return code. Main may accept an array of String objects as arguments.

A Simple C# Application To create the example program, you should first create a folder on your hard drive to hold the files. Call the folder something like "CSConsole." Then, using your favorite text editor, create a text file called *WebPageToConsole.cs* in the "CSConsole" folder. You will compile this C# program into a command-line executable called *WebPageToConsole.exe*.

When you run *WebPageToConsole* from the command line, you will include a URI (a Uniform Resource Identifier, which can be a URL or a file name) as a command-line argument, and *WebPageToConsole* will output the HTML from that Web page or the contents of that file on the console.

The code in your *WebPageToConsole.cs* should look exactly like the code in Listing 1-1. I copied and pasted this code directly from my own version of the *WebPageToConsole.cs* file, which compiles and runs without errors or warnings.

LISTING 1-1 *WebPageToConsole.cs*

```
using System;
using System.IO;
using System.Net;
class App {
   public static void Main(String[] args) {
      WebRequest myRequest = WebRequest.Create(args[0]);
      WebResponse myResponse = myRequest.GetResponse();
      Stream myStream = myResponse.GetResponseStream();
      StreamReader myStreamReader = new
      StreamReader(myStream);
      Console.WriteLine(myStreamReader.ReadToEnd());
      myResponse.Close();
   }
}
```

The three *using* directives in Listing 1-1 pull in the .NET Framework namespaces that we will need, so we don't have to type the fully qualified class names for the .NET Framework classes that are used in the program.

The *class App* line defines the class for the application. App is not a keyword. You could name this class anything you want.

The *Main* method is the entry point of the program. It is declared inside a class and must be static. It can either be void or return an int. This Main method is written with parameters to allow the program to read command-line arguments.

WebRequest is the abstract base class for the .NET Framework's request/response model for accessing data from the Internet. The *WebRequest.Create* method returns one of WebRequest's descendant classes, such as HttpWebRequest or FileWebRequest, based on the protocol specified in the URI that is passed in as an argument.

Calling the WebRequest's GetResponse method sends the request for the URI and returns a WebResponse object that holds the text of the response.

The WebResponse GetResponseStream method returns a Stream object. Stream is the abstract base class of all streams. A Stream is an abstraction of a sequence of bytes, such as a file, an input/output device, an inter-process communication pipe, or a TCP/IP socket.

The StreamReader class is designed for character input in a particular encoding, whereas the Stream class is designed for byte input and output. You use StreamReader for reading lines of text.

The Console class provides basic support for applications that read characters from, and write characters to, the console. The WriteLine method writes data to the standard output stream, followed by a line termination string.

The response stream must be closed to avoid running out of system resources. The response stream can be closed by calling Close on the Stream object or by calling Close on the Response object.

C++ programmers will probably notice that the code in Listing 1-1 does not free or release the myStreamReader instance and that it might look like a memory leak. In C#, it is unnecessary (and impossible) to release memory explicitly. The CLR garbage collector automatically frees memory that is referenced by variables that have gone out of scope.

You will find more detailed information about each keyword, class, and method in the .NET Framework SDK documentation, and you should spend some quality time studying it. It will be time well spent.

Compile the program using the following command line:

```
csc webpagetoconsole.cs /reference:mscorlib.dll
```

MSCORLIB.DLL is the name of the assembly that contains the classes from the .NET Framework Class Library that we are using. For instance, if you look at the

SDK documentation for the StreamReader class, you will see that it is part of the System.IO namespace and resides in the MSCORLIB.DLL assembly. Explicitly referencing MSCORLIB.DLL on the compile command line is unnecessary because the compiler implicitly references that assembly.

Any problems you encounter will be caused either by errors in your typing (remember that C# is a case-sensitive language) or by problems with your machine configuration, such as the environment variables not being set properly. Errors in the compile process will be displayed on the console.

The error messages from the C# compiler tend to be fairly descriptive. So if you encounter any errors, you should be able to figure out what the problem is by carefully considering the text of the error messages.

Note: Please forgive me as I ascend my author's soapbox for a moment. The code in this book does, in fact, compile and run successfully. However, you might encounter errors when trying to build and run this example program for the first time. Microsoft .NET is probably a new development environment for you, and you are likely to make some mistakes at first. If you are a developer, for your own benefit you need to stick with it and work through those mistakes. If you encounter any error messages, research them until you find the solution. Use the documentation. Use Visual Studio .NET and the debugger if you have to. You will learn a great deal about .NET by going through the process of making this example work. Okay—off my soapbox!

You can run the program using the following command line:

```
webpagetoconsole http://www.microsoft.com
```

The HTML of that Web page will scroll by on the console. You can also use a file-based URI such as this:

```
webpagetoconsole c:\test.txt
```

In this case, the contents of the *c:\test.txt* file will be displayed on the console (provided that there is such a file). If you were to specify a file name without a full path, you will get an error message:

```
webpagetoconsole test.txt
```

This is because the system can't resolve whether to use the HttpWebRequest or the FileWebRequest class, both of which are descendants of the WebRequest abstract base class.

This example teaches you several things about the .NET Framework: (1) It exposes you to a representative sampling of the .NET Framework Class Library; (2) it illustrates how to use classes from the .NET Framework Class Library; (3) it (hopefully) influenced you to become familiar with the developer documentation for .NET; (4) it shows you the syntax for the C# programming language; and (5) it familiarizes you with the command-line C# compiler.

Incidentally, I plan to put a program very similar to this one to practical use. As you may be aware, on each Web page for the books on Amazon.com, there is an "Amazon.com Sales Rank" list for that book. The sales rank indicates how well that particular book is selling compared to the other books on Amazon. For example, a book with a sales rank of "15" is the 15th-best-selling book on Amazon. For popular books, these sales ranks are recalculated every hour.

I plan to modify the code in Listing 1-1 so that it retrieves the Amazon page for this book and then seeks through the WebResponse's stream object to parse out the sales rank, which it will append to a table in a SQL Server database. I can schedule an automatic job in Windows to run my program every hour. Using this program, I can graph the sales ranking over time and watch the life cycle of my book. (Yes, I am a nerd.) However, you could use this idea to write a very simple program to retrieve periodically data that interests you from the Web.

1.4.2 .NET FRAMEWORK SDK SAMPLES

In the Preface, I recommended that you install the .NET Framework SDK Samples. I have found these samples to be very helpful in learning the .NET Framework. Before you can use the SDK samples, especially the ASP.NET samples, which are particularly helpful, you have to build them. The files for the SDK samples are in a collection of folders on the drive that contains the SDK. This is the folder on my machine:

```
C:\Program Files\Microsoft.NET\FrameworkSDK\Samples
```

There is a *StartSamples.htm* file in that folder that you can browse for a summary outline of the SDK samples. There is also a link to a configuration details document that describes the details of installing and building the SDK samples. It also points you to a configuration utility called ConfigSamples.exe, which installs the sample databases and creates the IIS virtual roots needed for the samples.

The SDK samples are built using the .NET command-line compilers and some make files. There is also a *buildall.bat* file in the Samples folder that will build the samples as a batch.

Your experience in compiling the previous WebPageToConsole sample should prepare you for any problems you might encounter in trying to build the SDK samples. After you build the SDK samples, you will be able to refer to the ASP.NET QuickStart Tutorial as you work through the samples in Chapters 3, 4, and 5.

Chapters 3, 4, and 5 will explain how to use ASP.NET Web Forms to build B2B apps that can handle requests from browsers. Chapter 6 will get you started building XML Web services to handle service requests from other applications and will introduce you to BizTalk Server for automating business processes.

Before delving into those ASP.NET topics, we must first explore a topic that is fundamental to B2B application development. That topic is security, or content access control, and it is the topic of Chapter 2.

SUMMARY

Web sites come in three basic flavors: static sites, dynamic sites, and sites that are business applications. Dynamic sites are more complex to build than static sites. Sites that are business applications are more complex to build than dynamic sites. B2B Web sites are in fact N-tier business applications. Hence the term *B2B application* is more descriptive than the term *B2B Web site*.

With the .NET Framework Class Library, you can implement the complex logic required by B2B applications in powerful programming languages and compile that code into business objects. Business objects provide the middle-tier platform for implementing B2B application logic.

Implementing Security in B2B Applications

This chapter gives details of security development in B2B applications, especially *how* to implement security and content access. Chapter 8 focuses on *why* security threats exist and *where* the threats come from. Chapter 8 also gives an introduction to encryption, public and private keys, digital certificates, and SSL. You may want to refer to that chapter for context on the implementation advice presented in this chapter. The key points for this chapter are the following:

- A B2B Web site aggregates multiple extranets into a single site.

- A B2B Web site provides the security context in which commerce between companies can be conducted online.

- Application software used by businesses today is typically not built to run in a B2B environment, so developers must somehow bolt security and content access control onto these applications.

- Role-based security is not sufficient for typical B2B Web sites.

- Developers can build a powerful, permission list-based access control system using a SQL database, and they can expose the security settings that are stored in the database to content managers with Web browsers.

2.1　SECURITY, A PRIMARY ROLE OF B2B WEB SITES

Every company has information and applications that it uses internally, as well as customers and partner businesses that it works with externally. When a company exposes its internal information to its external customers, it needs to do so in the right context. And when customers obtain information from a company, they need to obtain that information in the right context. A B2B Web site provides that context.

A primary function of a B2B Web site is to secure the flow of information between businesses. A B2B Web site provides the *security context* in which online commerce can be conducted.

2.1.1 A REAL-WORLD EXAMPLE OF A FUNDAMENTAL B2B DESIGN PATTERN

Recently I met some people from a Fortune 500 company who were very interested in implementing B2B Internet commerce. This company is a manufacturer in a particular industry, but their example is broadly applicable, so I'll refer to them with the generic name "Manufacturer A." In fact, their example is so broadly applicable, that it constitutes a fundamental design pattern that builders of B2B applications will encounter again and again.

Manufacturer A maintains numerous lucrative business relationships with several Fortune 500 companies. In some of these relationships, Manufacturer A is the buyer, and in others it is the seller. In all of these relationships, a large quantity of contextual information supplements each transaction. (Here I am not referring to computer science-type ACID transactions, but rather I am using the term *transaction* merely to mean a purchase or sale of goods or services.)

Information in diverse forms is exchanged between Manufacturer A and its business partners. Information is exchanged both in advance of each transaction and after each transaction is completed. Sometimes information is exchanged for the express purpose of keeping the relationship between the companies alive and healthy.

Information is exchanged on products, prices, designs, shipments, estimates, recommendations, proposals, contracts, clarifications, problems, replacements, questions, answers—you name it. And this information is exchanged through several different, and often inefficient, mediums, including fax, e-mail, telephone, voice mail, snail mail, and face-to-face.

It is important to note that information is exchanged in the context of the particular relationship between Manufacturer A and its individual business partners. For example, the information that Manufacturer A provides to Company B is tailored to Company B. Another company, such as Company C, should never see any of Company B's confidential information. Thus every relationship between businesses has its own *security context*, which defines what information is to be exchanged between the parties. (At this level of discussion, the security context is an abstract idea, and I am not yet referring to any concrete implementation of a security context in software.)

A manager I know at Manufacturer A realized that he could use the Internet to enhance greatly his company's relationships with its various business partners. This manager felt that if he could build an extranet site that is secure and tailored to Company B, he could use it efficiently to exchange information and perform transactions with Company B. He realized that a secure extranet site would be a more efficient medium in which to conduct business than the current mishmash of faxes, e-mails, phone calls, voice mails, letters, and meetings.

He decided that, ideally, Manufacturer A's extranet site should look and act like it is part of Company B's intranet. In other words, the site should be unique and tailored for Company B. Such a Web site would make it easier for the people at Company B to conduct business with his company.

He also realized that if he were to set up an extranet site for each of his company's business partners, they could all conduct business more readily with his company. This idea is illustrated in Figure 2-1.

As you can see in Figure 2-1, each extranet site provides a security context in which information is exchanged and transactions are conducted with each individual business partner. It is important to note again that information is exchanged in the context of the particular relationship between Manufacturer A and each individual business partner.

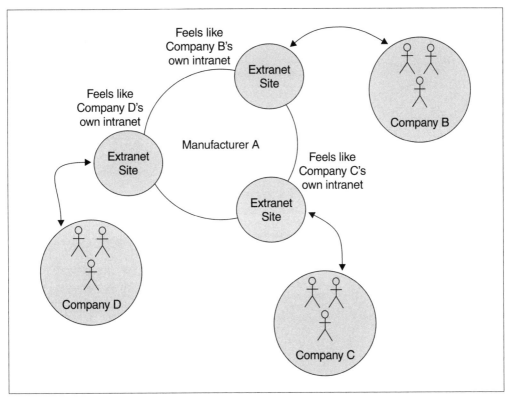

FIGURE 2-1 *Extranets Provide the Security Contexts for B2B Applications*

This is a prevalent design pattern in B2B commerce. The relationship between two businesses defines the security context in which information is exchanged.

Unlike the illustration in Figure 2-1, a company will probably not want to implement a separate extranet site for each of its customers and partners. Rather, the company will want a single Web site that can function like a chameleon and change its appearance based on its context. This is what a B2B Web site does, as illustrated in Figure 2-2.

A B2B Web site contains and aggregates multiple extranets. The idea is *one URL— multiple Web sites*. This means that a customer can visit the B2B Web site, and based on who they are, what they do, and what company they work for, the Web site dynamically changes its skin and its content to match that customer's context.

Therefore, when I say, "B2B Web site," think "extranet site that changes its skin and content to match the user who is viewing it."

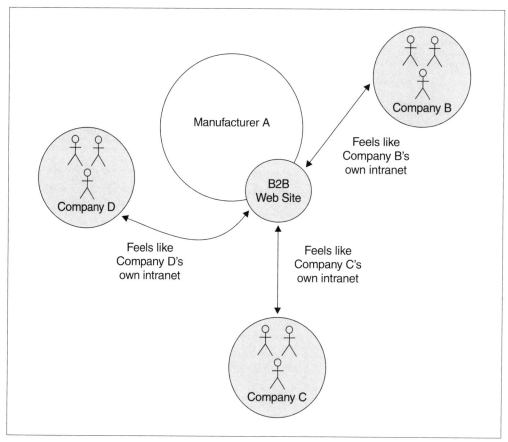

FIGURE 2-2   *A Single B2B Web Site Aggregates Multiple Extranet Sites*

When it comes to concrete implementations in the B2B world, a company can't deploy applications that don't work within the security context of each partner's relationship. For example, you can't buy an online product catalog system off the shelf and expect it to work in a B2B environment unless that product catalog system knows how to work within the proper security context. You don't want that product catalog application to take the specialized products and prices that you intended for Company B and expose them to Company C also. You want the products and prices for Company B to be accessible only to users from Company B.

If the product catalog is a complex application that was designed without any B2B-type security context in mind and if you don't have access to the source code for that catalog app, it might be difficult for you to bolt on that security context. For many applications, this security context must exist at the *schema* level, with the app designed and built using the security schema as its foundation. For a catalog application to expose certain products and prices only to certain companies, it needs a schema that enables a particular company or set of companies to be associated with each item in the catalog, or perhaps with each attribute of each item in the catalog.

Traditionally, software applications have been built for use only inside the protected walls of a business, with no thought given to the prospect of these applications being opened up for access by users outside the company. External access, and the requisite security that it demands, is typically not considered when designing the security features of software applications, and information systems in general are not constructed with external security in mind.

For a company to implement Internet commerce between businesses, it has to find a way to bolt access controls onto applications that were designed to work only inside the walls of the company. The company needs to provide secure, Web-based access to its backend applications for each of its relevant customers. Furnishing this security is a primary function of a B2B Web site.

When I talk to developers who are new to B2B development, a question I often hear is "Is all of this security really necessary?" The best answer I can give is to explain that in every one of the dozens of B2B development projects I have been involved with, the business managers, the people driving the design of the application, always pushed the envelope of the app's access control system. When it comes to opening up their sensitive business data to customers and partners outside the company, business managers always want robust and highly granular control of who has access to what.

It turns out that providing a highly granular level of content access control can be tricky to implement. I have noticed a common misconception among developers who assume that role-based security is the answer to virtually any security problem. In my experience, group- or role-based security is inadequate for typical B2B applications.

For example, a company that owns a B2B Web site might have a document that it wants to make available only to executives of their supplier companies. With role-based security, the company's content manager on the B2B site could create a role called Executives and another role called Suppliers. However, the problem is that you typically cannot do a logical *AND* between the roles with role-based security. Set-based operations between the roles are not available in typical role-based security systems.

The content manager might specify the Executive's role and the Supplier's role as having access to this document, but that would mean that anyone who is an executive, whether he or she works for a supplier or not, and anyone who works for a supplier, whether he or she is an executive or not, would be able to access this document. In other words, granting access to the Executive's role and the Supplier's role creates a logical *OR* between the roles, which is a union of the sets of Executives and Suppliers.

To create a logical *AND* between the roles, the content manager would have to hardwire it into another role called SupplierExecutives, which would be the intersection of the Executive's role and the Supplier's role. The problem with this approach is that the number of roles the content manager must create mushrooms as it becomes apparent how many logical *AND*s are required between their various roles. As the roles proliferate, they become difficult to manage. In addition, performing the security checks, whether at login time or each time a resource is accessed, can become a significant drag on performance.

There is another limitation with the role-based security found in operating systems and databases that makes it inadequate for B2B applications. Typically there is a requirement that content managers on the B2B Web site must be able to administer the content access settings. The problem is that content managers are generally not system administrators or database administrators or developers; they are nontechnical business users who are responsible for content on the site and who want to specify who can see what.

So B2B application developers cannot expect these nontechnical content managers to run any operating system administration utilities or database administration utilities to administer the content access control on the B2B Web site. I mention this not as a complaint about these utilities but rather to point out that developers of B2B applications cannot assume their users will be able to use them effectively. Therefore developers have to build administration screens for content access settings that are more elegant than those utilities based on the (lack of) technical savvy of the content managers.

The bottom line is that for B2B applications, developers must create application-level security that is more powerful than system-level group or role-based security and at the same time is easier to use than operating system and database administration screens.

Later in this chapter, I describe a *permission list*–based access control algorithm that enables security to be applied to distinct resources on a Web site. Those resources could be individual documents or pages. The granularity of the algorithm can be extended to apply security to portions of pages and to methods on Web services.

This permission list–based access control algorithm is implemented using a few tables and stored procedures in SQL Server, which could be exposed to nontechnical content managers on a B2B Web site using elegant and simple HTML forms. But before getting into the SQL schema and code, there are a few fundamental concepts on implementing security that must be clarified.

2.2 MECHANISMS FOR CONTROLLING ACCESS TO DATA AND APPLICATIONS

The whole process of providing the right information to the right people begins with two basic concepts: authentication and authorization.

2.2.1 AUTHENTICATION

Authentication is the process of identifying a user who is requesting access to an information system. Authentication is typically performed by taking the user through a login procedure of some sort. This user is called the *principal*. During the login process, principals present evidence of their identity so the system can be satisfied that they are who they claim to be. The proof of identity that a principal provides at login time is known as *credentials*.

For example, a principal could offer his or her knowledge of a user ID and a password or something like an access card or a digital certificate as proof of identity. They might also use a physical feature or a biometric such as a scan of their fingerprint, retina, face, or voice. If a principal offers the correct credentials, the authentication process assumes that the principal is who he or she claims to be.

It is important to remember that if a thief steals someone's credentials, the thief can then impersonate the victim. Because the authentication process can't tell that an imposter is presenting someone else's credentials, it might be impossible to discover that something is amiss until long after the thief has gained access to the system in the victim's name and has done whatever damage he or she intended to do. Therefore, in order for the authorization process to keep out unauthorized persons, users of information systems must judiciously guard their credentials.

2.2.2 AUTHORIZATION

Authorization is the process of deciding which resources a principal is permitted to access. In B2B applications, different principals will have different degrees of access.

The degrees of access in B2B applications, however are typically not limited to a single dimension.

The typical B2B application requires a matrix of authorization levels. Authorization must be granted based on multiple criteria, such as the following:

- Identity
- Employer
- Role
- Company type

The owners of the application must create a list of attributes that are relevant to their business and their B2B application. Based on my experience with B2B applications, the list of attributes should be kept to five or six at the most for performance and maintenance reasons and should include the attributes of identity, employer, and role.

Attributes such as these must be mapped and correlated to the way that the data is classified inside an organization. In other words, management has to decide which companies, users, and roles can have what type of access to which data inside the organization.

In order to put these decisions about data access and security into practice in B2B applications, the authentication and authorization mechanisms must be implemented using existing Internet-based technologies.

2.2.3 OPTIONS FOR IMPLEMENTING AUTHENTICATION AND AUTHORIZATION

Existing Web- and server-based technologies currently offer three techniques for implementing authentication and authorization: network operating system, third-party, and application-specific.

NETWORK OPERATING SYSTEM

Modern network operating systems typically offer some type of user authentication and authorization mechanism. Using a network operating system for authentication and authorization in B2B applications typically means representing the users of your B2B application in the user account management function of the server's network operating system (NOS). This user account management function might be a local user account database that is built into the NOS, or it might be an LDAP server, such as Microsoft Active Directory.

With this technique, you manage the users of your B2B application in the NOS user account database as if they were inside-the-enterprise users. However, this leads to a bit of a mismatch. Many, perhaps most, of the users of B2B applications are actually outside-the-enterprise users.

Keep in mind that many B2B users are actually *not* employees of the company that owns the B2B app. These users access the company's internal information systems only through the B2B Web site from *outside* the walls of the enterprise. You must also remember that your NOS user account management function was designed for managing employees of the company who are inside the walls of the enterprise, usually on a local area network.

An internal NOS user account database is not the right tool for managing external B2B application users. This mismatch between the tool and the job is manifest in two ways in B2B implementations.

The first mismatch is that you end up mixing internal and external users in the NOS user account database, which may make the maintenance process of the user database cumbersome. Having a large number of external, B2B app users in the NOS user account database could bog down the database and make it difficult to manage the enterprise's internal users in the same database. In addition, there is no tight coupling of the B2B application with the B2B user account management function. The user account management would happen with an administration tool that is provided by the NOS and that is separate from the rest of the B2B application.

Second, and more important, the granularity of the authorization mechanisms that NOS user account databases provide is typically not right for B2B applications. User account databases often provide a grouping function of some sort for users where the administrator can create groups or roles and then specify which users belong to these groups or roles. However, as explained earlier, a grouping mechanism like this is insufficient for B2B-type authorization, which needs to use attributes such as identity, employer, and role at a minimum In addition, most B2B applications need to keep a variety of application-specific user information. Many NOS user account databases have a limited ability to do this.

Active Directory provides some additional capabilities in that it enables users to be arranged in a hierarchy and enables additional attributes to be assigned to each user. However, Microsoft Active Directory has the following restrictions:

- There may be performance limitations when querying for users based on their attributes instead of their place in the hierarchy.

- There may be performance limitations when updating application-specific user information.

- There may be insufficient support for transactional updates of user information.

Of course, you will need to test the performance of Active Directory yourself for use in your own B2B applications. Depending on the requirements of your application, the performance of Active Directory may be adequate.

Limited support for transactional updates of user information could be a significant problem for B2B applications, depending on what user information is kept in Active Directory and how often and in what way it must be updated.

Even in B2B applications that use Active Directory, there is often a need to keep user-specific information in a relational database. In those applications, Active Directory can play a role in providing a single sign-on capability for users inside the enterprise. In applications that require authenticating the inside-the-enterprise users, the developer of the B2B application often has to write some code that handles the integration of B2B user information that is in the database with the information that is in Active Directory.

The other authorization mechanism provided by NOS is Access Control Lists (ACLs), which enable administrators to assign a list of authorized users and groups to each resource. As is the case with NOS user account databases and Active Directory, the granularity of the authorization is not quite right for use with B2B apps. In the case of ACLs, they are too granular. You end up having to assign an ACL to each resource and then having to keep ACLs updated as users, groups, and resources change over time. This becomes a prohibitively large maintenance task. The bottom line is that your NOS often may not provide the authentication and authorization capability that your B2B applications require.

Third-Party

Another approach is to rely on a third party to provide authentication and authorization services, several of which are available on the Web. For example, Microsoft "HailStorm," which is based on the Microsoft Passport authentication system, is one service Web application developers can use to authenticate and authorize users.

As of this writing, "HailStorm" is not yet in operation, and other services appear to provide authentication but little that could be used for authorization in B2B applications, so it is difficult to predict what implementation issues might arise when using "HailStorm" or other Web-based authentication and authorization services with B2B applications.

Application-Specific

Unfortunately, the NOS and/or Active Directory may not provide all of the authorization capabilities that your B2B applications need, and remote Web-based authentication and authorization are not a reality at this time. So, depending on the application requirements, your B2B applications will need their own authorization mechanisms.

Because typical B2B applications must keep a variety of application-specific user information, the app will usually use a customized database to hold that user information. In nearly all B2B applications, it makes sense to use this database for authentication and authorization of principals as well. Using an application-specific authentication and authorization process for B2B apps has the additional advantage of allowing other applications, not just users, to log in to the B2B application.

Security for Cross-Company Applications   Chapter 6 introduces the tools for building applications that span company boundaries using XML Web services and BizTalk Server. XML Web services leverage the SOAP protocol. SOAP stands for Simple Object Access Protocol, and it is a proposed standard for linking applications over the Internet. Simply put, SOAP is a remote procedure call (RPC) mechanism that is implemented via HTTP and XML.

The SOAP specification doesn't say anything about security. In fact, no security is required for HTTP, XML, or SOAP. In the absence of standards for securing messages, it's possible that SOAP is going to open up a whole new avenue for security vulnerabilities.

However, with an application-specific authentication and authorization process, you can implement user ID and password parameters in each of the methods and use SSL to keep them secure while they are traveling between client and server.

2.3 IMPLEMENTING SQL-BASED AUTHENTICATION AND AUTHORIZATION

Application-specific authentication and authorization can be implemented using a relational database server. The authentication process is simply a matter of prompting (forcing) the user to enter a user ID and a password and then looking up that user ID and password in the database to make sure they are valid. If a principal enters a valid user ID and password, they are authenticated. An invalid user ID and password are not authenticated, and the principal is denied access to any secure resources.

As already discussed in this chapter, typical B2B applications require a matrix of authorization levels, and the authority to access resources must be granted based on multiple criteria, such as the principal's identity, employer, role, and so on.

Resources can be Web pages, documents on the Web site, SOAP methods, portions of Web pages that display data from internal systems, and so forth. A resource could be anything on the B2B site to which you may want to control access.

An authorization process to control access to resources requires that all of the secured resources be listed in the database. In other words, there must to be a row in a database table for each resource that you want to protect.

In Chapters 3 through 5, you will work through an ASP.NET Web Forms example that secures access to documents on a Web site. This chapter contains the code that creates the database the Web Forms application uses.

To work through the Chapter 2 code, create a SQL Server database named "ManufacturerA," and execute the SQL commands in the code listings here. Then enter the data shown later in the chapter to test the database and get it ready for use in Chapter 3.

Run the SQL DDL (data definition language) code shown in Listing 2-1 to create in your "ManufacturerA" database a Documents table that will be used to control access to documents.

LISTING 2-1   *Table Linking Permission Lists and Documents*

```
CREATE TABLE Documents (
    DocID varchar (20) NOT NULL ,
    Name varchar (20),
    MimeType varchar (20),
    FilePath varchar (250)
)
```

The *DocID* field is the unique identifier, the key field, for each document. The *Name* field is the name of the document that is displayed on the Web page as a hyperlink, which users can click to see the document. The *MimeType* is the file type, and the *FilePath* field points to the location where each document can be accessed and sent out to browsers that request it.

The DocID field is also a foreign key that is used to link each document to Permission List records. A link table is used to link permission lists with documents. Run the SQL code shown in Listing 2-2 to create this table.

LISTING 2-2   *Table Linking Permission Lists and Documents*

```
CREATE TABLE PLDocument (
    PermissionListID int NULL ,
    DocumentID varchar (20)
)
```

A permission list is a collection of criteria. The PermissionLists table holds the permission lists. Create the PermissionLists table defined in Listing 2-3.

LISTING 2-3   *Permission List Table*

```
CREATE TABLE PermissionLists (
    PLKey int NOT NULL ,
    Company varchar (50),
    CompanyCategory varchar (50),
    Person varchar (50),
    Role varchar (50)
)
```

In Listing 2-3, the PLKey field is the primary key for the table and the unique identifier for each permission list. Each permission list is a unique combination of Company, CompanyCategory (which is used to classify companies), Person, and Role.

The intent is for each field to be AND'ed together to determine a unique level of access. For example, a permission list with "Viewstar" as the Company and "Executive Staff" as the Role means that a principal has to be both an employee of Viewstar *and* a member of the executive staff in order to qualify for that permission. In this case, the CompanyCategory and Person fields would be populated with some value, an "any" symbol of some kind that would indicate there are no restrictions on those fields.

These permissions are linked to documents using the PLDocument table. For example, if a particular document had the just mentioned Viewstar/Executive Staff permission as its lone permission, only principals who are executives of Viewstar would be authorized to access that document. If more than one permission is linked to a particular document, those permissions are OR'ed together, meaning that a principal need only qualify for one of the permissions to gain access to that document.

Permission lists are also associated with principals. This is implemented in the PLPerson table. Run the code to create the PLPerson table defined in Listing 2-4.

LISTING 2-4　*Table Linking Permission Lists and Persons*

```
CREATE TABLE PLPerson (
    PermissionListID int NULL ,
    PersonID varchar (20) NULL
)
```

There also needs to be a table that holds person data. Run the SQL code to create the table that holds person data that is shown in Listing 2-5.

LISTING 2-5　*Table Containing Person Data*

```
CREATE TABLE Persons (
    UserID varchar (20) NOT NULL ,
    Password varchar (50) NOT NULL
)
```

In Listing 2-5, the UserID field is the primary key for the table, and it is the unique identifier for each permission list. Of course, there would be several other fields in the Persons table of a real B2B application. These fields might include such information as each person's employer, role or roles, contact information, and so forth. The schema is simplified here for clarity.

The Password field holds the user's password. It is specified here as 50 characters in length to accommodate encrypted passwords. An even better idea than storing encrypted passwords is storing the passwords as hash values, which are more difficult to reverse.

You could use a message digest algorithm such as MD5 or SHA-1 to distill each password into a value of 128 or 256 bits in length, which you could store in the database instead of the password itself. Performing a search for "MD5" or "SHA-1" with a Web search engine will net you a long list of resources that will help you implement these message digest functions in your applications.

Note: In real B2B applications, the passwords should never be stored in clear text in the database. Ideally, passwords should be stored as Hash values, which would make the passwords extremely difficult to decipher.

Each user in the database could potentially be associated with several permissions. It is a matter of comparing each person's attributes—such as his or her employer, role, and so on— with the permission lists in the PermissionLists table and then putting a record in the PLPerson table for each permission for which the person qualifies.

Each person and each document are associated with permission lists. This is illustrated in Figure 2-3.

The SQL code to enforce these relationships in a Microsoft SQL Server database is shown in Listing 2-6. Run this code to create these constraints in your ManufacturerA database.

LISTING 2-6 *Constraints to Enforce Relationships with Permission Lists*

```
ALTER TABLE PermissionLists WITH NOCHECK ADD
    CONSTRAINT PK_PermissionLists PRIMARY KEY   CLUSTERED
    (
        PLKey
    )  ON [PRIMARY]
GO
ALTER TABLE Documents WITH NOCHECK ADD
    CONSTRAINT PK_Documents PRIMARY KEY   CLUSTERED
    (
        DocID
    )  ON [PRIMARY]
GO
ALTER TABLE Persons WITH NOCHECK ADD
    CONSTRAINT PK_Persons PRIMARY KEY   CLUSTERED
    (
        UserID
```
(continued)

```
     )   ON [PRIMARY]
GO
ALTER TABLE PLDocument ADD
    CONSTRAINT FK_PLDocument_Documents FOREIGN KEY
    (
        DocumentID
    ) REFERENCES Documents (
        DocID
    ),
    CONSTRAINT FK_PLDocument_PermissionLists FOREIGN KEY
    (
        PermissionListID
    ) REFERENCES PermissionLists (
        PLKey
    )
GO
ALTER TABLE PLPerson ADD
    CONSTRAINT FK_PLPerson_PermissionLists FOREIGN KEY
    (
        PermissionListID
    ) REFERENCES PermissionLists (
       PLKey
    ),
    CONSTRAINT FK_PLPerson_Persons FOREIGN KEY
    (
        PersonID
    ) REFERENCES Persons (
        UserID
    )
GO
```

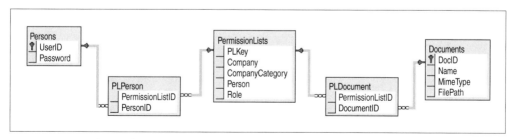

FIGURE 2-3   *Relationship Between Persons, Permission Lists, and Documents*

In a production application, there are no doubt other constraints that you would want to add. For instance, you might want to add a constraint on the PermissionLists table to enforce the uniqueness of the combination of the CompanyCategory, Person, and Role fields (recall that each record is a unique combination of those fields).

Given a person, it is easy to write a SQL query that returns the IDs of the documents that the person can access. The SQL SELECT statement in Listing 2-7 returns the documents that a principal is authorized to access. In Listing 2-7, the personID of 'SidSalesman' could be a parameter, which is passed into the query to generalize it for use with any person in the database. To make this example a bit more concrete, enter data into the PermissionLists table, as shown in Table 2-1.

LISTING 2-7   *Query to Return the Documents a Principal Can Access*

```
SELECT DISTINCT pldocument.documentid from pldocument, plperson
WHERE pldocument.permissionlistID = plperson.permissionlistID
AND plperson.personID = 'SidSalesman'
```

The example Data in Table 2-1 shows ten permission lists, each of which is a unique combination of the fields. The "0" in the fields indicates that there is no restriction on that field for that particular permission. For example, PermissionList 8 requires that the principal have a role of "Sales Staff," but there are no other restrictions. To qualify for that permission, the principal must have the "Sales Staff" role but could be employed by any company of any category.

TABLE 2-1   *Example Data in PermissionList Table*

PLKEY	COMPANY	CATEGORY	PERSON	ROLE
1	0	0	SamSiteAdmin	0
10	0	Gold	0	Executive Staff
2	0	0	0	Developer
3	0	Gold	0	0
4	T & R Tech	0	0	0
5	T & R Tech	0	0	Executive Staff
6	Viewstar	0	0	0
7	Viewstar	0	0	Executive Staff
8	0	0	0	Sales Staff
9	0	SiteOwner	0	0

PermissionList 9 is interesting because it uses a category of "SiteOwner." In this scheme, there is a company table that contains all of the information for each company. The company that owns the B2B Web site is given a category of "SiteOwner."

PermissionList 1 is a very restrictive permission. Only a principal with a Person ID of SamSiteAdmin qualifies for that permission.

Enter data in the PLDocument table so that it is populated as shown in Table 2-2. Because of the foreign key constraints, you will first need to add records in the Documents table that correspond to the DocID entries shown in Table 2-2. For now, you can just fill in the DocID field in the Documents table and leave the other fields blank. It goes without saying that you will enter each DocID only once in the Document table. After entering the DocIDs, enter the data in Table 2-2 in the PLDocument table. There is a one-to-many relationship between the Documents table and the PLDocument table, which is why there are duplicate DocIDs in Table 2-2.

You can see that GoldQuotas and GoldPaymentTerms are accessible only by Permission 10, which is only the executive staff of companies with a Gold category. You can also see that most of the admin documents are limited to Permission 1, which is restricted to PersonID SamSiteAdmin.

Enter data so that the PLPerson table is populated as shown in Table 2-3. Table 2-3 is sorted by PersonID so that you can see what is happening with each person.

TABLE 2-2   *Example Data in PLDocument Table*

DOCID	PERMISSIONLISTID
AdminProcedures	1
AdminPolicy	1
ContentCodes	8
ContentCodes	9
TRTechContract	5
ViewstarContract	7
DevHowTo	2
EastRegionProdInfo	4
EastRegionProdInfo	6
GoldPricing	3
GoldQuotas	10
GoldPaymentTerms	10
SalesLit	3
SalesLit	8

TABLE 2-3   *Example Data in PLPerson Table*

PERSONID	PERMISSIONLISTID
ElmerEmployee	9
EdTRExecutive	3
EdTRExecutive	4
EdTRExecutive	5
PeterProgrammer	2
SamSiteAdmin	1
SamSiteAdmin	10
SamSiteAdmin	2
SamSiteAdmin	3
SamSiteAdmin	4
SamSiteAdmin	6
SamSiteAdmin	8
SamSiteAdmin	9
SidSalesman	3
SidSalesman	6
ValViewStarExec	3
ValViewStarExec	6
ValViewStarExec	7
ValViewStarExec	8
VickiViewStar	6

Because of the foreign key constraints, you will first need to add in the Persons table records that correspond to the PersonID entries shown in Table 2-3. For now, you can just fill in the Password field in the Person table with "1234." After entering the PersonIDs in the Persons table, enter the data in Table 2-3 in the PLPerson table.

PersonID SamSiteAdmin has been given almost every permission in the system. This is because he is the system administrator and must have access to lots of places. The only permissions he doesn't have are 5 and 7, which are the Viewstar and T & R Tech executive staff permissions. (In a real implementation, the system administrator would probably qualify for those permissions as well.)

PersonID ElmerEmployee has only one permission, that of SiteOwner. He is apparently an employee of the company that owns the B2B Web site, but he hasn't been given much access to it.

TABLE 2-4   *Resources that PersonID EdTRExecutive Is Authorized to Access*

RESOURCEID
TRTechContract
EastRegionProdInfo
GoldPricing
SalesLit

PersonID EdTRExecutive is apparently an executive with T&R Tech. Running the SQL query in Listing 2-7 with PersonID = 'EdTRExecutive' yields the documents in Table 2-4.

A stored procedure can be created for SQL Server that takes the PersonID and DocumentID as input parameters and returns an output parameter indicating whether that person has access to that document. The stored procedure is shown in Listing 2-8. This stored procedure does a count of the documents that match this document ID and that are among the documents this person is permitted to access. Of course, there is only one document with this document ID, and it may or may not be among the documents this user is permitted to see, so the count will be either 0 or 1. That makes it handy to use in an *if* condition in C# code. You actually get to use this stored procedure in an ASP.NET Web page in Chapter 3.

LISTING 2-8   *Stored Procedure That returns 0 or 1 if the Principal Has Access*

```
CREATE PROCEDURE sp_UserHasAccessToDoc
@userid VARCHAR(20), @docid VARCHAR(20), @HasAccess INT OUTPUT AS
SELECT @HasAccess = COUNT(*) FROM documents
WHERE DocID = @docid AND DocID IN
(SELECT DISTINCT pldocument.documentid from pldocument, plperson
WHERE pldocument.permissionlistID = plperson.permissionlistID
AND plperson.personID = @userid)
GO
```

Using these tables and SQL queries to retrieve the documents that a principal can access is pretty straightforward. It would certainly also be possible to create HTML forms that enable content managers on the B2B Web site to manage the data in these tables using a Web browser.

To extend this scheme so it secures the data that is posted on the B2B Web site from internal information systems, developers will have to find a way to limit the data coming out of those internal information systems based on the permissions for each principal. Depending on the capabilities and limitations of those information systems, this may be easy, or it may be difficult.

SUMMARY

The primary roles of a B2B Web site are aggregating multiple extranets into a single Web site and providing the security context in which companies can safely conduct business online with other companies and individuals.

Application software used by businesses today is not built to run within a B2B security context. Therefore developers are forced to find a way to bolt security and content access control onto typical business applications.

Role-based security is typically not sufficient for the types of content access problems that B2B commerce presents. However, developers can build a powerful, permission list-based access control system using a SQL database and can expose its data to content managers with Web browsers so that nontechnical people can manage the content access settings on the site.

ASP.NET Web Forms and Authentication

In Chapter 2, you learned about a real-life manufacturer, Manufacturer A, and a manager who realized he could use B2B applications to enhance that company's relationships with suppliers and partners. In Chapter 3, you will begin working through ASP.NET source code that illustrates a practical way to implement a secure B2B Web site. A Web site such as this could serve as the genesis for complex B2B applications like the ones Manufacturer A uses.

Over the next four chapters, you will build for Manufacturer A a secure B2B Web site that offers sophisticated content access control using ASP.NET and the relational database tables and queries you worked with in Chapter 2. In this chapter, you will implement a login and logout facility, which is usually the first step in constructing such a Web site.

The key points for this chapter are the following:

- A secure Web site that enables users to log in and see information that is for their eyes only can be useful in many applications across several industries.

- Authentication, implemented through a login mechanism, is a prerequisite for controlling access to resources on a Web site.

- Cookie-based authentication is simple to implement in ASP.NET.

3.1   AUTHENTICATION IN ASP.NET WEB APPLICATIONS

Putting up a brochure-ware Web site that is public for anyone to browse can be easy. The technology is pretty straightforward, and the biggest challenges are creative, not technical. Putting in an intranet site where the whole Web site is protected by a firewall that can be accessed only by those inside the firewall can likewise be easy.

However, selectively granting access to content on a Web site so that certain pieces of content on the site are accessible only to particular people is not straight-forward. The first step in doing so is to build a login and logout facility.

In this chapter, you will learn to build a site where people must log in, and in subsequent chapters you will learn how to ensure that the content each person accesses is for his or her eyes only. This B2B Web site will enable Manufacturer A to publish secure content over the Internet by controlling who has access to the various resources on the site.

3.1.1   WHAT YOU CAN DO WITH A SECURE WEB SITE

A practical example of a secure site would be a Web site that provides product and pricing information to the resellers of a manufacturer's products. A site like this is sometimes called a *selling-chain management* site and is usually owned by a manu-facturer. Manufacturers almost always sell their products through other companies, which resell their products. A selling-chain management site enables these resellers to log in to the manufacturer's Web site and see product and pricing information that is unique for the reseller.

The content access control on a selling-chain management Web site has two dimensions. First, a manufacturer will typically grant better pricing and payment terms to certain resellers. The manufacturer will not want other resellers to see the prices and terms that it grants to its preferred resellers, so there is a separation of content based on company.

Second, within each reseller company, there may be employees with certain roles that enable them to see more privileged information than other employees. For example, a manufacturer might want to grant access to information on upcoming products only to the employees of a reseller who have signed a nondisclosure agree-ment. So there is a separation of content within each company based on each person's identity, role, or some other attribute. Note that this content access control is not hierarchical but matrixed.

In addition to selling-chain management, there are numerous examples of appli-cations where a secure Web site is expedient. Each of the following applications requires the secure flow of sensitive information between specific parties:

- Managing projects in the construction industry

- Publishing and gathering data during clinical trials in the pharmaceutical industry

- Providing collaboration between broker/dealers and their registered rep-resentatives in the financial services industry

- Giving secure access to a resume and job database for subscribers in the professional recruiting industry

- Optimizing production and inventory levels with supply-chain management applications in the manufacturing industry

This chapter illustrates a portion of the foundation that is required for selling-chain management sites as well as for B2B applications in general. There are lots of code for you to work through in this and subsequent chapters, but your reward will be an understanding of how to implement content access control in an ASP.NET Web site.

3.1.2   BUILDING THE MANUFACTURERA WEB SITE

You will need to install Visual Studio .NET and the C# compiler to work through the sample code in this chapter. You will also need to create the database tables and stored procedures described in Chapter 2, and that database must be accessible from your Visual Studio .NET development machine.

Run Visual Studio .NET. Create a new Visual C# project for an ASP.NET Web application. You do this by selecting the File, New, Project menu choice. Then in the New Project dialog, select "Visual C# Projects" in the left tree navigator and the "ASP.NET Web Application" icon in the right side of the window. Specify the name of the project as "ManufacturerA." Leave the default location. This is illustrated in Figure 3-1. Visual Studio .NET will churn for a while and finally present you with a blank page named WebForm1.aspx.

THE MANUFACTURERA HOME PAGE

The first page that you will create will be the Home page for the ManufacturerA Web site. The page will say something simple yet profoundly beautiful. It will say "Welcome to Manufacturer A's Home Page."

When you created the ManufacturerA project, Visual Studio .NET created a blank page named WebForm1.aspx. You will simply rename this page and use it as your Home page. To rename the page, click the WebForm1.aspx name in the Visual Studio .NET Solution Explorer to select it, and then click it again so that you can edit the name. Change the name from WebForm1.aspx to Home.aspx.

The Home page should be displayed in Design mode in the Visual Studio .NET integrated development environment (IDE). On the page, place a Label control, which you can find in the Visual Studio .NET Toolbox under the Web Forms tab.

There is also a Label control under HTML tab in the Visual Studio .NET Toolbox, but don't use it. You should use the ASP.NET Web Server Control version of the

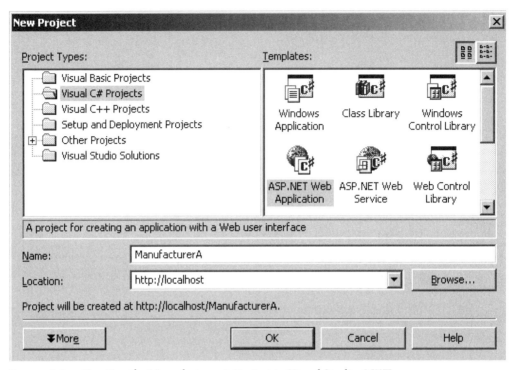

FIGURE 3-1   *Creating the ManufacturerA Project in Visual Studio .NET*

Label control, which is found under the Web Forms tab. For details on the different types of controls that are available in Visual Studio .NET, see "Introduction to ASP.NET Server Controls" section of the Visual Studio .NET documentation.

Set the Text property of the Label control to say "Welcome to Manufacturer A's Home Page." This is shown in Figure 3-2.

Save the page and build the project by selecting the Build, Build menu choice in Visual Studio .NET. If you try to browse the Home page before building the project, you will see an error message rendered in the browser. There is a code-behind page called Global.asax.cs that must be compiled before any pages on the site can be browsed. There is another code-behind page called Home.aspx.cs that also must be compiled before the Home page can be browsed. For your Manu-facturerA project, Visual Studio .NET will store these files on the system drive in Inetpub\wwwroot\ManufacturerA directory.

After building the project successfully, view the Home page in the browser. The URL for the page will most likely be *http://localhost/ManufacturerA/home.aspx*. If this is your first experience working with ASP.NET, take a moment to pat yourself on the back. You have just built and browsed your first ASP.NET page.

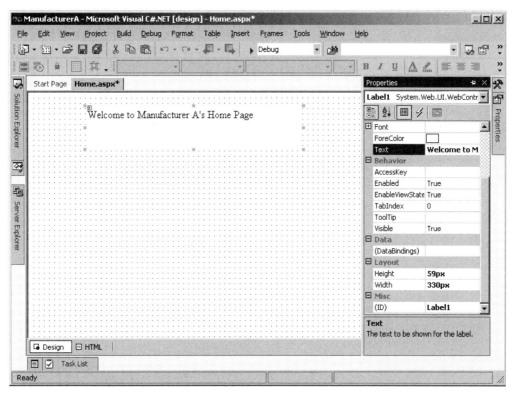

FIGURE 3-2 *The ManufacturerA Home Page*

Go back to Visual Studio .NET. Note that you can double-click anywhere on the Home.aspx page to bring up the Home.aspx.cs code-behind page in Visual Studio .NET. The code-behind page from an ASP.NET page that I created on my machine is shown in Listing 3-1 (with a few lines removed for brevity).

LISTING 3-1 *Home.aspx.cs Code-behind Page for Home.aspx Page*

```
using System;
using System.Collections;
using System.ComponentModel;
using System.Data;
using System.Drawing;
using System.Web;
using System.Web.SessionState;
using System.Web.UI;
using System.Web.UI.WebControls;
using System.Web.UI.HtmlControls;                        (continued)
```

```
namespace ManufacturerA
{
   public class WebForm1 : System.Web.UI.Page
   {
      protected System.Web.UI.WebControls.Label Label1;

      public WebForm1()
      {
         Page.Init += new System.EventHandler(Page_Init);
      }

      private void Page_Load(object sender, System.EventArgs e)
      {
         // Put user code to initialize the page here
      }

      private void Page_Init(object sender, EventArgs e)
      {
         //
         // CODEGEN: This call is required by the ASP.NET Web
            Form Designer.
         //
         InitializeComponent();
      }
   }
}
```

You can see in Listing 3-1 that there are several *using* directives. As you know, these using directives pull in the various .NET Framework namespaces, so you don't have to type the fully qualified class names for the .NET Framework classes that are used in the program.

The *Home.aspx.cs* file contains a class named WebForm1 that is derived from System.Web.UI.Page. You can also see that the WebForm1 class has a member that is defined by this line:

```
protected System.Web.UI.WebControls.Label Label1;
```

This Label1 object corresponds to the Label control that says "Welcome to Manufacturer A's Home Page." There are methods that correspond to events that occur when the page is initialized and loaded. As a developer, you can place your own application code within those methods. You will write some C# code in a code-behind page later.

So at design time with ASP.NET pages, there is the Web page itself, shown in HTML, and there is a code-behind page, which in this project is written in C#. This is quite different from Active Server Pages (ASP). In ASP, each page consisted of HTML text interspersed with code.

At runtime, the difference between ASP and ASP.NET is even more profound. The ASP processor read the page, extracted and interpreted the code, and then translated the results back into HTML before sending the results to the browser. In the ASP.NET Page class, the entire Web Form is a program whose output is HTML. The page goes through a series of processing stages, including *initialize*, *process*, and *dispose*. The Page class performs these stages each time the page is called. In other words, the page is initialized, processed, and disposed every time a browser requests the page from the server. The Page class also has a distinct stage named *render*, during which HTML is generated and that is unique to Page and Page-derived classes.

Go back to the Home.aspx page in Visual Studio .NET. Note that you can view the Home.aspx HTML page in a WYSIWYB (what you see is what you browse) Design mode or in HTML text mode by clicking on the tabs in the lower left portion of the window. So you can edit the HTML of an ASP.NET page by changing it in drag and drop Design mode or in HTML code editing mode.

Note also that changing the HTML does not force a recompile. If you change the HTML, you need only save the page and refresh it in the browser to see your changes. You must save and refresh the page in the browser, but you don't have to recompile. To see this for yourself, go back to the Design mode of the Home.aspx page, select the label, and bring up its properties. Modify the Font settings for the Label control by setting the font size to "large." Save the page and refresh it in your browser. You will see the font size of the label text change in your browser. If you were to change any of the C# code in the code-behind page, you would have to recompile. You will get lots of opportunities to do this as you work through the next few chapters.

AUTHENTICATION

As a developer, you can easily specify that people who browse the site must log in before they are able to access any resources on the site. The idea is that whenever users initially request a page on this site, they first will be presented with a Login page where they can enter their credentials. If their credentials are valid, they are logged in and redirected from the Login page to the page they originally asked for.

To specify that people must log in before accessing the resources on the site, you modify the Web.config file in your ManufacturerA project.

Open the *Web.config* file for your ManufacturerA project in Visual Studio .NET. You can find the *Web.config* file in the Solution Explorer window and open it by double-clicking it.

The *Web.config* is an XML file, which you can edit using XML parser or any standard text editor, such as the editor in the Visual Studio .NET IDE. You cannot access the file remotely using a Web browser. For security reasons, ASP.NET configures Microsoft IIS to prevent direct browser access to *Web.config* files. If you attempt to access a configuration file using a browser, you will get HTTP access error 403.

The *Web.config* file contains nested sections marked by tags. Listing 3-2 shows the *Web.config* file (with the comments removed) in a project that I created on my machine.

LISTING 3-2 *Web.config File*

```xml
<?xml version="1.0" encoding="utf-8" ?>
<configuration>
  <system.web>
    <compilation
        defaultLanguage="c#"
        debug="true"
    />
    <customErrors
    mode="Off"
    />
    <authentication mode="None" />
    <trace
        enabled="false"
        requestLimit="10"
        pageOutput="false"
        traceMode="SortByTime"
            localOnly="true"
    />
    <sessionState
            mode="InProc"
            stateConnectionString="tcpip=127.0.0.1:42424"
            sqlConnectionString="data source=127.0.0.1;user
            id=sa;password="
            cookieless="false"
            timeout="20"
    />
    <httpHandlers>
      <add verb="*" path="*.vb"
        type="System.Web.HttpNotFoundHandler,System.Web" />
      <add verb="*" path="*.cs"
        type="System.Web.HttpNotFoundHandler,System.Web" />
      <add verb="*" path="*.vbproj"
```
(continued)

```
        type="System.Web.HttpNotFoundHandler,System.Web" />
      <add verb="*" path="*.csproj"
        type="System.Web.HttpNotFoundHandler,System.Web" />
      <add verb="*" path="*.webinfo"
        type="System.Web.HttpNotFoundHandler,System.Web" />
    </httpHandlers>
    <globalization
            requestEncoding="utf-8"
            responseEncoding="utf-8"
    />
  </system.web>
  </configuration>
```

This *Web.config* file specifies such things as the default language for the code behind pages, whether debugging is on or off, how error handling is done, the authentication mode, and how session state is persisted. The httpHandlers section maps incoming requests to the System.Web.HttpNotFoundHandler class, which returns a page-not-found page so that the source code cannot be downloaded. Incidentally, you will write your own HTTP handler in Chapter 5.

An exhaustive explanation of the various tags in the *Web.Config* file is outside the scope of this book. Because this book is focused more on B2B commerce than on .NET, I will leave it to the reader to examine the ASP.NET documentation to find detailed explanations of the tags in the *Web.config* file.

Potentially, there can be several *Web.config* files in an ASP.NET Web application. The configuration settings in the *Web.config* are applied in a hierarchical manner, based on the directory structure under the Inetpub\wwwroot\<your project here> directory. Each *Web.config* file supplies configuration information to the directory in which it is located and to all of its child directories.

The *Web.config* files that reside in child directories can supply configuration settings in addition to those inherited from parent directories and can override or modify settings defined in parent directories. Therefore the configuration settings for any given Web resource are supplied by the *Web.config* file located in its directory and by all the *Web.config* files in all its parent directories.

There is a root configuration file, *C:\WINNT\Microsoft.NET\Framework\version\CONFIG\Machine.config*, which provides ASP.NET configuration settings for the entire Web server.

ASP.NET detects changes to the *Web.config* files and automatically applies new configuration settings to Web resources affected by the changes. The server does not have to be rebooted, nor does the Web service have to be stopped and restarted for the changes to take effect.

The ASP.NET configuration system is extensible. You can define new configuration parameters and write configuration section handlers to process them. You will experience some of this extensibility yourself in Chapter 4 when you learn how to place database connection information in the *Web.config* file.

The hierarchical nature of *Web.config* files offers some powerful possibilities for Web development. Unfortunately, the requirements for content access control in typical B2B applications don't fit into a simple hierarchy. The ability to place *Web.config* files in a hierarchy of directories doesn't quite give the B2B application developer all of the tools needed to control access to content in a B2B setting.

As I mentioned earlier in this chapter and also in Chapter 2, content access in B2B Web sites is matrixed, not hierarchical, and it depends at the very least on the user's employer, identity, and role. It is not possible to arrange a matrix of content access controls into a simple hierarchy.

The example code in this book modifies the *Web.config* file that applies to the ManufacturerA project as a whole, and it implements content access controls using the matrix technique specified in Chapter 2.

At this point, you will use only the *Web.config* file to specify that users must log in before they can access any resources on the site. To specify this, you change the mode attribute of the authentication tag. The possible modes are "Windows," "Forms," "Passport," and "None." For this application, you will use forms-based authentication. Windows and Passport authentication are often not appropriate for B2B applications for the reasons listed in Chapter 2.

Change the authentication section of the *Web.config* file in your ManufacturerA project so that it matches Listing 3-3.

LISTING 3-3 *Forms-based Authentication in the Web.config File*

```
<authentication mode="Forms">
   <forms loginUrl="login.aspx" name="AuthManufacturerA" />;
</authentication>
<authorization>
   <deny users="?" />
</authorization>
```

The forms element in the authentication section in Listing 3-3 specifies two attributes: the Login page and the name of the cookie. There is also a protection attribute that specifies whether the cookie is to be encrypted and validated. The default option is All, which means that the cookie is encrypted and validated so it cannot be easily read or modified in transit between the server and the browser. By default, the cookie will expire after 30 minutes of inactivity. See the ASP.NET documentation for details on these topics.

The deny users="?" element in the authorization section means that all anonymous users are denied access to the site. See "ASP.NET Authorization" in the *.NET Framework Developer's Guide* for details. It is possible to specify that certain users be granted access, but for this application we want to force everyone to log in before seeing anything on the site. The forms element in the authentication section is where you specify the Login page and the name of the cookie that will be sent to the browser.

Cookie-Based Authentication The cookie used in ASP.NET forms-based authentication can be a temporary or a persistent cookie. A temporary cookie lasts only as long as that browser instance is running. When the browser is closed, the cookie is automatically deleted. A persistent cookie is written to the browser machine's hard disk and persists between browser sessions.

Later in this chapter, you will implement code that lets the user specify the type of cookie that is used. You specify the cookie type by calling the SetAuthCookie method. The forms element in Listing 3-3 specifies a Login page named login.aspx.

Create a Login.aspx page in your ManufacturerA project. There are several ways to create a new ASP.NET page in Visual Studio.NET, but my personal favorite is to select the File, Add New Item menu choice. The Add New Item dialog appears with the Web Form icon selected, and you just have to change the name of the page to Login.aspx.

The Login page must prompt the user to enter a user ID and a password and to specify whether the user wants a persistent cookie that is saved across browser sessions. You will want the Login page to be nicely formatted. Placing an HTML table on the page to arrange the labels and input boxes will be helpful in formatting the page.

Add a table to the Login page by selecting the Table, Insert, Table menu. In the Insert Table dialog window, specify two columns and three rows. In Design mode on the Login page, move the table to the center of the page by dragging it with the mouse.

In the left-hand cell of the first row, type the text "User ID:." To do this, single-click in the cell to position the cursor inside the cell and then type. In the right-hand cell of the first row, place a TextBox with an ID of Username. To do this, single-click in the right-hand cell to position the cursor, and double-click the TextBox Web Server control, which is under the Web Forms tab in the Toolbox.

In the left-hand cell of the second row, type the text "Password:." In the right-hand cell of the second row, place a TextBox control with an ID of Password.

In the left-hand cell of the third row, type the text "Autologin next visit:." In the right-hand cell of the third row, place a CheckBox Web Server control with an ID of RememberMe.

Beneath the table, place a Button Web Server control with an ID of LoginButton and a Text property of Login.

Your Login page should look similar to the one in Figure 3-3.

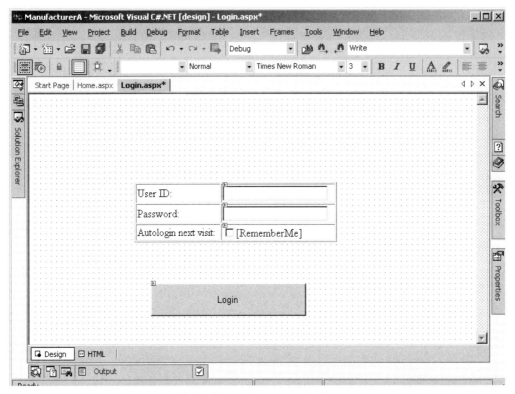

FIGURE 3-3 *Login Page in Visual Studio.NET Design Mode*

Save and compile the *Login.aspx* file by selecting the Build, Build menu choice in Visual Studio.NET. View the Login page in your browser. The URL will probably be *http://localhost/ManufacturerA/Login.aspx*.

TESTING AND DEBUGGING

To test the pages you have created and the code you have written so far, the first step is to try to view the page in the browser. If there are any errors, they will be described in detail in the browser. If there is an error in the *Web.config* file, the offending XML from the *Web.config* file will be rendered in the browser. If there is an error in your C# code, the source file name and the line number with the problem will be shown in the browser. Usually this information will be sufficient for you to track down the problem and solve it.

You can also run the Visual Studio.NET debugger to step through your C# code. All you have to do is set a breakpoint in your C# code and press the F5 key. An instance of Internet Explorer will be launched, which will point at the Start Page for your project. When your breakpoint gets hit, execution will stop inside the debugger in Visual Studio.NET. The Start Page should already be set to your Home.aspx page, but you can set the Start Page by bringing up the properties of your project, clicking Configuration Properties, Debugging, and then specifying the Start Page in the Start Action section of the dialog window. If you want to do it the easy way, right-click on the page name in the Solution Explorer and select the "Set As Start Page" menu choice.

Note that the debugger will run only if there are no errors in the *Web.config* file. If there are problems with your *Web.config* file when you press F5 to start debugging, you will get an error message. To track down problems in your *Web.config* file, just view a page from your site in the browser, and the offending XML from *Web.config* file will be rendered in the browser.

After successfully building and browsing the Login page, add to the top of the page a Label control that has an ID of LoginInvalid and a text of "Login invalid." You should see the "Login invalid" text at the top of the page in the browser.

Save the page and view it in browser. Set the Visible property to False on the LoginInvalid Label control, and save and view it in the browser again. The Login invalid text should no longer be visible in the browser.

ADDING A HIDDEN INPUT CONTROL

Go to the HTML view of Login.aspx and add the following line within the Form tags:

```
<INPUT id="RedirectUrl" type="hidden" name="RedirectUrl"
runat="server">
```

Double-click on the Login page outside of any controls to open Login.aspx.cs, and position the cursor at the Page_Load method. Add code to make the Page_Load method look identical to Listing 3-4.

LISTING 3-4   *Storing the ReturnUrl in the RedirectUrl Hidden Control*

```
private void Page_Load(object sender, System.EventArgs e)
{
    if (!IsPostBack)
    {
        RedirectUrl.Value = Request.QueryString["ReturnUrl"];
    }
}
```

The IsPostBack is the property of the Page class that indicates whether the page is being loaded in response to a client postback or it is being loaded and accessed for the first time. When a request for a protected resource comes into the Web server from an unauthenticated browser, the forms authentication module redirects the request to the Login page to collect credentials from the user. When the browser is redirected to the Login page, the original page that the user requested is placed in a query string variable named ReturnUrl. In Listing 3-4, the page that the user requested is placed in the RedirectUrl hidden control.

So far, you have made only the hidden control an HTML control. To make it a .NET Web Server control, add the following line to login.aspx.cs. Make the hidden input control a member of the Login class by placing this line inside the Login class definition in Login.aspx.cs:

```
protected System.Web.UI.HtmlControls.HtmlInputHidden RedirectUrl;
```

LOGGING IN

Add code to the LoginButton_Click method so it looks like the code in Listing 3-5.

LISTING 3-5   *LoginButton_Click*

```
private void LoginButton_Click(object sender, System.EventArgs e)
{
    if (Username.Text == "guest")
    {
        FormsAuthentication.SetAuthCookie(Username.Text,
        RememberMe.Checked);
        string redirectUrl = Request.Form["RedirectUrl"];
        if (redirectUrl.Length > 0) Response.Redirect(redirectUrl);
        else Response.Redirect("ErrorPage.htm");
    }
    else
    {
        LoginInvalid.Visible = true;
    }
}
```

The code in Listing 3-5 is executed at the server when the user clicks the login button. If the user entered "guest" for the user ID, he or she is logged in. The line that calls the FormsAuthentication.SetAuthCookie method sends a cookie to the browser so that any subsequent requests that the browser makes during this session will be authenticated. If the user has checked the checkbox indicating that he or she wants to be logged in automatically in future browser sessions, the second parameter of SetAuthCookie method makes the cookie a persistent one so it is durable between browser sessions.

You will note that the code in Listing 3-5 does not contain any exception or error handling code. This is the case for the other code samples in this book as well. For your development work, you will need to add the error and exception handling code that is appropriate for your application.

The lines following the call to SetAuthCookie redirect the user's browser to the original page requested. The following line handles the case when the user browses the Login page directly, enters a valid user ID and password, and clicks the login button:

```
Response.Redirect("ErrorPage.htm");
```

There is no page to go to after logging in, so ErrorPage.htm is displayed.

To compile the Login page, you need to add the following line to the top of the *Login.aspx.cs* file:

```
using System.Web.Security;
```

Create in your ManufacturerA project an HTML page named ErrorPage.htm that says, "You logged in without requesting a page." Alternatively, you could redirect them to your Home page. Build the project and point your browser to the Home page. You should see the Login page first.

With a User ID of anything other than "guest," the Invalid login Label control should become visible. With a User ID of "guest," the browser should be redirected to the Home page.

Point the browser to other Web pages (off this site), and then point it to the Home page again. You should see the Home page come up without the Login page. This is because of the cookie that was sent to the browser at login.

Close the browser, and run another browser instance and browse the Home page. You should see that the Login page comes up before the Home page. This is because the cookie was a temporary one and was removed when the browser was closed.

Check the Autologin next, visit checkbox, and click the Login button. You should see that you get automatically logged in now and are taken immediately to the Home page, even when you close the browser and run a new browser instance. This is because the cookie was saved by the browser and persists even when the browser is closed.

LOGGING OUT

To make it easy for users to remove the persistent cookie, you should create a logout process. Create a page named Logout.aspx. Add a Label control to the center of the page that says, "Logged out." Add a Hyperlink Web Server control to the Logout page. Be sure to use the Hyperlink control that is under the Web Forms tab, not the HTML tab, of the Visual Studio .NET Toolbox. Make the text of the hyperlink say, "Home Page," with the NavigateURL property pointing to the Home.aspx page. The Page_Load method in Logout.aspx.cs should look like Listing 3-6.

LISTING 3-6 *Logout Page_Load*

```
private void Page_Load(object sender, System.EventArgs e)
{
        FormsAuthentication.SignOut();
}
```

The FormsAuthentication.SignOut method removes the cookie from the user's browser. Add the following line to Logout.aspx.cs:

```
using System.Web.Security;
```

Add a Web Forms Hyperlink control to the Home.aspx page, and make it point to the Logout page. Build your ManufacturerA project, and then test it in your browser.

TESTING YOUR LOGIN/LOGOUT SYSTEM

When you test your login/logout system, it is important to know that your browser will cache pages in order to avoid the necessity of requesting the pages from the server each time. This browser caching could make it falsely appear that you have direct access to the Home page after you have logged out, when in fact you do not.

To ensure that page caching by the browser doesn't interfere with your testing of when the Home page is accessible from the server and when it's not, you need to change the browser settings so your browser does not used a locally cached version of the Home page.

In Internet Explorer, select the Tools, Internet Options menu. In the Temporary Internet files section of the Internet Options dialog, click the Settings button. In the Settings dialog, under Check for newer versions of stored pages, select the "Every visit to the page" radio button, and click the OK buttons to close the dialogs.

This actually forces the browser to request the page from the server each time and enables you to test when the server is actually serving up the Home page and when it only appears to because the browser is using its own local copy of the page.

As you test your logout facility, you should see that after you log out, you cannot access the Home page until you log in again. When using a temporary cookie, closing the browser has the same effect as logging out.

SUMMARY

Authentication is the first step to being able to control access to content on a Web site. ASP.NET provides a forms-based authentication mechanism that forces users to provide credentials, a user ID and password, at a Login page before seeing content on the site.

In ASP.NET, forms-based authentication is straightforward to implement. It is simply a matter of changing the authentication section of the *Web.config* file and creating a Login and a Logout page, each with a few controls and a little bit of code.

CHAPTER 4

ASP.NET Web Forms and Database Access

In Chapter 3, you implemented the forms authentication mechanism of ASP.NET. In this chapter, you will use data from a database for authenticating users and for determining what they are authorized to see.

The key points for this chapter are the following:

- A relational database can provide an ideal place to store user information for your ASP.NET applications.

- The ASP.NET HttpApplication class provides events that you as an application developer can tap into to implement sophisticated authorization logic.

- You can replace the intrinsic User object in ASP.NET with your own Person class that you can extend as needed to implement the authorization mechanism of your applications.

4.1 USING A RELATIONAL DATABASE SERVER FOR ASP.NET SECURITY

A relational database server can provide a robust store for a Web site's security and content access information. Now you will work through the code to access data from a relational database for use in the authentication and authorization mechanisms of an ASP.NET Web site.

4.1.1 PLACING DATABASE CONNECTION INFORMATION IN THE *WEB.CONFIG* FILE

You can store the list of users of your B2B applications in an ASP.NET configuration file. You will find an example in the ASP.NET documentation that demonstrates storing user IDs and passwords in an XML file.

In my humble opinion, however, it is more desirable to store the list of users in a database than in an XML file. Call me old-fashioned, but I think that the robustness a relational database server provides through transactions, concurrency control, high-volume data handling, and data integrity constraints makes a database a more industrial-strength data store.

Of course, with ADO.NET and the modern XML interfaces that are available in Microsoft SQL Server, the question of where the list of users is actually stored could be of little consequence to the developer. The code to store the list in a relational database could be nearly identical to the code in an XML file—all the more reason to store the list in a relational database server instead of in a text file on the hard disk. You still get the robustness of a database server without having to write a lot of extra code.

Instead of user IDs and passwords, it is better to put the database connection information in an XML configuration file. Placing the database connection string in the *Web.config* file makes it possible to change the database to which the application connects without having to change the source code and recompile the application.

To place the database connection information in the *Web.config* file, add the following tags near the beginning between the <configuration> and the <system.web> tags, as shown in Listing 4-1.

LISTING 4-1 *Placing Database Connection Information in the Web.config File*

```
<configuration>
   <configSections>
      <section name="dsnstore"
         type="System.Configuration.NameValueSectionHandler,
         System" />
   </configSections>
   <dsnstore>
      <add key="dbconnection" value=
         "server=localhost;uid=sa;Initial
catalog=ManufacturerA"/>
   </dsnstore>
   <system.web>
```

The XML in Listing 4-1 adds an application-specific configuration section to the *Web.config* file. The name of the section is dsnstore, the type attribute specifies a class to handle the processing of the XML in that section. Listing 4-1 uses the System.Configuration.NameValueSectionHandler class, which can process and expose name-value pair configuration information from the *Web.config* file. See the ASP.NET documentation for details.

As you can see in the dsnstore section, Listing 4-1 assumes a SQL Server user of sa. This is done only for simplicity. In a real application, you would want to create in SQL Server a user who can perform only the minimum set of tasks needed for the application and log in as that user instead of sa.

The Initial catalog=ManufacturerA is the portion of the connection string that specifies the database. You will recall that ManufacturerA is the name of the database that you created in Chapter 2.

4.1.2 LOGGING IN USING VALID USER IDS IN THE DATABASE

It is important to note here that we do not intend to use the SQL Server list of users for the Web site. Rather, we log into SQL Server as the SQL Server user *sa*, the system administrator and then query an everyday, average, run-of-the-mill user table named Persons that we created, which holds the list of users for the Web site.

You will recall from Chapter 3 that the LoginButton_Click method in Listing 3-5 had an *if* statement that simply compared the user ID with *guest*. You must change that so the list of valid users resides in a database table and is not hard coded within the LoginButton_Click source code.

Make the *if* condition in the LoginButton_Click method in the *Login.aspx.cs* file in your Visual Studio .NET ManufacturerA project call a method named UserIsValid, as shown here:

```
if (Username.Text == "guest" || UserIsValid(Username.Text,
Password.Text))
```

After adding the call to the UserIsValid method, add the UserIsValid method to the Login class in *Login.aspx.cs* in your ManufacturerA project, as shown in Listing 4-2. You can see that the first several lines are comment lines that begin with

LISTING 4-2 *UserIsValid Method in the Login Class*

```
/// <summary>
/// Determine if the credentials supplied by the user are valid.
/// Run a stored procedure to see if the specified userid and
/// password are in the Persons table the database.
/// </summary>
/// <param name="username">the user supplied username</param>
/// <param name="password">the user supplied password</param>
private bool UserIsValid(string username, string password)
{
    bool isValid = false;
    SqlParameter[] sqlParams = {
                                                        (continued)
```

```
        new SqlParameter("@userid", SqlDbType.VarChar, 20),
        new SqlParameter("@password", SqlDbType.VarChar, 50)
    };
    sqlParams[0].Value = username.Trim();
    sqlParams[1].Value = password.Trim();
    SqlHelper helper = new SqlHelper("sp_ValidateUser", sqlParams,
        CommandType.StoredProcedure);
    SqlParameter validParam = new SqlParameter("@IsValid",
        SqlDbType.Int);
    validParam.Direction = ParameterDirection.Output;
    helper.Execute(ref validParam);
    if (1 == ((int)validParam.Value)) isValid = true;
    return isValid;
}
```

triple slashes. In C#, you can document your code using XML. C# is the only .NET programming language that has this feature. For a tutorial on creating an XML file containing documentation comments, see the *XML Documentation Tutorial* in the Visual Studio .NET documentation.

The code in Listing 4-2 creates an array of SqlParameter objects, which represent parameters to a SqlCommand object. The SqlCommand object represents a stored procedure in a relational database. The code also creates an instance of a class called SqlHelper, which you will see in Listing 4-4.

LISTING 4-3   *sp_ValidateUser SQL Stored Procedure*

```
CREATE PROCEDURE sp_ValidateUser @userid VARCHAR(20), @password
VARCHAR(50), @IsValid INT OUTPUT AS
SELECT @IsValid = COUNT(*) FROM Persons WHERE userid = @userid
AND password = @password
```

The Listing 4-2 code calls a stored procedure named sp_ValidateUser, whose code is shown in Listing 4-3.

You will notice that the sp_ValidateUser stored procedure returns the COUNT(*), or the number of records in the Persons table that have the right user ID and password. Because the user ID is unique, this query will return either 1 or 0 in the output parameter. This makes it easy to use in an *if* condition in the C# source code.

Run the SQL code in Listing 4-3 to create the sp_ValidateUser stored procedure in the ManufacturerA database. To avoid replicating the C# code needed to execute stored procedures, it is worthwhile to create a C# class that handles the details of the database work for you. This is the purpose of the SqlHelper class that is instantiated in Listing 4-2.

Create a new C# class in your ManufacturerA project, and name the file SQL-Helper.cs. Insert the code shown in Listing 4-4.

LISTING 4-4 *SqlHelper Class*

```
namespace ManufacturerA.Sql.Utility
{
   using System;
   using System.Data;
   using System.Data.SqlClient;
   using System.Web;
   using System.Collections.Specialized;

   public class SqlHelper
   {
      string _executableCode = null;
      CommandType _cmdType = CommandType.Text;
      SqlParameter[] _sqlParameters = null;

      public SqlHelper(string exeCode)
      {
         _executableCode = exeCode;
      }

      public SqlHelper(string exeCode, SqlParameter[] inParams)
      {
         _executableCode = exeCode;
         _sqlParameters = inParams;
      }

      public SqlHelper(string exeCode, SqlParameter[] inParams,
         CommandType cmdType)
      {
         _executableCode = exeCode;
         _cmdType = cmdType;
         _sqlParameters = inParams;
      }

      public void Execute()
      {
         NameValueCollection nvc = (NameValueCollection)
            HttpContext.Current.GetConfig("dsnstore");
         String dsn = nvc.Get("dbconnection");
         SqlCommand myCommand = new SqlCommand();
         myCommand.Connection = new SqlConnection(dsn);
         myCommand.Connection.Open();
         try
         {
```
(continued)

```
            myCommand.CommandText = _executableCode;
            myCommand.CommandType = _cmdType;
            if (null != _sqlParameters)
            {
                for (int i=0; i<_sqlParameters.Length; i++)
                {
                    myCommand.Parameters.Add(_sqlParameters[i]);
                }
            }
            myCommand.ExecuteNonQuery();
        }
        finally
        {
            myCommand.Connection.Close();
        }
    }

    public void Execute(ref SqlParameter outParameter)
    {
        NameValueCollection nvc = (NameValueCollection)
            HttpContext.Current.GetConfig("dsnstore");
        String dsn = nvc.Get("dbconnection");
        SqlCommand myCommand = new SqlCommand();
        myCommand.Connection = new SqlConnection(dsn);
        myCommand.Connection.Open();
        try
        {
            myCommand.CommandText = _executableCode;
            myCommand.CommandType = _cmdType;
            if (null != _sqlParameters)
            {
                for (int i=0; i<_sqlParameters.Length; i++)
                {
                    myCommand.Parameters.Add(_sqlParameters[i]);
                }
            }
            myCommand.Parameters.Add(outParameter);
            myCommand.ExecuteNonQuery();
        }
        finally
        {
            myCommand.Connection.Close();
        }
    }
  }
}
```

You can see in Listing 4-4 that the SqlHelper class resides in the ManufacturerA.Sql.Utility namespace, which is a new namespace created for this class. You can also see that the SqlHelper class has three constructors and two Execute methods. The three constructors enable SqlHelper instances to be created for executing SQL statements, stored procedures, or stored procedures with parameters.

The two Execute methods run SQL UPDATE, INSERT, and DELETE statements and stored procedures either with or without an output parameter. The Execute methods call HttpContext.Current.GetConfig("dsnstore") to get a NameValueCollection to retrieve the database connection information from the *Web.config* file. The Execute methods run the SqlCommand.ExecuteNonQuery method, which does not return any rows but does return the number of rows affected and populates output parameters with data. Later in this chapter you will add an Execute statement that runs a query, either as a stored procedure or SQL SELECT statement, and returns an ADO.NET DataSet containing rows from the database.

In a sophisticated B2B application, it is often desirable for developers to delegate the database operations to business objects that are designed for that purpose. You could think of the SqlHelper class as a very simple example of this. For the B2B applications that you build, you may require business objects that are more capable and sophisticated than this SqlHelper class.

Before you can build your ManufacturerA project, you need to add the two lines shown in Listing 4-5 to the *Login.aspx.cs* file. The using directives in Listing 4-5 enable the UserIsValid method to use the SqlParameter, SqlCommand, and SqlHelper classes without having to specify their fully qualified class names.

LISTING 4-5 *Additional Namespaces in Login.aspx.cs*

```
using System.Data.SqlClient;
using ManufacturerA.Sql.Utility;
```

Build your ManufacturerA project. The code should compile without errors or warnings.

To test your code, try browsing the Home page and logging in as "guest" to make sure that still works. Then look in the Persons table in your ManufacturerA database. If you entered records into the Persons table, as specified in Chapter 2, you will have several users with passwords of 1234 whom you can log in to the site.

Try logging in as one of the users in the Persons table. If you think good thoughts, enjoy clean living, and have correct code, you will be able to log in to the site successfully.

As mentioned in Chapter 3, if there are any errors, they will be described in pretty good detail in the browser. Errors in your *Web.config* file will be rendered in the browser, as will errors in your C# code. Usually this information will be sufficient for you to track down the problem and solve it. If necessary, you can also run the Visual Studio .NET debugger to step through your C# code by setting a breakpoint in your C# code and pressing the F5 key.

After you successfully log in, I recommend that you take several minutes to savor your accomplishment and revel in your mastery of this technology.

4.1.3 SHOWING THE RIGHT INFORMATION TO THE RIGHT PEOPLE

Now that you have enabled users listed in the Persons database to log in to the Web site, you need to make sure that they see only the content that they are authorized to see.

As you will recall from Chapter 2, authorization is based on the attributes of the user. However, with the source code you have implemented so far, you have authenticated only the user. In other words, you know the user is a valid user, but you don't know any of the user's attributes, so you can't determine what content on the site he or she is authorized to access.

USING THE AUTHENTICATEREQUEST EVENT OF THE HTTPAPPLICATION CLASS
There are events that occur at the application level of your ASP.NET Web site. Some of these events fire when requests for pages are received and when those requests are authenticated and authorized.

You will recall that when you create a new ASP.NET page, a code-behind page that contains C# code is created. This C# code derives a new class from the .NET Page class. Therefore each page on your site consists of a class that is derived from the Page class. The Page class has methods that fire when certain events occur, such as Page_Load. You can add your own code to these methods to perform tasks that are necessary for your application.

In addition to classes for each page, there is a class for the overall ASP.NET application called HttpApplication. There is a page that contains the HttpApplication-derived class for your application called *Global.asax*.

The *Global.asax* file resides in the root directory of an ASP.NET application. This file is not like a normal ASP.NET page in that it is configured so that any direct URL request for it is automatically rejected. External users cannot download or view the code written within it.

Use the Visual Studio .NET Solution Explorer to open the *Global.asax* file in your ManufacturerA project. The page will be opened in Design mode, which isn't very interesting because it's an empty page. Double-click on the page in Design mode to bring up the *Global.asax.cs* file, which is much more interesting because it shows the code for the HttpApplication-derived class for your application. The *Global.asax.cs* file from my machine is shown in Listing 4-6.

LISTING 4-6 *Global.asax.cs File*

```csharp
using System;
using System.Collections;
using System.ComponentModel;
using System.Web;
using System.Web.SessionState;

namespace ManufacturerA
{
    /// <summary>
    /// Summary description for Global.
    /// </summary>
    public class Global : System.Web.HttpApplication
    {
        protected void Application_Start(Object sender,
            EventArgs e)
        {
        }
        protected void Session_Start(Object sender,
            EventArgs e)
        {
        }
        protected void Application_BeginRequest
            (Object sender, EventArgs e)
        {
        }
        protected void Application_EndRequest
            (Object sender, EventArgs e)
        {
        }
        protected void Session_End(Object sender,
            EventArgs e)
        {
        }
        protected void Application_End(Object sender,
            EventArgs e)
        {
        }
    }
}
```

In Listing 4-6, you can see the class named Global that is derived from System.Web.HttpApplication. You can also see methods that fire when certain events occur, such as Session_Start.

The HttpApplication has more events than those in Listing 4-6. See the documentation on the HttpApplication class for details of these events. The events that we are interested in are *AuthenticateRequest* and *AuthorizeRequest.* In order to find out when these events fire and in what order, add the code in Listing 4-7 to the Global class in your *Global.asax.cs* file.

LISTING 4-7 *AuthenticateRequest and AuthorizeRequest Events*

```
protected void Application_AuthenticateRequest(Object sender,
    EventArgs e)
{
    Response.Write("AuthenticateRequest<BR>");
}

protected void Application_AuthorizeRequest(Object sender,
    EventArgs e)
{
    Response.Write("AuthorizeRequest<BR>");
}
```

Build your ManufacturerA project and browse your Home page. You should see the text "AuthenticateRequest" followed by "AuthorizeRequest" at the top of each page in your browser. This illustrates the fact that before each page is rendered, the Application_AuthenticateRequest method executes and then the Application_AuthorizeRequest method executes. You can also use the Visual Studio .NET debugger to see when these methods execute. All you have to do is put a breakpoint on the closing curly bracket of each method and press F5.

The interesting thing about this event code in your HttpApplication-derived class is that the Application_AuthorizeRequest method executes for every request for any resource that comes into the site. You do not have to replicate the code that does access control and put it in every single page that you want to make secure, nor do you have to write an ISAPI DLL in C/C++ to handle the requests as they come into the server. In the HttpApplication-derived class, you have easy access to these events in your favorite .NET programming language, and the code need reside only in the *Global.asax.cs* file.

The Authentication stuff is already taken care of, so you don't need to be concerned any further with the AuthenticateRequest event. But there is some work left to do on the AuthorizeRequest event.

FINDING INFORMATION ABOUT THE CURRENT USER

Each request that comes into your application has a context that you can examine. This contextual information is encapsulated in objects that you can access through the HttpApplication object.

The HttpApplication object includes members such as the *Request* object, which is an instance of the HttpRequest class; the *Response* object, which is an instance of the HttpResponse class; and the *User* object, which implements the IPrincipal interface. Consult the documentation for additional detail about these objects.

For this application, the User object is not very helpful until after the user has been authenticated. After authentication, the User.Identity.Name property will contain the name under which the user logged in. Add some code to your Application_AuthorizeRequest method so that it looks like Listing 4-8.

LISTING 4-8   *User and Request Information in the Application_AuthorizeRequest Method*

```
protected void Application_AuthorizeRequest(Object sender,
    EventArgs e)
{
    Response.Write("AuthorizeRequest<BR>");
    if (Request.IsAuthenticated)
    {
        Response.Write(User.Identity.Name + "<BR>");
        Response.Write(Request.PhysicalPath + "<BR>");
    }
}
```

As you can see in Listing 4-8, the HttpApplication.Request object has an IsAuthenticated property that indicates whether authentication has happened yet. If the user is authenticated, the first Response.Write call paints the user's name on the browser page, and the second Response.Write call paints the physical path of the resource they are requesting.

AUTHORIZATION WITH GUSTO

Now you have everything you need to implement a robust authorization mechanism. You have the current user's login ID in the User.Identity.Name property, the resource the user is asking for in the Request.PhysicalPath property, and a place—the Application_AuthorizeRequest method—where you can put an authorization checking code to determine whether the user should gain access to whatever resource he or she is requesting.

At this point, you can implement the authorization check using the relational database, your own programming logic, or some combination of database logic and your own code.

Authorization Using a Relational Database Server   Authorizing requests for re-sources using a relational database server is a matter of calling a stored procedure that takes two parameters, the user ID, and the resource the user is requesting. This stored procedure can return yea or nay on whether that user is allowed to see that resource.

The sp_UserHasAccessToDoc stored procedure does just that. You can see the code for sp_UserHasAccessToDoc in Listing 2-8 in Chapter 2. You will use that stored procedure in Chapter 5.

Authorization Using Your Own C# Code   To perform authorization using your own programming logic, you must have more information about the user than just the login ID.

In ASP.NET, there is a User object that implements the .NET IPrincipal inter-face. You have easy access to this User object in the ASP.NET code throughout your site. However, to do any matrix-based authorization, you will need to extend the attributes of the User object beyond those defined in the IPrincipal interface.

To extend the attributes of the User object, we will create a class called Person that will be derived from IPrincipal and then will add some attributes that are needed for this application. A public attribute that we will add is the name of the company for which the user works.

To get the data needed to test this code, add a CompanyName field to the Per-sons table in the ManufacturerA database. Make the CompanyName field a VarChar of 50 characters in length. Add a FirstName field and a LastName field to the Per-sons table, too, and make them VarChar 50 as well.

Fill in the CompanyName, FirstName, and LastName fields with whatever data you think would be appropriate for each record in the Persons table. This is just test data, so it doesn't need to be fancy, but each of the records should have unique data in these fields for testing purposes.

To begin implementing the code, add another overload of the Execute method to the SqlHelper class in the *SqlHelper.cs* file. This additional Execute method is shown in Listing 4-9.

LISTING 4-9   *Additional Execute Method for the SqlHelper Class*

```
public void Execute(ref DataSet outSet)
{
   NameValueCollection nvc = (NameValueCollection)
      HttpContext.Current.GetConfig("dsnstore");
   String dsn = nvc.Get("dbconnection");
   SqlDataAdapter myCommand = new SqlDataAdapter();
   myCommand.SelectCommand = new SqlCommand();
```
(continued)

```
myCommand.SelectCommand.Connection = new SqlConnection(dsn);
myCommand.SelectCommand.Connection.Open();
try
{
    myCommand.SelectCommand.CommandText = _executableCode;
    myCommand.SelectCommand.CommandType = _cmdType;
    if (null != _sqlParameters)
    {
        for (int i=0; i<_sqlParameters.Length; i++)
        {
            myCommand.SelectCommand.Parameters.
                Add(_sqlParameters[i]);
        }
    }
    myCommand.Fill(outSet);
}
finally
{
    myCommand.SelectCommand.Connection.Close();
}
}
```

The Execute method in Listing 4-9 returns an ADO.NET DataSet object in an output parameter. This Execute method is called by the code in Listing 4-10.

Create a new C# class in your ManufacturerA project, and name the file *Person.cs*. Then insert the Person class code, which is shown in Listing 4-10.

LISTING 4-10 *Person Class*

```
using System;
using System.Collections;
using System.Data;
using System.Data.SqlClient;
using System.Security.Principal;
using System.Text;
using System.Web;
using ManufacturerA.Sql.Utility;
using ManufacturerA.Security;

namespace ManufacturerA.BusinessObject
{
    /// <summary>
    /// Class that represents a person in our system.
```

(continued)

```
/// It implements IPrincipal so it can be used as
/// the User object in the http context object,
/// which we extend for our application
/// </summary>
public class Person : IPrincipal
{
    /// <summary>
    /// The company that the person works for.
    /// </summary>
    private string _company;
    public string Company {
        get { return _company; }
    }
    /// <summary>
    /// The data from the database that represents this person.
    /// </summary>
    private DataRow _personData = null;

    /// <summary>
    /// Default constructor is private to hide it from the
    /// outside world.
    /// </summary>
    private Person()
    {
    }

    /// <summary>
    /// Constructor for the person object.  It just keeps
    /// a reference to the passed in IIdentity object and
    /// then gets information about the user from the
    /// database. The HttpContext.User property is replaced
    /// with a Person object on each (authenticated) page hit.
    /// The Person object is cached in the global cache after
    /// it is first created so it doesn't need to be recreated
    /// on each page hit.
    /// </summary>
    /// <param name="identity">the identity of the person</param>
    public Person(IIdentity identity)
    {
        _identity = identity;
        GetPersonData();
        GetCompanyData();
    }
```

(continued)

```
/// <summary>
/// Expose the identity of the person as a property for
/// the IPrincipal interface.
/// </summary>
private IIdentity _identity;
public IIdentity Identity {
   get { return _identity; }
}

/// <summary>
/// Return this person's full name (firstName + lastName).
/// </summary>
public string FullName {
   get {
      if (null != _personData) {
         return _personData["FirstName"] + " "
            + _personData["LastName"];
      } else if (null != Identity) {
         return Identity.Name;
      }
      return "Anonymous";
   }
}

/// <summary>
/// Query the database for the user info for this person.
/// For now we just store the DataRow that we query out.
/// </summary>
protected void GetPersonData()
{
   DataSet ds = new DataSet();
   SqlParameter[] sqlParams
      = { new SqlParameter("@userid",
      SqlDbType.VarChar, 20) };
   sqlParams[0].Value = Identity.Name;
   SqlHelper helper = new
      SqlHelper("sp_GetPersonInfo", sqlParams,
      CommandType.StoredProcedure);
   helper.Execute(ref ds);

   DataTable table = ds.Tables[0];
   if (table.Rows.Count >= 1) _personData = table.Rows[0];
}
```

(continued)

```
/// <summary>
/// Query the database for the Company of this Person.
/// Store the Company name in the _company field.
/// </summary>
protected void GetCompanyData()
{
    DataSet ds = new DataSet();
    string selstr =
        "select CompanyName from Persons where UserID = '"
        + Identity.Name + "'";
    SqlHelper helper = new SqlHelper(selstr);
    helper.Execute(ref ds);
    DataTable table = ds.Tables[0];
    if (table.Rows.Count >= 1) _company =
        table.Rows[0]["CompanyName"].ToString().Trim();
}


/// <summary>
/// We don't use role-based security, so return false.
/// </summary>
/// <param name="role">role we are checking for</param>
public bool IsInRole(string role)
{
    return false;
}
    }
}
```

The comments for the Person class are embedded in the source code. The idea is that we've created this Person object that gets its data from the database. The Person class exposes properties that we can access, and the class can be extended to provide any properties or methods that might be needed for your applications.

In previous chapters, I explained the concept of a *security context* for each user who visits a B2B Web site. This Person class is where you put the data you need to manage the security context for each user.

The GetPersonData method uses the new Execute method in the SqlHelper class and calls a stored procedure named sp_GetPersonInfo. The code for sp_GetPerson-Info is shown in Listing 4-11.

LISTING 4-11 *sp_GetPersonInfo SQL Stored Procedure*

```
CREATE PROCEDURE sp_GetPersonInfo @userid VARCHAR(20) AS
SELECT * FROM persons WHERE UserID = @userid
```

You can see that Listing 4-11 uses a *SELECT* * statement. In real applications, you should not use SELECT * but instead should specify the list of fields for robustness sake.

Now that you have your own Person object, you need to replace the intrinsic ASP.NET User object with this Person object of yours. The code to that is shown in Listing 4-12. Create a new C# class in your ManufacturerA project, and name the file *SecurityModule.cs.* Put in the code in Listing 4-12.

LISTING 4-12 *SecurityModule Class That Replaces the User Object with Our Person Object*

```
using System;
using System.Web;
using ManufacturerA.BusinessObject;

namespace ManufacturerA.Security
{
    /// <summary>
    /// Class that implements IHttpModule.  This class is
    /// specified in web.config so it gets called on each
    /// http hit.
    /// Its purpose is to replace the User object in each
    /// HttpContext with a Person object. Person is our
    /// class that implements IPrincipal and enables us to
    /// add our own attributes, beyond those in the User
    /// object.
    /// </summary>
    public class SecurityModule : IHttpModule
    {
        /// <summary>
        /// The name of this IHttpModule.
        /// </summary>
        public String ModuleName {
            get { return "SecurityModule"; }
        }

        /// <summary>
        /// Initialize this module.  Add event handlers for
```

(continued)

```
/// authentication and ending the request.
/// </summary>
/// <param name="app">current application object</param>
public void Init(HttpApplication app)
{
   app.EndRequest += new EventHandler(this.OnLeave);
   app.AuthenticateRequest +=
      new EventHandler(this.OnEnter);
}

/// <summary>
/// Handle cleanup of this object.
/// Nothing to do at the moment.
/// </summary>
public void Dispose()
{
}

/// <summary>
/// Handle the authenticate request.  If the user has
/// already been authenticated, then we can replace the
/// User object in the current context with a Person
/// object that represents the authenticated user.
/// </summary>
/// <param name="source">originator of the event</param>
/// <param name="eventArgs">event data</param>
public void OnEnter(Object source, EventArgs eventArgs)
{
   // Get the current HTTP context
   HttpApplication app = (HttpApplication)source;
   HttpContext context = app.Context;

   // If we've been authenticated, then replace the
   // context User object with a Person instance.
   // If not, then there is nothing to do.
   if (context.Request.IsAuthenticated) {
      // First check to see if we've cached a Person
      // object for this user. If so, we can just use
      // it; otherwise we have to create a
      // new one (and cache it for later use).
      Person p = (Person)context.
         Cache[context.User.Identity.Name];
      if (null == p) {
         context.User = new                      (continued)
```

```
                    Person(context.User.Identity);
                context.Cache[context.User.Identity.Name] =
                    context.User;
            } else {
                context.User = p;
            }
        }
    }

    /// <summary>
    /// Handle the end request event.
    /// Don't do anything for now.
    /// </summary>
    /// <param name="source">originator of the event</param>
    /// <param name="eventArgs">event data</param>
    public void OnLeave(Object source, EventArgs eventArgs)
    {
    }
    }
}
```

The Init method in the SecurityModule class makes its OnEnter method an event handler for the HttpApplication's AuthenticateRequest event. This causes the SecurityModule.OnEnter method to fire before the HttpApplication.AuthenticateRequest method does. The OnEnter method assigns the Person object to the User property of the HttpApplication's HttpContext object. When the HttpApplication .AuthenticateRequest method fires a few nanoseconds later, the HttpApplication object has a Person object where its User object used to be.

You need to make another addition to the *Web.config* file to make this Security-Module work. Create an httpModules section *Web.config* file, and specify your SecurityModule in the add subtag, as shown in Listing 4-13.

To test your code, make your Application_AuthorizeRequest method look like the code in Listing 4-14.

LISTING 4-13 *Additions to Web.config for the SecurityModule Class*

```
<httpModules>
   <add
       type="ManufacturerA.Security.SecurityModule, ManufacturerA"
       name=" ManufacturerA " />
</httpModules>
```

LISTING 4-14   *Additions to Application_AuthorizeRequest to test the Person Class*

```
protected void Application_AuthorizeRequest(Object sender,
EventArgs e)
{
   Response.Write("AuthorizeRequest<BR>");
   if (Request.IsAuthenticated)
   {
      Response.Write(User.Identity.Name + "<BR>");
      Response.Write(Request.PhysicalPath + "<BR>");
      Response.Write(
         ((ManufacturerA.BusinessObject.Person)User).Company
         + "<BR>");
      Response.Write(
         ((ManufacturerA.BusinessObject.Person)User).FullName
         + "<BR>");
   }
}
```

To test this, browse a page or two on your ManufacturerA site. At the top of each page, the Person's company name and full name should be rendered.

The significance of all this is that you can now access the attributes of your own Person object wherever the ASP.NET User object used to be. The Person object gets its data from the database, which is easy to extend, and gets its functionality from your own C# source code, of which you are now a prolific writer.

As you consider ways to extend your Person class, you might consider adding attributes to your Person class, such as those shown in Listing 4-15.

LISTING 4-15   *Additional Attributes That Might Be Useful in the Person Class*

```
/// <summary>
/// A hashtable of the roles this person has.  The key is the ///
/// name
/// of the role.  The value is the bitmask offset of the role in
/// case we eventually want to use bitmasked role checking for
/// speed.
/// </summary>
private CaseInsensitiveHashtable _roles = null;
/// <summary>
/// Return the roles that this person is in.  The returned value
/// is a collection of names (strings) that specify the roles.
/// </summary>
```

(continued)

```
public ICollection Roles {
    get { return (null != _roles)? _roles.Keys : null; }
}

/// <summary>
/// A list of the specific permissions that the user has.
/// </summary>
private ArrayList _permissions = null;
/// <summary>
/// Accessor for the permission list for this person.
/// </summary>
public ICollection Permissions {
    get { return _permissions; }
}
```

Inside the Application_AuthorizeRequest, you can write whatever logic you need to determine whether current users are authorized to access the resources they are requesting. If they are authorized to access a given resource, your code need do nothing more. If they are not, then you can use the HttpApplication's Response object to redirect their browser to an error page of some sort, as shown here:

```
Response.Redirect("PageNotFound.htm");
```

In any of the Web Form pages on your site, you can access your Person object with code that is identical to the code shown in Listing 4-14. As an experiment, try adding the Response.Write calls that are inside the Application_AuthorizeRequest to the Page_Load method of your Home page. You should see that you can access your Person object with your Page code as well as your HttpApplication code. After you are done experimenting, comment out the Response.Write calls in your Home page and in your *Global.asax.cs* file.

If you are displaying data that is queried from a company's internal information systems in the pages of its B2B Web site, you can use the attributes of your Person object to ensure that the data the Web site is displaying is for the right company, the right role, and the right person.

SUMMARY

A relational database provides an ideal place to store user authentication and authorization information for your ASP.NET applications. The ASP.NET HttpApplication class provides events such as AuthorizeRequest that you can tap into to implement sophisticated authorization logic.

You can replace the intrinsic User object in ASP.NET with your own Person class that you can extend as needed to implement the authorization mechanism of your applications. The Person object can be extended with attributes that are simple data types or collections and with methods that contain complex logic for your applications.

ASP.NET and Database-Driven Content Access Control

Content and collaboration on a B2B Web site usually involves documents. Much of the content on a B2B site is in the form of documents, and users collaborate with each other by reading, changing, and posting documents.

The key points for this chapter are the following:

- Documents constitute the unstructured data of a Web site.

- The ability to provide selected users with secure access to documents is a fundamental requirement of a B2B Web site.

- The security mechanism for documents can be implemented in .NET using a C# class that accepts requests for documents and performs the content access control.

- In addition to reading documents, users also need to be able to upload them to the server. The processing and storage of these uploaded documents can be implemented in at least three different ways, depending on the requirements of the application.

5.1 DOCUMENTS

Most B2B Web sites publish some combination of structured information and unstructured information. The structured information comes primarily from databases and information systems. It usually consists of data that is queried from databases and then rendered in HTML tables on Web pages. The unstructured information on a

B2B Web site comes primarily in the form of documents that are stored and published on the site. These documents are typically stored as files on the Web server. On the site there are usually Web pages that contain hyperlinks that point to these documents. When a user browses one of these Web pages and clicks on one of these hyperlinks, the document is sent to and displayed in the browser.

It is important to understand that there is a clear distinction between a *document* and a *page*. Documents are files. The documents could be text files, graphics files, HTML files, PDF files, or application files such as Word doc files or Excel spreadsheet files. Documents are typically created by people other than the developers of the site.

Pages, on the other hand, are ASP.NET aspx Web pages. Pages are ASPX files with their associated code-behind page. Pages are not data on the site but are part of the site itself. Pages are incorporated into the site's navigation system and information architecture, while documents are not. Pages are created by the developers of the site.

So whenever you read the word *page*, think ASPX file that is part of the site and was created in Visual Studio.NET. Whenever you read the word *document*, think text file, graphics file, PDF file, HTML file, or application file that is data on the site and was created by someone other than a developer of the site.

5.1.1 SECURITY FOR PUBLISHING DOCUMENTS

Not everyone who visits a B2B Web site will be allowed to see the documents published there. Some documents will contain sensitive information, such as exclusive prices or advanced product information. A document might be a contract that must be kept confidential, or it might contain information that would violate someone's privacy if the documents were exposed to the wrong people.

You will recall that in the ManufacturerA database in Chapter 2, each user in the Persons database has access to only certain documents. Run the query shown in Listing 5-1 against the ManufacturerA database to find out which documents are accessible for the site administrator, SamSiteAdmin.

LISTING 5-1 *Documents Accessible to the Site Administrator, SamSiteAdmin*

```
SELECT DISTINCT pldocument.documentid from pldocument, plperson
WHERE pldocument.permissionlistID = plperson.permissionlistID
AND plperson.personID = 'SamSiteAdmin'
```

Based on the data from Chapter 2, SamSiteAdmin is authorized to see several documents. If you run this query for other users in the Persons table, you will see what documents they are authorized to access.

In this chapter you will create an ASP.NET page that contains hyperlinks to some of the documents on the site. When a user brings up the page in his or her browser and clicks on one of the hyperlinks, the system will verify whether the user is authorized to access that particular document. If the user is authorized to access the document, the contents of the document will be displayed in the user's browser. If the user is not authorized to access that document, he or she will receive a "Page Not Found" message in his or her browser.

5.1.2 BUILDING AN ASP.NET PAGE THAT CONTAINS HYPERLINKS TO DOCUMENTS

To enable users to access documents on a Web site, it is usually necessary to create a Web page or two that contain hyperlinks to the documents. Before doing this, however, you must create the document files for testing, and you will need to populate the ManufacturerA database with some test data.

The first thing to do is create a directory on the hard disk to hold the document files. Create a new directory under the "Inetpub\wwwroot\ManufacturerA" directory, and name it "Corpus." (According to the *Random House College Dictionary,* a *corpus* is a large or complete collection of writings, so the name is appropriate for a collection of documents.) Then in the "Corpus" directory, create a few text files that correspond to the documents listed in the Documents table in your ManufacturerA database. At the very least, you should create three text files named *AdminPolicy.txt, ContentCodes.txt,* and *EastRegionProdInfo.txt,* which correspond with records in the Documents table as shown in Chapter 2. Make each of these files contain its file name and whatever random text you want to place in the files.

Next, you will need to add some data to the ManufacturerA database so the server can send these files to the browsers of authorized users who request them. In the Documents table in the ManufacturerA database, fill in the Name, MimeType, and FilePath fields. You can make the contents of the Name field identical to the contents of the DocID field, or you can use something fancier if you like. Fill in the MimeType field of each record in the Documents table with *text/plain.* In the FilePath field, specify the full pathname to the file. For example, on my machine, the full pathname to the AdminPolicy.txt file I created is

```
D:\Inetpub\wwwroot\ManufacturerA\Corpus\AdminPolicy.txt.
```

Fill in the FilePath field for every document for which you have created a file.

After you have created the document files and have filled in the data in the database so that the app can serve up those files, it is time to build the ASP.NET page that provides access to those documents.

In your ManufacturerA project in Visual Studio.NET, create a new ASP.NET page and call it something poetic, such as "ListOfDocuments.aspx." At the top center of the page place a Label control that says "Available Documents." Place three Hyperlink Web Server controls on the page. Make the Text properties of each of these hyperlinks correspond to the Name or DocID of a document in the Documents table in the database. In other words, each hyperlink should say the name of the document to which it points. On my ListOfDocuments page, I created a hyperlink whose text is AdminPolicy, another whose text is ContentCodes, and a third whose text is EastRegionProdInfo.

Copy the Logout hyperlink control from the Home.aspx page, and paste it onto the ListOfDocuments page. This enables users easily to logout from the ListOfDocuments page. You might want to place on the Home page a hyperlink that points to the ListOfDocuments page to enable easy navigation between the pages.

TEST YOUR LISTOFDOCUMENTS PAGE

There is an easy way for you to test the work you have done so far. On each hyperlink control on the ListOfDocuments page, there is a NavigateURL property that indicates the page or document to which the hyperlink points. To test your work so far, specify the full path name of each document as the NavigateURL property for each hyperlink control. You can simply copy the contents of the FilePath field from the appropriate records in the Documents table and paste it into the Property window of each hyperlink control in Visual Studio.NET.

Do a build in Visual Studio.NET, and then view the ListOfDocuments.aspx page in your browser. When you click on each hyperlink, the contents of the file should be displayed in the browser.

THE ASP.NET TRACE FACILITY

As you know, if there are problems with your code at runtime, the errors will be described in your browser. You can also use the debugger to track down any hard-to-find problems. In addition, ASP.NET has Trace functionality.

In the *Web.config* file of your ManufacturerA project, you will find the trace tag. Set the enabled attribute to true and save the *Web.config* file. Browse a few pages on the ManufacturerA site, and then browse the following URL:

```
http://localhost/manufacturera/Trace.axd
```

This page will show a summary of the requests that came into the application after tracing was enabled. You can click on the View Details link for each request to see a plethora of tracing information on each request. Incidentally, if you set the pageOutput attribute of the trace tag in the *Web.config* file to true, this detailed tracing information will be rendered on every page on the site. Tracing information plastered onto every page is not usually what you would want, but it might be helpful in certain circumstances.

With tracing enabled and pageOutput disabled, add the following line to the Page_Load method of your ListOfDocuments page and build your ManufacturerA project:

```
Trace.Write("MyPageLoadCategory","My trace message");
```

Hit your ListOfDocuments page again in your browser, and then look at the Trace.axd page. When you view the details of your latest request for the ListOfDocuments page, you should see your trace message listed under the "Trace Information" heading.

You do not need to remove trace statements from your code prior to your site going live. In an ASP.NET site, tracing is disabled by default. Even though trace statements exist in the code, tracing must be enabled on the site before trace statements or the trace stack will be displayed by a requesting browser.

5.1.3 Authorization for Documents

Now it is time to add the content access code to make sure that the user is authorized to see each document. As you know, each hyperlink on the ListOfDocuments.aspx page points directly to the document file, and the file is sent to the browser when the user clicks on the hyperlink. Instead of pointing at each file directly, if each hyperlink pointed to a particular ASP.NET page, code on that page could perform the security check that ensures that the user is authorized to access the requested document. Next, you will write the code to implement this approach.

Creating Your Own C# Class

To implement document security, you can use the HttpApplication.AuthorizeRequest event to authorize all requests, document requests, and requests for aspx pages. You could also use the HttpApplication.AuthorizeRequest event to authorize requests for aspx pages and then create a special aspx page that authorizes the requests for documents.

You learned how to use the HttpApplication.AuthorizeRequest event in Chapter 4. Now you will see how to create a special aspx page to authorize requests for documents. You can do it either way, so it is a matter of prototyping the software for your own application and then deciding which approach works best for your particular application.

To create an aspx page that authorizes requests for documents, in your ManufacturerA project create a new C# class named DocumentHandler in a file named DocumentHandler.cs, and insert the code in Listing 5-2.

LISTING 5-2 *DocumentHandler Class*

```
using System;
using System.Data;
using System.Data.SqlClient;
using System.Web;
using System.Web.Security;
using ManufacturerA.Sql.Utility;
```
(continued)

```
namespace ManufacturerA
{
    /// <summary>
    /// DocumentHandler is a class that implements the
    /// IHttpHandler interface. It constitutes the page
    /// that document requests can be funneled through
    /// to check whether a given user is authorized to
    /// access a given document.
    /// </summary>
    public class DocumentHandler : IHttpHandler
    {
        public DocumentHandler()
        {
        }

        /// <summary>
        /// Implementation of the IHttpHandler interface method
        /// that tells ASP.NET whether we can reuse
        /// instances of this class.  In this case we can,
        /// so we return true.
        /// </summary>
        public bool IsReusable
        {
            get { return true; }
        }

        /// <summary>
        /// Implementation of the IHttpHandler method to process
        /// the http request. The query string contains the id of
        /// the document we want to serve up.  If the current user
        /// has access to that document, then we set some http
        /// headers and serve up the file.
        /// </summary>
        /// <param name="context">the current http context</param>
        public void ProcessRequest(HttpContext context)
        {
            string docid = context.Request.QueryString["doc"];
            if (UserHasAccessToDoc(docid, context))
            {
                DataRow docRow = GetDocumentRow(docid);
                string fileName =
                ((string)docRow["filePath"]).Trim();
                context.Response.ClearHeaders();
                context.Response.ContentType =            (continued)
```

```
                     ((string)docRow["MimeType"]).Trim();
          context.Response.WriteFile(fileName, false);
       }
       else
       {
          context.Response.Redirect("FileNotFound.htm");
       }
    }


    /// <summary>
    /// Return the DataRow that represents the document
    /// with the specified ID.
    /// </summary>
    DataRow GetDocumentRow(string docid)
    {
       DataSet ds = new DataSet();
       SqlParameter[] sqlParams =
       { new SqlParameter("@id", SqlDbType.VarChar) };
       sqlParams[0].Value = docid;
       SqlHelper helper = new SqlHelper("sp_GetDocByID",
          sqlParams, CommandType.StoredProcedure);
       helper.Execute(ref ds);
       return ds.Tables[0].Rows[0];
    }


    /// <summary>
    /// Document security check.  Return true if the current
    /// users have access to the specified document.  Return
    /// false if they don't.
    /// </summary>
    /// <param name="Doc">Doc to check access for</param>
    /// <param name="context">the HttpContext object</param>
    private bool UserHasAccessToDoc(string Doc,
       HttpContext context)
    {
       bool HasAccess = false;
       if (context.Request.IsAuthenticated)
       {
          SqlParameter[] sqlParams = {
             new SqlParameter("@userid", SqlDbType.VarChar,
             20),
             new SqlParameter("@docid", SqlDbType.VarChar, 20)
          };
```

(continued)

```
                sqlParams[0].Value = context.User.Identity.Name;
                sqlParams[1].Value = Doc;
                SqlHelper helper =
                    new SqlHelper("sp_UserHasAccessToDoc", sqlParams,
                    CommandType.StoredProcedure);
                SqlParameter validParam =
                    new SqlParameter("@HasAccess", SqlDbType.Int);
                validParam.Direction = ParameterDirection.Output;
                helper.Execute(ref validParam);
                if (1 == ((int)validParam.Value)) HasAccess = true;
            }
        return HasAccess;
        }
    }
}
```

What is happening here is that the DocumentHandler class acts like a Web page. The ProcessRequest method processes the http request and sends the requested file to the browser using the HttpContext.Response.WriteFile method, provided that users are authorized to see the document they are requesting.

You will probably notice that there is no DocumentHandler.aspx page, just the DocumentHandler C# class in a *DocumentHandler.cs* file. Because the Document-Handler C# class implements the IHttpHandler interface, the class can handle http requests as if it were an aspx page. However, you have to indicate this in the *Web.config* file. Add the XML shown in Listing 5-3 to the *Web.config* file inside the <httpHandlers> tags.

LISTING 5-3 *Web.config httpHandler Subtag for the DocumentHandler Class*

```
<add verb="*" path="DocumentHandler.aspx"
    type="ManufacturerA.DocumentHandler, ManufacturerA" />
```

The UserHasAccessToDoc method takes the document ID and the HttpContext object as parameters. It uses the HttpContext object to get at the User object to obtain this user's name. It then runs the sp_UserHasAccessToDoc stored procedure to determine whether this user is authorized to see this document. You can see the code for sp_UserHasAccessToDoc in Listing 2-8 in Chapter 2.

A technique that might be useful here to improve performance is caching the security information in the User object at login time. For example, you might cache the list of documents that the user is authorized to access as a RAM-based collection that is an attribute of the User object. Then, instead of running the sp_UserHas-AccessToDoc stored procedure everytime anyone tries to access a document, you could avoid that round trip to the database by looking up the information in the collection in the User object. Reading from local memory is usually much faster than running a stored procedure, so this could be a nice optimization for a busy application.

Unfortunately, this type of caching has a downside. If the permissions for a document or for a user are modified, those modifications will not immediately take effect on users who are currently logged in. The list of documents a user is authorized to access is calculated and cached at login time; it is recalculated only when that user logs out and then logs in again. Caching makes the system a little less real-time. However, this problem is typically not too egregious, and the benefits of caching typically outweigh the loss of real-time responsiveness to modifications of settings for the currently logged in users.

You can see that the GetDocumentRow method calls a stored procedure named sp_GetDocByID. Execute the SQL code that is shown in Listing 5-4 in the ManufacturerA database to create the sp_GetDocByID stored procedure.

LISTING 5-4 *sp_GetDocByID Stored Procedure*

```
CREATE PROCEDURE sp_GetDocByID @id VARCHAR(20) AS
SELECT * FROM documents WHERE DocID = @id
```

After you write the C# code and execute the SQL code to create the stored procedure, build your ManufacturerA project in Visual Studio.NET. It should build without errors or warnings.

On each hyperlink control on the ListOfDocuments page, change the NavigateURL property so that it points to DocumentHandler.aspx. Include a query string variable named *doc* that has a value of the DocID for the document to which the hyperlink points. For example, on my ListOfDocuments page, the hyperlink that points to my AdminPolicy document has a NavigateURL property that looks like the following:

```
DocumentHandler.aspx?doc=AdminPolicy
```

Build your ManufacturerA project in Visual Studio.NET. After successfully building the code in Visual Studio.NET and saving the Web.config file, you should be able to browse the ListOfDocuments page and view the documents that the user under whose name you logged in can access.

You will notice that if you log in as SamSiteAdmin, you are able to access all three of the documents that I suggested using: AdminPolicy, ContentCodes, and EastRegionProdInfo. If you log in as EdTRExecutive, you will see that you have access only to EastRegionProdInfo. When you click on the hyperlinks for Admin-Policy and ContentCodes, you get a Page Not Found, HTTP 404 message. This 404 message actually applies to the *FileNotFound.htm* file, which we have not created yet, but that's probably okay for the prototyping that we are doing here.

5.1.4 PREVENTING SECURITY BYPASS

One security breach still possible at this point is that any user who figures out the URL for a document in the corpus can browse it without the authorization check being activated. For example, the following URL could enable a user to browse the *adminpolicy.txt* file without authorization:

```
http://localhost/manufacturera/corpus/adminpolicy.txt
```

Test this by trying this URL in your browser. You should be able to bring up your documents from the Corpus directory in your browser, whether or not you are logged in as a valid user on the ManufacturerA site.

To solve this problem, you can instruct IIS to disallow the Read, Write, and Directory access in the Corpus directory. To do this, run the Control Panel and Administrative Tools applet and double-click the Internet Services Manager. (On my machine, I located the Corpus directory in the Internet Services Manager under the ManufacturerA Web site, which is under the Default Web Site.) You should bring up Corpus directory's properties and uncheck Read, Write, and Directory browsing, and click the OK button.

After disallowing Read, Write, and Directory access in the Corpus directory, you should no longer be able to bring up the files in your browser by using a URL that bypasses the DocumentHandler page. However, you should be able to access the documents using URLs that use the DocumentHandler page on the ManufacturerA Web site, such as this URL:

```
http://localhost/manufacturera/DocumentHandler.aspx?doc=
AdminPolicy
```

When using a URL that requests the DocumentHandler page, the user is forced to log in to the site, and requests for documents are properly authenticated and authorized.

There is, however, one thing about the ListOfDocuments page that is somewhat inelegant: When users click on a hyperlink to a document that they are not authorized to see, they get a rather ugly "file not found" message.

For some highly sensitive applications, if users don't have access to a document, they shouldn't even be told of the document's existence. In some applications, letting users know that certain documents exist could be considered a security breach.

Ideally, if users are not authorized to view a document, they should not be presented with a hyperlink to that document. In the ListOfDocuments page, the document hyperlinks are hard-coded into the page, regardless of whether the current user is authorized to see those documents.

5.1.5 SHOWING CONFIDENTIAL HYPERLINKS

Now you will create a page that shows hyperlinks only to those documents a user is allowed to see. On this new page, if a user isn't authorized to see a given document, he or she will not see a hyperlink either.

You will recall that Listing 5-1 contains a SQL query that returns the IDs of the documents that a given user is allowed to see. It is fairly straightforward to extend that query to return the document name and its URI for those documents that a given user is allowed to see. The document name could then be used as the Text property of a hyperlink control, and the URI could be used as the NavigateURL property. Then it is possible to create a page that shows hyperlinks only to documents that a user is allowed to see.

As is frequently the case in building these pages, the first thing you need is some test data. Add a column named "URI" to the Documents table in your ManufacturerA database. On each document record for which you have created files, fill in the URI field with the values that you used for the NavigateURL property of the hyperlink controls on your ListOfDocuments page. For example, the URI field of my AdminPolicy document contains the following string:

```
DocumentHandler.aspx?doc=AdminPolicy
```

In your ManufacturerA database, create a stored procedure named sp_DocsICanSee, as shown in Listing 5-5.

LISTING 5-5 *sp_DocsICanSee Stored Procedure*

```
CREATE PROCEDURE sp_DocsICanSee @userid VARCHAR(20) AS
SELECT DISTINCT documents.name, documents.uri
FROM documents, pldocument, plperson
WHERE documents.docid = pldocument.documentid
AND pldocument.permissionlistID = plperson.permissionlistID
AND plperson.personID = @userid
```

Test your sp_DocsICanSee stored procedure using the SQL Server Query Analyzer, or your favorite query tool, against the data you have entered into your ManufacturerA database. Make sure that you can get some document names and meaningful URIs out of the query. Some of the document records will not have URIs, which is okay as long as some of the records do.

Create a new aspx page named DocsICanSee.aspx, and on it place a Repeater control, which you will find in the Toolbox under the Web Forms tab. With the Repeater control, explicitly declare all HTML layout, formatting, and style tags within the control's templates. To do this, you have to dive into some HTML.

Switch from Design mode to HTML mode in the DocsICanSee.aspx page. Add the HTML code between the asp:Repeater tags, as shown in Listing 5-6.

LISTING 5-6   *HTML View of DocsICanSee.aspx*

```
<asp:Repeater id="Repeater1" runat="server">
   <HeaderTemplate>
      <h3><font face="Verdana">Documents I Can See</font></h3>
      <table border="1">
   </HeaderTemplate>
   <ItemTemplate>
      <tr>
      <td>
         <asp:HyperLink runat="server"
            Text='<%#
            DataBinder.Eval(Container.DataItem, "Name") %>'
            NavigateUrl='<%#
            DataBinder.Eval(Container.DataItem, "URI") %>'
            ID="Hyperlink1">
         </asp:HyperLink>
      </td>
      </tr>
   </ItemTemplate>
   <FooterTemplate>
      </table>
   </FooterTemplate>
</asp:Repeater>
```

This way the HTML code inside the HeaderTemplate tags gets rendered once, as does the HTML inside the FooterTemplate tags. We will feed the Repeater control a DataSet, and the HTML code inside the ItemTemplate tags will render once for each row in the DataSet. That means we will get one hyperlink control for each record in the DataSet. The Repeater control will fill in the hyperlink's Text property with the contents of the Name field from the DataSet. It will fill in the hyperlink's NavigateUrl property with the contents of the URI field from the DataSet.

Save the DocsICanSee page, and then bring up the *DocsICanSee.aspx.cs* file. Note the line in the file that declares the Repeater control:

```
protected System.Web.UI.WebControls.Repeater Repeater1;
```

Make the Page_Load method look like the code in Listing 5-7.

LISTING 5-7   *Page_Load Method in DocsICanSee Class*

```
private void Page_Load(object sender, System.EventArgs e)
{
   DataSet ds = new DataSet();
   SqlParameter[] sqlParams =
   { new SqlParameter("@userid", SqlDbType.VarChar) };
   sqlParams[0].Value = User.Identity.Name;
   SqlHelper helper = new SqlHelper("sp_DocsICanSee",
      sqlParams, CommandType.StoredProcedure);
   helper.Execute(ref ds);
   Repeater1.DataSource = ds;
   Repeater1.DataBind();
}
```

You can see that the SqlHelper class executes the sp_DocsICanSee stored procedure to return a DataSet of document names and URIs that the current user is authorized to see. That DataSet gets set as the DataSource of the Repeater control.

Add the lines shown in Listing 5-8 to the top of the *DocsICanSee.aspx.cs* file.

LISTING 5-8   *Page_Load Method in DocsICanSee Class*

```
using System.Data.SqlClient;
using ManufacturerA.Sql.Utility;
```

Finally, copy logout hyperlink control from your Home page, and paste it onto the DocsICanSee page. This will make it easier for you to test your page with different users. Build the page and give it a browse.

When you browse the page, if you are logged in as a user who can see lots of documents, like SamSiteAdmin, you will see an HTML table that contains hyperlinks. Those hyperlinks for which there is no file (where the URI field is blank) are not activated. Those hyperlinks that are activated should take you to their document when you click on them.

Storing the URIs in the database might be problematic in cases where more than one Web application needs to use the documents table. To add more flexibility to this scheme, you could build URIs/links on the fly in the ASP.NET code, based on the document name or ID. This would put the onus on each Web application to resolve the location of the files and would make the document table more universally accessible. Once you get this working, you will have reached another milestone in your conquest of .NET and B2B development.

5.1.6   UPLOADING DOCUMENTS

So far, you have written code to handle content access control for the reading of doc-uments. However, many B2B applications require collaboration features. Collabora-tion means that users not only log in to the site and see documents that are for their eyes only, but they also upload documents to the site for other users to see. These uploaded documents might go through an approval process where a content manager reviews the document before it is exposed to other users on the site. And certainly these documents would need to have permissions assigned to them so only the right users could view them.

The code to upload documents to the server is straightforward, and you can search the ASP.NET documentation and the .NET SDK samples for *HtmlInputFile* to locate code samples that illustrate how to do it.

The tricky part for the developer is not writing the code that uploads the file from a browser but figuring out where to store the file and how to process it, which must be based on the requirements of each application. Often, the processing of doc-uments involves some definition and execution of workflows.

I wish I could give you a code sample that covers 80 percent of the cases for storing and processing uploaded documents, as I did with the permission list-based security system. However, my advice on handling uploaded documents cannot be that clear-cut. The best I can do is paint with a broad brush to illustrate what choices you have for your own implementations.

SAVING FILES IN THE CORPUS

Your first alternative is to store the uploaded documents in the Corpus directory. This is probably the most straightforward option from a coding standpoint. How-ever, this option has some limitations that make it somewhat inelegant for certain applications.

On the upside, as I said, this option is easy to code. To save the file in the Corpus, you just call the SaveAs method of the HtmlInputFile class. You can use the Indexing Service to index the contents of the documents to provide a full-text search capability, which would no doubt be a popular feature. SQL Server even offers extended SQL syntax for performing file system searches in conjunction with searches inside the database, so there is potential here for some powerful implementations.

On the downside, you end up with files in the Corpus directory that are refer-enced by records in the Documents table in the database. For each file in the Corpus directory, you will want a corresponding record in the Documents table to hold its Meta data, such as the document's ID, name, URI, author, activation and expiration dates, permission lists, and so on. So you basically have two separate data stores: the tables in the database and the Corpus files. Now you have to write the code to make sure they stay in sync with each other. The problem is that files in the Corpus could be deleted or renamed, and there is no automatic mechanism that ensures that the data in the database gets updated to reflect that.

Another inelegant area is backing up the site. You will of course want to provide an automated backup facility for your application so the administrator can perform backups easily. Remember that a backup process that is a headache means that backups will not occur very often, so you will want to create an easy backup process. The tricky part for the developer is to ensure that, if an administrator has to restore the site using a previous backup, the restored database and the restored Corpus are in sync with each other. That means it is difficult to write the code for an online backup because during the backup you don't want changes to the database or Corpus, which could make the database backup and the Corpus backup inconsistent with each other. I am sure you will agree that this issue is ungainly—not a showstopper, perhaps, but it is an issue that requires some thought.

SAVING FILES IN SQL SERVER

Another alternative is to store the document files in an Image (BLOB) field in the Documents table in SQL Server. This makes certain tasks more elegant, but the documents have to live within the limitations of SQL Server and the Image data type.

On the upside, there is a tight coupling between the database and the documents. You can use transactions and constraints in the database to ensure that the Meta data about each document is always in sync with the document itself. In addition, SQL Server does all of the work of providing an easy online backup facility and can even provide replication to other servers if you need it.

On the downside, in SQL Server 2000, each document must be less than 16 megabytes in size and must not contain more than 256 kilobytes (KB) of filtered text in order for full-text search to work. See the SQL Server Books Online, *Filtering Supported File Types* section, for details. There may also be performance considerations. I have not tested the relative speeds of reading/writing Image data in SQL Server and reading/writing files in a Corpus directory, but you would want to do some prototyping and testing early to know what you are up against there.

SAVING FILES IN SHAREPOINT PORTAL SERVER

Yet another alternative is to use Microsoft SharePoint Portal Server as your document repository. As of this writing, SharePoint is a new product, but it promises some interesting capabilities in the area of document content management.

On the upside, SharePoint promises robust document management, search, subscriptions, and in-line discussions for document management and collaboration processes. SharePoint also offers a Digital Dashboard and Web Parts, which is a nice implementation of a Web site that can show data from other internal information systems. You can browse the Microsoft Web site for more details at *http://www.microsoft.com/sharepoint/*.

On the downside, SharePoint is built for intranets only. There is no B2B security built into SharePoint at all. This means a potentially large development effort to bolt B2B security onto a SharePoint site.

5.1.7 BUILDING A SEARCH PAGE

Whatever you ultimately decide for your document repository, your users will want a full-text search feature. You will need to construct on your site a Search page that has input fields for searching the structured Meta data as well as the unstructured file data on the site. The results of the Search page will need to be intersected with the list of resources that the current users are authorized to see, to ensure that they can't access resources through the search feature that they couldn't access otherwise.

The implementation of the Search page will be different for each of the three document repository options I just described. The best advice I can give is to keep both the Search UI and the Search code as simple as possible.

SUMMARY

Providing content management and secure collaboration between users is a fundamental requirement for typical B2B Web sites. You can implement sophisticated content access control in .NET with a SQL database to store the security settings and a C# class to process the requests for documents.

In order for a Web site to provide collaboration, its users need to be able to upload as well as download documents securely. You have some choices when it comes to ways to handle the storage and processing of uploaded documents for your site's collaboration features.

XML Web services and BizTalk

Some developers who are new to the B2B world mistakenly assume that credit card processing is an important part of all e-commerce Web sites. However, you must realize that B2B commerce is very different from B2C commerce. Commerce between businesses is typically not conducted with credit cards but with business documents, particularly purchase orders and invoices.

In this chapter you will learn how businesses can exchange documents, such as purchase orders and invoices, and thereby conduct commerce over the Internet.

The key points for this chapter are the following:

- XML Web services provide a way for application logic to be invoked remotely over the Internet.

- XML Web services can be used to send the contents of documents programmatically across the Internet.

- BizTalk Server can use XML Web services or other, more traditional approaches to send and receive documents across the Internet.

- BizTalk Server can automate long-running business processes and provides a unique programming language and transaction model to enable this capability.

6.1   REAL WORLD B2B COMMERCE

The two primary tools for implementing B2B commerce on the Windows platform are XML Web services and BizTalk Server. With these tools, you can send and receive business documents and make them part of applications that perform commercial transactions.

Using XML Web services and BizTalk Server, you can invoke application logic from across the Internet, send documents between applications and between companies, and automate high-level business processes that take documents as input and produce other documents as output.

6.1.1 XML WEB SERVICES

There is not enough room in a single chapter for a complete discourse on Microsoft's XML Web services. Therefore this chapter provides just enough information to get you started building XML Web services in Visual Studio.NET and provides an example of how and when to use them in a B2B environment.

XML Web services enable applications to exchange messages and invoke application logic remotely using XML. These services are designed for the loosely coupled environment of the Internet. They use standard protocols such as HTTP, XML, and SOAP.

SOAP stands for Simple Object Access Protocol. Simply put, SOAP is a remote procedure call (RPC) mechanism that is implemented via HTTP and XML. The SOAP protocol specification defines an RPC-style message exchange pattern. XML Web services often combine SOAP messages to enable the exchange of structured information, such as purchase orders and invoices, which can be used to automate internal and external business processes.

There are two parties in a typical Web service setting: the server application that hosts or exposes the Web service and the client app that calls the methods that are exposed by Web service.

Web service discovery is the process of a client finding a Web service and locating the documents that describe it. Web services are made known over the Internet to their potential clients in Web services directories, such as the UDDI (Universal Description, Discovery, and Integration) Directory. Web services directories help potential clients to find Web services.

If Web service clients know the location of the service, they can bypass the discovery process. In the B2B application world, B2B apps are typically written for particular clients and are not usually intended to appeal to clients who are unknown to the authors of the service.

A B2B Web service will typically be a component of a larger B2B application that provides secure content, commerce, and collaboration to a particular set of users. The private and secure nature of B2B applications means that Web services in the B2B world are often not meant for public consumption, so there is usually little need to publish discovery information for them in Web service directories.

Using a Web service directory to find Web services is typically not necessary in the B2B world, but Web service clients must know how to interact with a Web service before they can use it. Therefore a clear description of what the Web service supports is necessary.

Each Web service must provide a service description, which is a document that is written in an XML grammar called Web Service Description Language (WSDL). The WSDL for each Web service defines the format of messages the Web service understands. The service description is a contract that spells out the behavior of a Web service and tells clients how to interact with it.

6.1.2 BUILDING AND USING XML WEB SERVICES IN VISUAL STUDIO.NET

Now you will create an XML Web service that returns a custom product catalog to clients who have the right credentials. Visual Studio.NET abstracts away much of the tedium involved in creating Web services. It provides code that handles the processing of Web service requests and takes care of the parsing and creation of SOAP messages.

First you will create a Web service named InventoryList. After creating and testing your InventoryList Web service, you will create a Windows app that is a client of the InventoryList Web service.

First open your ManufacturerA project in Visual Studio.NET. Select the File, New, Project menu choice. This brings up the New Project dialog. Specify a Visual C# Project, and select the Web Service icon. Change the Name to InventoryList.

Select the radio button labeled Add to Solution so that this new project is part of your ManufacturerA solution. Click the OK button. Visual Studio.NET will churn for a few seconds and then present you with a blank page named Service1 .asmx.cs[Design].

In Visual Studio.NET, each XML Web service consists of an .ASMX file and a Web service class file. In the project you just created, the .ASMX file is named Service1.asmx, and the Web service class file is named Service1.asmx.cs.

The Service1.asmx.cs[Design] page is the design view of the Service1.asmx.cs file. View the file by double-clicking on the Service1.asmx.cs[Design] page. In the file, the Web service class Service1 is public, has a public default constructor, and contains a commented-out public HelloWorld method that is marked with the WebMethod attribute.

The .ASMX file contains a WebService processing directive that references the Web service class. View the contents of the Service1.asmx file by right-clicking the .ASMX file in Solution Explorer and then selecting Open With on the shortcut menu. In the Open With dialog box, select Source Code (Text) Editor and then click Open. The contents of the Service1.asmx file are shown in Listing 6-1.

LISTING 6-1 Service1.asmx *Files*

```
<%@ WebService Language="c#" Codebehind="Service1.asmx.cs"
Class="InventoryList.Service1" %>
```

As you can see, the WebService directive and its attributes in the .ASMX file tell the system where to find the implementation of the Web service.

The Language attribute indicates the programming language used to develop the Web service. You can create XML Web services in any .NET-compatible language. This attribute exists to help Visual Studio manage the XML Web service project and is not actually required at runtime.

The Class attribute indicates that the Service1 class is the code-behind class that implements the functionality of the XML Web service. If you change the name of the class, be sure to change the class name in the Class attribute accordingly.

Turn your attention back to the Service1.asmx.cs file, shown in Listing 6-2. A few lines have been removed for brevity.

In the Service1.asmx.cs file, note that the Service1 class is derived from the System.Web.Services.WebService class. This is an optional base class for XML Web services that Visual Studio.NET uses for you. It provides direct access to useful ASP.NET objects, such as the Application, Context, and Session objects. For more information, see *System.Web.Services.WebService Class* in the documentation.

LISTING 6-2 Service1.asmx.cs *File*

```
using System;
using System.Collections;
using System.ComponentModel;
using System.Data;
using System.Diagnostics;
using System.Web;
using System.Web.Services;

namespace InventoryList
{
    public class Service1 : System.Web.Services.WebService
    {
        public Service1()
        {
            InitializeComponent();
        }

        /// <summary>
        /// Clean up any resources being used.
        /// </summary>
        protected override void Dispose( bool disposing )
        {
        }
```

(continued)

```
//      [WebMethod]
//      public string HelloWorld()
//      {
//          return "Hello World";
//      }
    }
}
```

ASP.NET will create an instance of your Service1 class to process incoming Web service requests. To do this, ASP.NET needs the Service1 class to be public, and the class must contain a public default constructor.

TESTING YOUR WEB SERVICE
The easiest way to test your InventoryList Web service is to add a WebMethod to the Service1 class and run it in the debugger. In the Service1.asmx.cs file, remove the comments from the lines of the HelloWorld method, including the [WebMethod] line. Right-click on the InventoryList project in Solution Explorer, and select the Select as StartUp Project menu choice. This makes your InventoryList project the project in your solution that runs when you start the debugger.

After setting your InventoryList project as the startup project, press the F5 key. The projects will be built, and then your browser will be launched. Here is the URL:

```
http://localhost/InventoryList/Service1.asmx
```

The page in the browser shows the Service help page. Click on the *HelloWorld* hyperlink. This is the URL to the Service help page:

```
http://localhost/InventoryList/Service1.asmx?op=HelloWorld
```

Click the Invoke button. Another instance of your browser will be launched and will point to the following URL:

```
http://localhost/InventoryList/Service1.asmx/HelloWorld?
```

This page displays the results of the HelloWorld method, with its Hello World in XML.

You may recall that the Service help page complained about Service1 using http://tempuri.org/ as its default namespace and recommended that the default namespace be changed before the Web service is made public.

Apply the optional WebService attribute to the Service1 class to specify the namespace and provide a brief description for the Web service. The brief description will appear on the Service help page.

Close the browser instances to end the debugging session, and add the WebService attribute to the Service1 class, as shown in Listing 6-3.

LISTING 6-3   *WebService Attribute*

```
[WebService(Namespace="http://manufacturera/webservices",
Description="A brief description of Manufacturer A's Web
service.")]
public class Service1 : System.Web.Services.WebService
{
```

Press F5 to launch the browser again. You will see that the Service help page no longer does as much whining about your Web service's namespace. Of course, Web services are not typically accessed by people using browsers. The browser interface is simply a convenient way to test them.

BUILDING A USEFUL WEB SERVICE

Next you will add another Web method that is a bit closer to what a Web service would do in a real B2B application. This method will return the list of products that are intended for each particular client who calls it. The method you will add is named GetProductList.

The idea with the GetProductList method is that Manufacturer A wants to make it easy for its resellers to place orders for its products. These products, their prices, descriptions, and availability change frequently, so it is necessary to place that information on the Web where it can be updated easily.

Unlike a typical B2C e-commerce site, however, ordering the products from Manufacturer A is not simply a matter of using a browser-based shopping cart and filling in an HTML form with credit card information. Rather, a purchase order (PO) with the right information in the right format needs to be generated and approved by the reseller's management. Then the PO needs to be submitted to Manufacturer A, which has a multistep process of its own for handling the PO once it is received.

Because B2B commerce is not one-step shopping, Manufacturer A has created a Windows application that its resellers can use to view the current catalog and generate purchase orders. This Windows app will be a client of the GetProductList method you are about to create. Add the method shown in Listing 6-4 to your Service1 class.

LISTING 6-4   *GetProductList Web Method*

```
[WebMethod(Description="Returns the catalog for the user in XML.")]
public DataSet GetProductList(string uid, string pw)
{
    DataSet ds = new DataSet();
    SqlParameter[] sqlParamsForValidate = {
        new SqlParameter("@userid", SqlDbType.VarChar, 20),
        new SqlParameter("@password", SqlDbType.VarChar, 50)
```

(continued)

```
    };
    SqlParamsForValidate[0].Value = uid.Trim();
    SqlParamsForValidate[1].Value = pw.Trim();
    SqlHelper validate = new SqlHelper("sp_ValidateUser",
        sqlParamsForValidate,
        CommandType.StoredProcedure);
    SqlParameter validParam = new SqlParameter("@IsValid",
        SqlDbType.Int);
    validParam.Direction = ParameterDirection.Output;
    validate.Execute(ref validParam);
    if (1 == ((int)validParam.Value))
    {
        SqlParameter[] sqlParamForProds =
            { new SqlParameter("@userid", SqlDbType.VarChar) };
        SqlParamForProds[0].Value = uid.Trim();
        SqlHelper prodlist = new SqlHelper("sp_ProdsICanSee",
            sqlParamForProds, CommandType.StoredProcedure);
        prodlist.Execute(ref ds);
    }
    return ds;
}
```

The GetProductList method returns an ADO.NET DataSet, which holds an XML representation of data from a database. The GetProductList method also performs authentication and authorization.

6.1.3   XML Web services Security

The current SOAP specification does not include specs on security, so for now the implementation of XML Web services security is up to each developer.

In implementing security in your Web service, you will of course be unable to use browser cookie-based authentication because the client of a Web service is typically not a browser. ASP.NET does not provide classes that handle Web service security right out of the box like the ASP.NET FormsAuthentication class does for browsers. You have to do a bit of coding yourself to implement authentication and authorization in a Web service.

The authentication code in Listing 6-4 is a fairly rudimentary way of authenticating a client of a Web service; the code is crude but effective. The GetProductList method takes a user ID and a password as parameters. Of course, if this Web service were exposed over an HTTP connection, the user ID and password could be seen by prying eyes. So if you were to use similar code in an actual B2B implementation, you would want to use HTTPS instead of HTTP. To authenticate the user, the GetProductList method runs the sp_ValidateUser stored procedure that you used in Chapter 4.

A more sophisticated approach would be to expose a Login Web method that returns a numeric key if the user is authenticated. Subsequent calls to other Web methods could take the numeric key as the first parameter. To authenticate the request, the Web method code could look up the key in some RAM-based collection to determine whether the key is valid. The keys could expire and be removed from the collection after a certain period of inactivity or when a Logout method is called.

After authenticating the user, the GetProductList method in Listing 6-4 runs the sp_ProdsICanSee stored procedure to retrieve the product information that this user is authorized to see. If you implement the more sophisticated Login method for authentication just described, you will have to map the numeric key to a particular user to perform your authorization check. In the code in Listing 6-4, the user ID is used for both authentication and authorization. Again, it is crude but effective.

6.1.4 COMPLETING THE WEB SERVICE CODE

The GetProductList method uses the SqlHelper class that you used in the ManufacturerA Web site in the previous chapters. Add the using directives shown in Listing 6-5 to your Service1.asmx.cs file.

LISTING 6-5 *Using Directives*

```
using System.Data.SqlClient;
using ManufacturerA.Sql.Utility;
```

In addition, add a reference to your ManufacturerA project in your InventoryList project. Right-click on the References folder of your InventoryList project in Solution Explorer, and select the Add Reference menu choice. On the Add Reference dialog, click the Project tab and then click the ManufacturerA project. Click the Select button, then the OK button.

At this point, you should be able to build your solution successfully. However, you will not be able to run your InventoryList Web service yet because the SqlHelper class expects to get its database connection information from the Web.config file.

The InventoryList Web service has its own virtual root under the Inetpub\ wwwroot directory, so it also has its own Web.config file. Add the configSections and dsnstore sections to the Web.config file for the InventoryList project, as shown in Listing 6-6. The configSections and dsnstore sections should be placed between the configuration and system.web start tags as shown.

LISTING 6-6 *Additions to the Web.config File for the InventoryList Project*

```
<configuration>
   <configSections>
      <section name="dsnstore"
         type="System.Configuration.NameValueSectionHandler,
         System" />
   </configSections>
   <dsnstore>
      <add key="dbconnection"
         value="server=localhost;uid=sa;Initial
         catalog=ManufacturerA" />
   </dsnstore>
   <system.web>
```

The code for the sp_ProdsICanSee stored procedure is shown in Listing 6-7.

LISTING 6-7 *sp_ProdsICanSee Stored Procedure*

```
CREATE PROCEDURE sp_ProdsICanSee @userid VARCHAR(20) AS
SELECT * FROM Products
```

Yes, sp_ProdsICanSee *is* simple. In a real application, the sp_ProdsICanSee stored procedure would retrieve product information from perhaps several tables and would retrieve the information about the user. Since we are only prototyping here, this simple version will work fine. In your ManufacturerA database, create a Products table containing whatever data makes sense to you for testing.

Test your GetProductList Web method by pressing F5 and then clicking the Invoke button in the browser for the GetProductList method. You should see the XML representation of the data from your Products table in the browser.

6.1.5   CREATING A WEB SERVICE CLIENT

Now it is time to create the Windows application that Manufacturer A provides for its resellers, which will be the Web service client for the GetProductList method. You can create the Web service client on the same machine on which the Web service was created, or you can use a different machine if they are networked.

Create a new project in Visual Studio.NET. Make it a C# project that is a Windows Application. Make sure you create a Windows Application because you are in fact building a fat client application. Name the project ACatalog, and do not make it part of the ManufacturerA solution. In other words, in the New Project dialog, select the Close Solution radio button. This causes the ManufacturerA solution to be closed and a new solution named ACatalog to be created to house the ACatalog project.

Visual Studio.NET will present you with the design view of the *Form1.cs* file. On this form, place a DataGrid control from the Toolbox. Make the DataGrid take up most of the area of the form, except for a strip along the bottom. In the bottom area of the form, place a Button control.

Bring up the properties of the DataGrid control. In the Anchor property, which is in the Layout category, specify that it should be anchored on all sides to the borders of the form. Make the Button control anchored to the bottom and right borders of the form.

Build the project and then run the application to make sure it works okay so far. When you resize the window, the DataGrid should resize with the window, and the Button control should stay anchored to the bottom right of the window.

In Visual Studio.NET, double-click on the Button control to bring up the Form1.cs page. The button1_Click method is where you will place the code to call the GetProductList method of the InventoryList Web service. However, first you have to add a reference to the InventoryList Web service to your ACatalog project.

In Solution Explorer, right-click on the References folder that is beneath the ACatalog project, and select the Add Web Reference menu choice. You are presented with the Add Web Reference dialog.

If you are building your client app on the same machine as the Web service, you can click the Web References on Local Web Server link to see the Web services that are on that machine. If you are building your client app on a different machine from the Web service, you can enter the IP address of the server machine in the address field at the top of the dialog.

In the Available References area of the dialog, you should see a hyperlink that says something very similar to this one:

```
http://localhost/InventoryList/InventoryList.vsdisco
```

If you are building the Web service client on a different machine, the hyperlink will look something like this:

```
http://192.168.1.101/InventoryList/InventoryList.vsdisco
```

Click the InventoryList.vsdisco link, and you will see further information about that Web service. The Add Reference button on the Add Web Reference dialog should be enabled now, so click it to add a reference to the Web service in your ACatalog project.

You will see in the Solution Explorer that a Web References folder is added under your ACatalog project. Also, if you look in the file system, you will see that a directory named Web References is created under the ACatalog directory. This Web References directory contains a directory with a file named *Service1.cs*. Visual Studio generates the Service1.cs file for you automatically, based on the WSDL for the InventoryList Web service. Double-click on the Service1.cs file in Windows Explorer to open the Service1.cs file in Visual Studio.NET.

The Service1 class in the Service1.cs file is a proxy class that the client can use to interact with the InventoryList Web service. The Service1 class is derived from System.Web.Services.Protocols.SoapHttpClientProtocol and contains the methods that correspond to the Web methods in the Web service.

In Service1.cs, do a search for GetProductList, and you will see that there is a GetProductList method declared in the file. There are also BeginGetProductList and EndGetProductList methods that are used for calling the GetProductList method asynchronously, which you will get to do later in this chapter.

After adding the Web Reference, add the lines shown in Listing 6-8 to the button1_Click method. As you type the code for the lines, Visual Studio's IntelliSense should be effective for you. This is one way for you to know that the Web Reference was added successfully.

LISTING 6-8 *Button1_Click Code to Call Web service*

```
ACatalog.localhost.Service1 CatalogSvc =
    new ACatalog.localhost.Service1();
dataGrid1.SetDataBinding(
    CatalogSvc.GetProductList("samsiteadmin","1234"),"");
```

Build and run your ACatalog application. When you click the button on the form, after a moment of hesitation, while the Web service proxy class gets instantiated and calls the InventoryList Web service, the DataGrid should get populated with data from your Products table.

Use your favorite database access tool to change some of the data in the Products table, and press the button in your ACatalog application again. You should see the DataGrid get redrawn and include the updated data from the database.

6.1.6 CALLING WEB METHODS ASYNCHRONOUSLY

The problem with calling a Web method in a synchronous manner is the fact that the application's main thread blocks until the Web method returns. Given that the Web is sometimes referred to as the World Wide Wait, it would be better to call the Web service method asynchronously so the app can continue to be responsive while waiting for the Web method to return.

One way to do this is to have the ACatalog application spawn another thread that makes the call to the Web method, waits patiently for it to return, gets the data, and then dies a peaceful death. All the while, the application's main thread can be responsive to other requests coming into the app.

It is important to note that an XML Web service does not have to have any special code to handle asynchronous requests. The proxy class that Visual Studio.NET creates for your client with the Web Services Description Language tool, Wsdl.exe, automatically creates methods for calling the Web service method asynchronously.

Implement an asynchronous call by adding the following line near the top of the *Form1.cs* file:

```
using System.Threading;
```

Add the lines shown in Listing 6-9 as members of the Form1 class.

LISTING 6-9   *New Members of the Form1 Class*

```
private ACatalog.localhost.Service1 CatalogSvc;
private Thread CatalogSvcThread;
private EventHandler onSvcComplete;
private IAsyncResult AsyncResult;
```

CatalogSvc will hold an instance of the proxy class that is created to interact with the Web service. We also create Thread, EventHandler, and IAsyncResult objects to use when we spawn a new thread to call the Web service. Add the lines shown in Listing 6-10 to the Form1 constructor.

LISTING 6-10   *Initialization Code in the Form1 Constructor*

```
CatalogSvc = new ACatalog.localhost.Service1();
onSvcComplete = new EventHandler(OnSvcComplete);
```

Change the button1_Click code so that it looks like the code shown in Listing 6-11.

LISTING 6-11   *Button1_Click method for Asychronous Call to Web service*

```
private void button1_Click(object sender, System.EventArgs e)
{
    button1.Text = "Please wait";
    button1.Enabled = false;
    dataGrid1.Enabled = false;
    CatalogSvcThread = new Thread(new ThreadStart(ThreadProcedure));
    CatalogSvcThread.Start();
}
```

The code in Listing 6-11 spawns a new thread and tells it to start. It also disables the button so that users can't press it while the app is waiting for a previous call to the Web method to return.

Add the two methods shown in Listing 6-12 to the Form1 class.

LISTING 6-12 *Additional Methods to Handle Asychronous Call to Web Service*

```
private void ThreadProcedure()
{
   // Begin the Async call to GetCatalog
   AsyncResult = CatalogSvc.BeginGetProductList(
      "samsiteadmin","1234", null, null);
   // Wait for the asynchronous operation to complete
   AsyncResult.AsyncWaitHandle.WaitOne();
   // Raise the OnSvcComplete using BeginInvoke so that
   // EndGetProductList can get the data from the Web method
   // and have it marshaled appropriately between threads
   BeginInvoke(onSvcComplete, new object[] {this,
   EventArgs.Empty});
}
private void OnSvcComplete(object sender, EventArgs e)
{
   // Get the completed results
   dataGrid1.SetDataBinding(
      CatalogSvc.EndGetProductList(AsyncResult),"");
   dataGrid1.Enabled = true;
   button1.Text = "Get Products";
   button1.Enabled = true;
}
```

The ThreadProcedure method runs on the new thread that was created in the Button1_Click method in Listing 6-11. It calls the BeginGetProductList method to begin the asynchronous call to the Web method. The BeginGetProductList method in the proxy class calls the .NET Framework BeginInvoke method to start an asynchronous invocation call to the Web service method.

The BeginGetProductList method returns immediately. The call to AsyncResult.AsyncWaitHandle.WaitOne(); causes the worker thread to wait until the Web method returns. As soon as it does, the worker thread raises an event by calling BeginInvoke so that EndGetProductList can be called by the main thread and the results can be marshaled between threads appropriately. The EndGetProductList method calls the .NET Framework EndInvoke method to complete the asynchronous invocation call to the Web service method and get the results.

6.1.7 BUILDING A WEB SERVICE THAT RETURNS FILES

A straightforward way of building a Web service method that returns a file, such as an invoice or PO that was generated by an accounting app, would simply be to read the file and return its contents as a string. The code for this is shown in Listing 6-13.

LISTING 6-13 *A Web service Method That Returns the Contents of a File*

```
[WebMethod]
public string ReturnPO()
{
    FileStream fs = new FileStream(
        "D:\\Inetpub\\wwwroot\\MyWebService\\PO.txt",
        FileMode.Open, FileAccess.Read);
    StreamReader reader = new StreamReader(fs);
    reader.BaseStream.Seek(0, SeekOrigin.Begin);
    string filecontentstr = reader.ReadToEnd();
    return filecontentstr;
}
```

To make this work, you will need to add the following using directive to the code-behind file that contains the method:

```
using System.IO;
```

The Web service client would parse the string to get the relevant information from the PO and do whatever is required to process the B2B commerce transaction. Listing 6-13 does not do any error checking or catch exceptions, and you would, of course, need to add that code in any application that you deploy.

UNTOUCHED BY HUMAN HANDS
The ACatalog application illustrates how to begin building a fat client application that calls a Web service for people to use. Another, perhaps more common scenario is where automated applications call Web services with little or no human interaction.

For example, a Manufacturing Resource Planning application could automatically query the resellers' inventory levels using Web services that they expose to do forecasting for the manufacturing process. These automated Web services fall into the domain of BizTalk Server, to which you will be introduced later in this chapter. Another area of concern before introducing BizTalk Server, however, is the need for transactions.

6.2 TRANSACTIONS IN XML WEB SERVICES

Often the automated invocations of Web services will involve changes to data in multiple systems. The risk of changing data in multiple systems is that something will fail in the hardware, software, or network somewhere, and only part of the data changes will happen. This could leave the systems in an inconsistent state. Hence, there is a need for Web services to use transactions.

Classes written using the .NET Framework Class Library can make use of COM+ Services, including automatic transactions, using classes in the System.EnterpriseServices namespace. The ContextUtil class is the best method for a .NET app to obtain information about the COM+ 1.0 object context. For further information on COM+ Services and transactions in .NET applications, see *System.EnterpriseServices, ContextUtil class,* and *Automatic Transactions* in the .NET documentation.

Transactions are meant to ensure that all interactions with other systems maintain the ACID properties (Atomicity, Consistency, Isolation, and Durability) that are required for robust distributed applications.

XML Web services provide the option of running Web method code within the scope of a transaction. You can declare an automatic transaction by using the *TransactionOption* property of the WebMethod attribute, as follows:

```
[WebMethod(TransactionOption=TransactionOption.Required)]
public int MyWebServiceMethod()
{
```

To use the TransactionOption property, you must add a reference to System.EnterpriseServices in your XML Web services project, and you must add the following using directive to your Web service code-behind page:

```
using System.EnterpriseServices;
```

Setting the TransactionOption property to TransactionOption.Required causes the system to share a transaction if one exists or to create a new transaction if necessary. Each time a Web service client calls the Web service method. See *TransactionOption Enumeration* in the documentation for details.

If a Web service method is participating in a transaction and an exception occurs, ASP.NET automatically aborts the transaction and backs out all of the changes that are within the scope of the transaction. If no exception occurs, then the transaction is committed automatically. You can also explicitly abort a transaction by calling the System.EnterpriseServices.ContextUtil.SetAbort() method.

6.2.1 SCOPE OF TRANSACTIONS IN XML WEB SERVICES

The key idea to glean from the previous paragraph is that for a given change to be backed out during an aborted transaction, the change must have occurred within the scope of the transaction.

The scope of a transaction in a Web service method is limited to the code inside the method and only that code that calls components and resource managers (such as Microsoft SQL Server) that support COM+ transactions. If a Web service method uses a component that does not support COM+ transactions, the changes made by that component are not automatically backed out if the transaction aborts.

In addition, due to the stateless nature of the HTTP protocol, if a Web service method calls another Web service, each Web service participates in its own transaction. You cannot nest transactions in cases where one Web service calls another Web service because a Web service method can act only as the root object in a transaction.

Imagine a scenario where a Web service method calls another Web service method across the Internet. The Web service method that is the callee makes some change to the state of a system to which it has access. The changes are successful, and the callee's transaction commits. The Web service that is the caller then executes some of its own code that tries to change some state in a system to which it has access but encounters a problem and must abort its transaction. When the transaction aborts, the caller's changes are backed out, but the callee's changes are not, and the systems end up in an inconsistent state. There is no automatic mechanism that causes the callee Web service to back out its changes when the caller Web service's transaction aborts. Each Web service method runs in a separate and unrelated transaction.

6.2.2 LENGTH OF TRANSACTIONS

As you may know, ACID transactions are resource-intensive because they usually require the locking of records in databases. For a server application to provide a reasonable level of scalability, it is necessary to keep transactions as brief as possible. In server applications, the magnitude of the duration of typical transactions is seconds or fractions of a second.

A problem arises, however, in the area of transactions for B2B applications. The problem is that individual transactions in the B2B world often have a length of days, weeks, or months—not seconds.

For example, suppose a company submits a PO to a manufacturer for a specific quantity of goods and stipulates that the goods must be delivered by a certain date. The manufacturer accepts the PO, which sets off several state changes in various information systems at the manufacturer. These could include state changes in the manufacturer's internal financial, production, and distribution applications. Now suppose that a week into the production process for these goods, a supplier notifies the manufacturer that it cannot provide the needed quantity of raw materials in time. Because the manufacturer cannot provide the required goods by the appointed date, the order must be canceled.

The cancellation of the order means that some of the state changes that were made to the financial, production, and the distribution applications need to be backed out. Had this transaction succeeded, it would have run from the time that the PO was accepted to the time that the products were delivered and the customer was invoiced, which could have been a period of several weeks. The scope of a transaction like this is not suitable for the ACID transactions found in COM+ Services, which are designed to have a duration of seconds.

6.2.3 GETTING THE RIGHT TRANSACTIONS

To implement B2B commerce, you must be able to perform transactions that have (1) a broad scope, meaning that they are not limited to the code in a single method, and (2) a long duration, meaning that they can take days, weeks, and months to complete and can be backed out at any point in the process.

One way to get transactions with sufficient scope and length for B2B commerce is to build the transaction infrastructure yourself. This would entail writing the code for compensating transactions, whose purpose is to back out the work of failed transactions. You would also need to build a mechanism for calling your compensating transactions at the right time.

Another way to get transactions with sufficient scope and length for B2B commerce is to use BizTalk Server. BizTalk Server provides support for long-running transactions that have broad scope. And it provides additional tools that developers of B2B commerce applications will find useful.

6.3 BIZTALK SERVER

BizTalk Server provides a development environment that is quite unique. BizTalk Server's development tools enable developers to build applications that are very broad in scope. BizTalk applications can serve as the glue that binds other applications together into far-reaching business processes.

Building these applications requires very high-level programming language. In BizTalk, business processes are not written in traditional programming language code but in a higher-level language, and they are easy to modify and rewrite.

BizTalk Server includes a unique programming language that is tailor-made for broadly scoped applications. The language is unique in that it has only nine commands.

1. *Begin*, which is the starting point of a business process that you write with this language.

2. *End*, which is the completion of one process flow. One business process can use multiple End commands if it includes Decision, While, or Fork commands (explained following).

3. *Action*, which defines an activity within a process. This activity could be a simple task, such as receiving or sending a document, either synchronously or asynchronously, perhaps using a Web service. Or it could

define a more complex task, such as creating an invoice or a PO and sending it off.

4. *Decision*, which selects one of two or more flows within the process. Each flow is associated with a rule that evaluates to TRUE or FALSE. The first rule that evaluates to TRUE is the one that gets selected. If no rules evaluate to TRUE, the Else flow is followed.

5. *While*, which enables a flow to be repeated. Each While command is associated with one rule. If the rule evaluates to TRUE, the flow is executed. The flow is terminated with an End command. When the End command is reached, the rule is evaluated again. If the rule evaluates to FALSE, there is a Continue flow that is then followed.

6. *Fork*, which enables two or more flows to be executed concurrently and independently of each other. For example, in a business process, you may have a flow that generates an invoice at the same time that another flow is arranging for the shipment of the goods. All of the flows from a single Fork command must end with a Join command or End command.

7. *Join*, which is the synchronization point for parallel flows. The Join command also rejoins flows after a decision has been made.

8. *Transaction*, which specifies a collection of actions, all of which are executed or none is. There are three types of transactions: short-lived (ACID) transactions, long-running transactions, and timed transactions. Transactions are explained in further detail following.

9. *Abort*, which aborts a transaction. This enables either an On Failure of Transaction or Compensation for Transaction process to be executed.

Because of the small number of commands, the editor that developers use to write programs in BizTalk is graphical. The editor is in fact Microsoft Visio, the flowcharting software. Each of these commands is represented by a shape in Visio. BizTalk Orchestration Designer provides eight flowchart shapes that are available on the Visio Flowchart stencil. You use these shapes on a Visio page to define your business process.

ORCHESTRATION

Building business processes that tie applications together is called Orchestration. Developers use the BizTalk Orchestration Designer, which uses Visio, to create BizTalk processes. The processes are compiled into XLANG (pronounced "exlang") schedules. The BizTalk Scheduler Engine executes these XLANG schedules. I will explain how these XLANG schedules get launched in a moment.

TRANSACTIONS IN BIZTALK

BizTalk Server enables transactions that are lengthy and involve many participants. As I mentioned previously, there are three types of transactions in BizTalk Orchestration: short-lived (ACID) transactions, long-running transactions, and timed transactions.

Short-lived (ACID) transactions are dependent on the underlying transaction support from COM+ and the Microsoft Distributed Transaction Coordinator (DTC).

One of the properties of ACID transactions is *isolation*. Isolation means that a transaction's intermediate results cannot be seen by other transactions. For a transaction to achieve isolation, it requires hard locks on all resources that are involved in the transaction. Therefore ACID transactions must of necessity be brief. A transaction cannot hold locks on resources for any significant length of time without seriously degrading the application's overall performance.

When a Transaction shape is placed on a schedule in the BizTalk Orchestration Designer, it defaults to the short-lived transaction type. Action shapes can be placed inside the transaction to ensure that they are executed as a unit. The code that implements these actions must support and participate in DTC type transactions or the work they do will not be undone if the transaction is aborted.

If the actions within a transaction might execute over a period of minutes, hours, days, or longer, then short-lived transactions cannot be used because they would block the work of other transactions in the system. Until recently, there was no support on the Windows platform for long-running transactions. BizTalk's long-running transactions fulfill this need.

Long-running transactions are made possible by two things. First, the requirement for isolation in long-running transactions is relaxed. The lack of isolation means that other transactions can see the intermediate results of long-running transactions. This isn't ideal, but to make an omelet, you can't keep the eggs isolated.

Second, the work of an aborted long-running transaction gets undone by a compensating transaction. The developer creates the actions and code for the compensating transaction, which gets called when and if the original transaction aborts.

A long-running transaction can surround short-lived transactions. In other words, multiple short-lived transactions can be nested inside a long-running transaction. Note that transactions can be nested only two levels deep in BizTalk, but this is sufficient for creating robust business processes.

Imagine a business process that is initiated when a manufacturer receives a PO from a customer. This process has a long-running transaction that contains two short-lived transactions. The first short-lived transaction checks the customer's credit status to determine if the customer is approved to make this purchase. If so, a PO acknowledgment is sent to the customer, and the first short-lived transaction commits.

Imagine that the second short-lived transaction performs some action that arranges for the goods to be picked from the warehouse and shipped to the customer. Now suppose that second short-lived transaction aborts for some reason. The work of the second short-lived transaction is undone automatically when the transaction aborts, but the first short-lived transaction has already committed, so it can't be undone.

However, the surrounding long-running transaction will also abort, and it will execute a compensating transaction that undoes the work of the first short-lived transaction. In BizTalk, this is called compensation.

Timed transactions are long-running transactions that abort if they have not committed in a specified amount of time. For example, a timed transaction can be used to group short-lived transactions and to wait for the arrival of a message within a specified time period. If the message arrives in time, the timed transaction commits. Otherwise, the timed transaction aborts and causes the short-lived transactions to execute their compensation code.

DEHYDRATION AND REHYDRATION

To run XLANG schedules, the BizTalk Scheduler Engine, of course, has to load them into memory. If an XLANG schedule has any long-running transactions, that schedule could be in memory for a long, long time. It simply is not feasible to keep an XLANG schedule in memory for days, weeks, and months on end. There needs to be a way to persist the state of an XLANG schedule to disk and then reinstantiate that schedule at the appropriate time. This process in BizTalk is called Dehydration and Rehydration.

When a schedule instance becomes idle for some period of time, it is dehydrated to the Orchestration Persistence database. Dehydration happens automatically after a configurable period of time, provided that the schedule instance is in an inactive state, with no actions or short-lived transactions being executed.

The XLANG schedule instance will remain dehydrated until it is either rehydrated or explicitly terminated by an administrator. Rehydration is performed by the XLANG Schedule Restart Service, which is a Windows service. The Schedule Restart Service watches for events that trigger an XLANG schedule to begin executing again and sees that they are fired up. This is the ultimate asynchronous execution model. It enables long-running functionality to be implemented in B2B applications.

TRACING AND DEBUGGING BIZTALK SCHEDULES

The execution model for BizTalk schedules is very slow compared to the execution model for traditional Windows applications, so tracing and debugging schedules could be a challenge. However, BizTalk does provide a tracing facility for BizTalk schedules.

When the XLANG Scheduler Engine executes a schedule, it generates events that can be trapped and displayed. There is a tool, XLANG Event Monitor, that traps and displays these events. In addition, any errors raised by the XLANG Scheduler Engine appear in the Event Viewer.

LAUNCHING AND RUNNING SCHEDULES

Schedules can be instantiated as COM+ components through COM monikers. However, a more common approach is for schedules to be instantiated by a message from the BizTalk Messaging Service.

A message can come into the BizTalk Messaging Service through an MSMQ message queue or simply as a document in a directory on the hard disk that is specified as an input directory. This document could be a PO, which could contain information that determines its destination. The document would be processed, the appropriate schedule instantiated, and its process executed.

OTHER COOL THINGS ABOUT BIZTALK SERVER

BizTalk contains a useful collection of tools for automating business processes. The BizTalk Messaging Service enables the secure sending and receiving of documents between applications and between companies. Because of BizTalk's ability to process documents, any application that can produce and consume data in files can work with BizTalk without modification. This means

- A company does not have to rebuild its venerable mainframe applications to use them in current and future business processes.

- Microsoft Office is the ubiquitous BizTalk client. For example, you can use Excel in Office XP to save documents in xml and post them over the Internet to BizTalk.

SUMMARY

XML Web services and BizTalk Server are highly effective tools for implementing B2B commerce with XML Web services, you can invoke application logic from across the Internet and send documents between applications and between companies.

Using BizTalk Server, you can send documents between applications and between companies, and you can make that transfer of documents part of automated high-level business processes.

Advanced B2B Applications with Webridge

The previous chapters illustrate for developers some of the basics of writing B2B applications using the .NET Framework. The .NET Framework provides, right off the CD, a portion of the infrastructure that B2B applications require. Chapters 2 through 6 of this book teach developers how to begin extending the .NET Framework for use in B2B applications.

As you contemplate extending the .NET Framework and building a B2B infrastructure yourself, you might consider a framework that provides the entire infrastructure right off the CD. A B2B development framework lets you concentrate directly on the features of your own B2B applications, without writing a lot of plumbing code first.

In this chapter, I would like to give you a thorough understanding of all the B2B development frameworks that are available on the Microsoft platform. Development frameworks can be a critical part of building B2B applications, and I would do my readers a disservice if I did not cover them. However, on the Microsoft platform, there is one particular B2B framework that is an order of magnitude more complete and capable than any of the others, and that is Webridge Extranet.

Webridge Extranet stands alone on the Microsoft platform in terms of the depth and breadth of the B2B infrastructure it provides. The capabilities of Webridge Extranet make it the prototypical B2B development framework, and I therefore concentrate exclusively on it in this chapter.

Webridge Extranet is in many ways a heavyweight framework. It costs thousands of dollars and has a significant learning curve that developers who use it must climb. The value proposition for Webridge Extranet is that the cost of the framework plus the cost of climbing the learning curve is less than the cost of building the infrastructure for your B2B applications from scratch. The remainder of this chapter is intended to help you decide if that is the case for you.

This chapter introduces you to the Webridge Extranet software. The key points for this chapter are the following:

- To make B2B applications useful in diverse situations, they must have a long list of features that are not simple to write.

- Webridge Extranet is a software framework that provides the infrastructure for B2B applications.

- Webridge Extranet enables developers to create quickly the features that customers want for their own deployments.

- Webridge Extranet also empowers business users to handle much of the administrative work in their own B2B applications.

7.1 INTRODUCTION TO WEBRIDGE EXTRANET

Webridge Extranet consists of a framework for creating B2B applications, with a secure Web site and several Web-based B2B applications that can be deployed out of the box. Webridge Extranet is the Leatherman® of the B2B application world and is one framework with a couple of thousand uses.

7.1.1 B2B INFRASTRUCTURE FOR RAPID DEVELOPMENT PROJECTS

Webridge Extranet is built to reduce the amount of plumbing code that developers must write. Because Webridge Extranet is built from the ground up as a B2B development environment, it enables developers to concentrate almost exclusively on the features of their applications. The infrastructure that B2B applications require is explained later in this chapter.

Using Webridge Extranet, developers can add features to their B2B applications in a series of short, 90-day projects that are easier to manage than longer, more complex development projects. A lightweight, 90-day methodology that has proven to be very effective for B2B projects is explained in Chapter 11 of this book.

Webridge Extranet includes a B2B Web site that companies can deploy out of the box, so they don't have to build their own B2B Web sites from scratch. This Web site is unique in that business managers can modify existing pages and can author new pages using their Web browser. This has the welcome effect of freeing developers from the tedium of creating Web pages for business users. With Webridge Extranet, developers can concentrate on programming. In addition to the Web site, Webridge Extranet includes several finished B2B apps that developers can modify and extend as needed.

7.1.2 MANAGING CONTEXT

A primary function of Webridge Extranet is user context management. By this I mean that Webridge Extranet manages the security context for every user who visits a Webridge Extranet-based B2B Web site.

As you learned in the previous chapters, each user of a B2B Web site has some relationship with the company that owns the site. That relationship is based on the users' characteristics, such as their roles, their employer, their location, their position, and so forth. Based on who they are and the role they fill in their work with the company that owns the site, each user is granted access to particular resources on the site. The users, then, have their own context in which they visit the B2B Web site, and Webridge Extranet manages that context for each user.

Developers who worked through the code examples in Chapters 2 through 5 of this book learned some of the basics of implementing context management using the .NET Framework. Webridge Extranet leverages .NET to provide a more complete implementation of user context management.

With its context management capability, Webridge Extranet enables companies to deploy multiple extranets for its customers. But instead of having to deploy a separate extranet site for each of its customers, a company can deploy one Webridge Extranet-based Web site that dynamically morphs itself into an extranet that is tailored for individual users as they log into the site, depending on who they are, what company they work for, and what their job is. Webridge Extranet provides multiple extranet sites from a single URL.

7.1.3 A PORTAL FOR INTEGRATING AND EXTENDING INTERNAL INFORMATION SYSTEMS

Because Webridge Extranet manages user context so effectively, a Webridge Extranet-based Web site can serve as a platform for integrating and extending a company's backend applications. Webridge Extranet can bring information together from multiple internal systems, such as SAP systems, MRP applications, inventory databases, accounting programs, and so on, and it can display information from these diverse backend systems using individual Web pages.

Webridge Extranet applies security to its Web pages so that people see only the information they are authorized to see. In this way, Webridge Extranet can serve as a portal into a company's internal information systems, which enables people outside the company to obtain the sensitive information they need and are authorized to access.

Developers can use Webridge Extranet to process the data from these backend systems using the .NET managed programming languages. This means that a

Webridge Extranet-based Web site can process information and integrate applications across departments and across company boundaries.

Webridge Extranet can therefore be used to "Web-ify" a company's backend systems. Using Webridge Extranet, a company can breathe new life into old mainframe applications and legacy systems, enabling them to be used by employees in remote locations and by customers in a secure way. In summary, Webridge Extranet provides a way to integrate and extend a company's internal applications to its external users, with a secure, Web-based user interface.

INDUSTRIAL-STRENGTH PLATFORM FOR B2B APPLICATIONS

Webridge Extranet is built to provide scalability on the middle tier. Chapter 1 of this book explained that B2B Web sites are actually three-tier applications, typically with a Web browser front end, a database back end, and a middle tier for the programming logic. Webridge Extranet does two things to provide high scalability on the middle tier.

First, Webridge Extranet enhances the in-memory caching provided by the .NET Framework. This caching enables a middle tier machine to process requests from clients without having to make frequent calls to the backend servers, which means higher performance and scalability for Webridge Extranet-based applications.

Second, Webridge Extranet enables multiple middle-tier machines to be clustered for use in a single application. Technology to do clustering of backend database machines has been around for several years, but the ability to cluster middle-tier machines (with software components that maintain state) is unusual and noteworthy.

7.1.4   HOW AND WHERE TO USE WEBRIDGE EXTRANET

The history of software is a history of increasing levels of abstraction. With Webridge Extranet, you work at a higher level of abstraction than you do when using the .NET Framework alone. The features described in this chapter illustrate the features you can build when working at a higher level of abstraction.

At this high level of abstraction, you can build Web applications that business users can configure and modify using their Web browsers. Providing businesspeople the ability to administer and modify their B2B Web site using a browser is a fundamental feature of Webridge Extranet.

BizTalk Server was introduced in the previous chapter. You might wonder how Webridge Extranet and BizTalk Server relate to each other. The bottom line is that in your B2B applications, you use Webridge Extranet for the human-computer interactions, and you use BizTalk for the computer-computer interactions and for automating workflows.

7.2 B2B INFRASTRUCTURE AND FUNCTIONALITY

B2B applications can be complicated. To get an idea of their potential complexity, glance at the features of the typical B2B applications that are described in Chapters 12, 13, and 14. The functionality that is required in sophisticated B2B apps can make building them a big project.

There are three different categories or levels of functionality in B2B applications. A typical instance or deployment of a B2B application must provide the following:

1. Infrastructure-level functionality for commerce, collaboration, and content

2. Industry-specific functionality, such as selling-chain management for manufacturers or clinical-trial management for pharmaceutical companies

3. The specific features, the business logic, and the particular look and feel that are required by the company that owns this particular deployment of the application

In summary, each deployment of a B2B application has infrastructure, industry, and individual functionality.

7.2.1 INFRASTRUCTURE CODE THAT IS NEEDED FOR B2B APPLICATIONS

The *infrastructure* functionality of a B2B application consists of plumbing code that provides the ability to do the following:

1. Dynamically generate HTML that is sent to browsers so that the skin and content of the site changes dynamically for each user who visits the site

2. Interface with specific backend databases and applications

3. Implement effective security and content access controls

4. Cache each user's content access settings appropriately so that authorization checks do not become a drag on the system's performance

5. Save the appropriate state from Business Objects in the database and handle the object-to-relational mapping

6. Save documents to and retrieve documents from a robust and secure document repository

7. Make method calls that invoke application logic and that transfer data and documents over networks and across the Internet

8. Perform all of these tasks inside of transactions, so that all of the participating information systems remain consistent with each other

Certainly, the .NET development tools make it easier to write this code than the Windows DNA tools did. As you learned in Chapter 3, the .NET Framework Class Library provides a Page class, and Page-derived objects generate the HTML that is sent to the browsers, which begins to address item 1 in the preceding infrastructure list.

As explained in Chapter 6, XML Web services and BizTalk Server enable remote method calls and the transfer of documents across the Internet, which handles item 7 in the infrastructure list. And the .NET Framework, COM+ Services, and BizTalk Server provide a robust transaction infrastructure, which handles item 8.

In addition, the .NET Framework provides partial implementations of the following:

- The code to interface with applications and databases, in ADO.NET, which partially addresses item 2 in the infrastructure list

- The event system for content access controls, using the Authenti-cateRequest event in the HttpApplication Class, which partially addresses item 3

- The hooks needed to cache each user's content access settings, using the extensible ASP.NET User object, which partially addresses item 4

- Some of the code for object-to-relational mapping, again in ADO.NET, which partially addresses item 5

- At least three possibilities for building a robust repository in which to store documents, using a Corpus directory, SQL Server, or SharePoint Portal Server, which partially addresses item 6

The previous chapters of this book show you how to get started writing your own code to build out this infrastructure.

7.2.2   THE CHALLENGE OF BUILDING B2B INFRASTRUCTURE CODE

Building the software at the infrastructure level can be a significant challenge. The challenge is not that the developers cannot conquer the technology. Rather, the challenge is that, in my experience, companies generally are not anxious to pay developers to write infrastructure-level software. Customers want features that they can use themselves, and they don't like to use their limited budgets to pay developers to write the plumbing code that enables those features.

Customers generally don't like to pay for groundbreaking development work on industry-specific functionality either. They want industry-specific functionality, but they don't relish the thought of paying a developer to build it from scratch. From my experience, customers generally expect to pay only for the development of their individual application features, their business logic, and their look and feel, all of which are specific to their own individual deployment.

In B2B applications that are relatively simple and that have a narrow scope, the infrastructure-level software potentially can be written quickly using the .NET Framework development tools. If those costs are low enough, the development costs of the software at the infrastructure level can be included in the project, without too much discomfort on the part of the person who writes the check.

The same can be said of the industry-specific functionality. If the logic is simple and if the tasks the application performs are few in number, developers can generally write the required software without too much heartburn coming from the sponsor of the project.

A simple application with a narrow scope would be one that provides, for instance, content access only, without commerce or collaboration capabilities. Of course, what often happens is the owners and users of the application sooner or later begin to ask for features that are outside of the original scope. To fulfill those feature requests, the developers are faced with the task of expanding the infrastructure of the application to support the new features. Expanding an application's infrastructure after the first version of the app has been developed can be tricky. To avoid having to do so, developers should start with an infrastructure that supports present and future feature requests.

Developers have to find a way to build this B2B infrastructure themselves, or they need to look to a B2B framework, such as Webridge Extranet, to provide that broad infrastructure for them.

7.3   THE WEBRIDGE EXTRANET FRAMEWORK

Webridge Extranet Framework compliments and enhances the .NET Framework for building B2B applications. At its heart, the Webridge Extranet Framework consists of a set of special .NET Framework classes. These classes are special in that they always run inside of transactions, and they automatically persist their state into a SQL Server database at the end of each transaction.

Back in the days of Windows DNA, the Webridge Extranet Framework classes were COM+ objects written in Visual J++. Now with the advent of .NET, the Webridge Extranet Framework classes have been converted to .NET Framework classes. Because the Webridge Extranet Framework classes were originally developed in the days of Windows DNA, there is some overlap between the .NET Framework classes and the Webridge Extranet Framework classes. However, Webridge is resolving that overlap over time in the course of the company's normal cycle of upgrades to the Webridge Extranet Framework.

At its foundation, the Webridge Extranet Framework is a set of classes that run inside of automatic transactions. Objects of these classes persist themselves in a SQL Server database at transaction commit-time whenever their state changes.

Webridge has also implemented a way for software objects to be saved in and retrieved from a relational database server. The objects in Webridge Extranet automatically save their state in a SQL Server database if their state changes during a transaction. If you have ever had to write a layer of software that handles object-to-relational mapping, you know that this is not easy to do in a robust way.

With these persistent objects, Webridge could offer a pretty decent object database that is built on the Microsoft .NET Servers. However, Webridge is not in the object database business; they are in the framework and B2B application business. They used their own object database to create a framework that provides further functionality that is required for commerce, collaboration, and content management in B2B applications.

Webridge has also exposed the underlying objects in such a way that they are easily accessible to .NET developers. These objects make it easy for developers to write *industry*-specific functionality, as well as the *individual* look and feel that the owners of each deployment will want for themselves.

As I mentioned earlier, included with the Webridge Extranet Framework is an off-the-shelf B2B Web site that developers can use as a starting point for building their own B2B apps. Webridge Extranet fully implements security and content access controls for B2B applications. Webridge Extranet also caches each user's content access settings, so authorization checks do not become a drag on the system's performance. And Webridge Extranet saves documents to and retrieves documents from a robust and secure document repository, which is described in more detail later in this chapter.

To add industry-specific functionality, developers can use the .NET Webridge Extranet classes and their favorite .NET Framework-managed language to build that functionality. A developer can take the Webridge Extranet site, change the colors and graphics, and have a complete B2B Web site that provides commerce, collaboration, and content management.

7.3.1 BEST OF SUITE

When it comes to B2B application development, most companies do not realistically consider building complex B2B apps from the ground up. They tend to want to start with a proven solution that gets them part or most of the way there and then use their developers to get them over the top with a custom development project that is small and manageable.

In the not-so-distant past, this meant company executives would pick what they thought was the best-of-breed content management app, and the best-of-breed security platform, and the best-of-breed online product catalog, and so on. Then they would task their developers with integrating these disparate best-of-breed applications into a unified solution to solve the company's B2B needs. This integration project was supposed to be the small and manageable development project I mentioned earlier that would get them over the top.

However, experience has demonstrated that these integration projects turn out to be neither small nor manageable, nor completely successful. This is because integrating sophisticated software applications that were not originally designed to be integrated with each other is a difficult development problem.

Every so often, there seems to be a cluster of new integration initiatives. Also, new middleware products and integration technologies are introduced with some frequency. This tends to nurture a belief that it is feasible to integrate a collection of disparate best-of-breed applications to build a B2B infrastructure, but this is a mirage. Even if the initial integration project is in some degree successful, every time the company's needs change, and every time one of the apps gets upgraded, the developers have to be called back in for more integration work.

Remember the early days of the Intel-based PC, when you would choose among the best-of-breed desktop apps? I remember choosing Word Perfect as my word processor, Lotus 1-2-3 as my spreadsheet, and dBase III as my database. I also remember wondering how to integrate these applications with each other, never really figuring out how to do it. I also remember how expensive it was to buy three separate applications.

Eventually the Microsoft Office suite came along, and then I could get a spreadsheet, a database, and a word processor (and a few other apps that I may or may not need right away), all in a nice package for the price of one or two of the separate applications. The integration between the applications became easier, too. I was able to put spreadsheet cells directly into my word processing documents, and I could pull data from my database directly into my spreadsheets. And over time, the applications in Office became just as good as or better than the old best-of-breed apps.

Now, in your mind, add three zeros onto the price tag of each desktop application. Also, imagine that each individual app is composed of tens of millions of lines of code instead of hundreds of thousands of lines. Now you are thinking about the relative cost and complexity of B2B apps. Webridge Extranet is the Microsoft Office of the B2B application world.

7.3.2 WEBRIDGE EXTRANET

Webridge Extranet includes a B2B Web site that implementers can customize and deploy easily. Webridge Extranet also includes the Webridge Extranet Application Suite, which consists of several integrated business applications that provide useful B2B functionality.

The Webridge Extranet Web site has some additional infrastructure-level features that are important to site owners and users and that are difficult for developers to build from scratch. These features include delegated administration and the ability for business owners to define their own information architecture and layout for their site.

The Webridge Extranet Application Suite includes B2B apps such as a secure online product catalog, a document management system, a process tracking system (for human-driven processes, as opposed to the computer-driven processes in BizTalk), secure threaded discussions, an e-mail–based notification system, and some other apps that can be useful in B2B implementations.

Finally, Webridge Extranet provides development tools that make it easy for programmers to build additional applications or modify or extend the existing ones.

The Webridge Extranet Web Site
Here I will hit the highlights of the Webridge Extranet Web site, that make it unique in the B2B world and that make it useful to implementers of B2B applications.

The remainder of this chapter reads more like a specification than a tutorial. If you do not have an immediate need for this type of software, the rest of this chapter might be a lot of detail for you to slog through. However, it will acquaint you with how high the bar is set for application functionality in the B2B world.

Delegated Administration   The first feature we will examine is Delegated Administration. The need for and application of Delegated Administration is best illustrated by a real-life example.

A company I know—I'll call it *Manufacturer B*—owns a B2B Web site that is used to conduct business with companies with which Manufacturer B has ongoing relationships. A sticky situation arose when one of the companies that uses its B2B site—I'll call it *Company D*—had to fire one of its employees. This employee at Company D had a user account on Manufacturer B's Web site and was authorized to access some of Company D's sensitive information on that site.

Company D contacted Manufacturer B and wanted the fired employee's account on the Web site disabled immediately. Manufacturer B was not able to respond immediately, and Company D viewed this as a serious problem with Manufacturer B's Web site. After this incident, Company D demanded the ability to administer the user accounts of its own employees on Manufacturer B's Web site.

Of course, this posed a problem for the site administrators at Manufacturer B. They had to find a way to grant a user or two from Company D the ability to administer the user accounts of the employees of Company D. However, they did not want these administrators from Company D to have access to the information or user accounts that belong to any other companies. They needed a way to grant selectively certain administrative capabilities to particular users.

The Webridge Extranet Web site enables site administrators to delegate some of their authority to particular users on the site. The idea is to grant certain individuals at other companies the authority to maintain the user account database for users who are employees of their own company. These individuals are called Delegated Administrators.

The authority that site administrators can selectively grant to Delegated Administrators includes the authority to create, edit, and delete data of any or all of the following types:

- Users

- User roles

- Companies

- Company categories (which are used to designate types of companies)

- Authorities

The ability to create, edit, and delete Authorities gives a Delegated Administrator the ability to delegate authority to yet other Delegated Administrators. System Administrators can specify whether a Delegated Administrator has the ability to delegate further his or her authority.

In Webridge Extranet, the ability to edit and delete data is always based on the hierarchy of Authorities. The *Root* Authority, which is the authority held by the System Administrator, can edit and delete any and all data on the site. Administrators in Authorities that are under the Root Authority are not able to edit and delete data that was created by the Root Authority, and they can edit and delete only data that was created in their Authority or in an Authority that is its child.

This creates natural barriers so that Delegated Administrators from various companies cannot affect each other's information on a site, while enabling higher-level Administrators to control and manage all of the data within their areas of responsibility.

Page Layout and Information Architecture Created by Authorized Users   In Webridge Extranet, Web pages are called Folders. The term *Folder* is used because it illustrates the fact that pages in Webridge Extranet are secure containers for content and functionality and that each Folder can contain links to other Folders, which can likewise contain content, functionality, and links to yet other Folders. You can view examples of Folders and see what kind of a browser UI they create by visiting the Webridge Web site at *www.webridge.com.*

Folders in Webridge Extranet are arranged in a hierarchy. Each Folder has a parent Folder and potentially several child Folders. Each child Folder may contain other child Folders, and those children may contain still other children. There is no fixed limit to the depth of the Folder hierarchy in Webridge Extranet.

The parent/child relationship of Folders on a Webridge Extranet-based site creates a hierarchy for the site. Note that each Folder has one and only one parent

Folder, except the Home Folder, which is the root of the hierarchy and has no parent. Note also that each Folder may contain zero, one, or many child Folders.

A site's Information Architecture (IA) refers to the organization and classification of content on the site, as well as the user interface that enables users to locate the content they are seeking.

The challenges of IA include creating effective and descriptive content labels and organizing those labels to maximize the usability of the site. As the content on the site changes over time, it is necessary to change the IA to match it. Webridge Extranet enables nonprogrammers and business users to modify the IA so it easily keeps pace with changes to the content and functionality on the site.

In a Webridge Extranet site, each Folder is given a name. The Folder name becomes the label for the content in that Folder. Administrators and content managers are able to create Folders and assign the name of each Folder on the site.

The IA of a Webridge Extranet site is made up of hyperlinks to the various Folders in the site. The names of the Folders are used as the text of hyperlinks that appear in the top navigation bar of each Web page. Hyperlinks to the Home Folder and to other top-level Folders appear in the Top Navigator of the Webridge Extranet site. Clicking a hyperlink that points to a Folder causes the browser to render that Folder. When a Folder is displayed, the child Folders it contains appear as hyperlinks inside the page.

Web Canvas for Page Layout If you have ever personalized your own home page on a site such as MSN or MyYahoo, you are familiar with the process of modifying a Web page using a browser. Webridge Extranet expands on this concept to enable business managers to specify the information that will appear in each folder on a Webridge Extranet-based site.

Folders display both content from the site and selected information from the company's internal applications. Administrators and Folder owners can specify the content and layout of each Folder. Items of content in a Webridge Extranet-based site are called *Resources*. Examples of resources are documents, URLs, messages, and data from other information systems. Resources are displayed in Folders using Components. A *Component* is a portion of a Web page that displays a particular type of Resource. For instance, a Document Component displays hyperlinks to documents.

Included with Webridge Extranet are several standard Components that accommodate frequently used Resource types, such as documents, URLs, messages, and calendar events. A complete list of the standard Components that are available with Webridge Extranet is available from Webridge.

Administrators and Folder owners can specify which Components appear in each Folder. Each Folder is a canvas on which authorized users can place Components that display information and provide functionality. The user interface for specifying these Components is similar to the personalization features for content and layout on the MSN and the MyYahoo Web sites.

Components can also serve as the user interface for application functionality. For example, a Component can display information from a process that securely integrates a company's Webridge Extranet-based applications with its backend information systems.

Content Ownership and Access Control　In every Webridge Extranet-based site, a few users (perhaps two or three) are designated as the administrators of the site. These users are assigned the role of *Site Manager*. In addition, the Webridge Extranet site is shipped with a particular user account named *System Administrator*, that is assigned the role of Site Manager and that is also an owner of all of the Folders that exist in the Webridge Extranet site.

The System Administrator can authorize other users on the site to create and own Folders. Folder owners can create child Folders within the Folders they own. When someone creates a Folder, he or she automatically become an owner of that Folder. The Webridge Extranet delegation model enables owners of a Folder to designate additional users to be owners of that Folder as well.

Content Access Control　Folders are used to segregate information and target it to distinct users and groups of users. Owners of a Folder can assign the access control settings for the Folder to control who has access to it.

The user interface for assigning the access control settings for the Folder is a simple browser-based form, which allows nontechnical business users to manage access without requiring help from people in IT. Access control in Webridge Extranet is based on a user's attributes.

- Identity
- Company
- Company category (which is used to designate types of companies)
- Role
- Group
- Authorities

Ownership of Content　Folder owners can create the look and feel for their Folder. Owners can control the content of the Folder by adding or removing Components (each of which displays a particular type of Resource) in the Folder. They can modify the name of the Folder and define its layout, including the display of an image and description. They can specify the number of columns in which Components are rendered inside the Folder. A Folder owner can also designate in which column and at what position each Component should be rendered.

Folder owners can designate a Folder as being Open, Closed, or Moderated. In an Open Folder, any user who can access the Folder can publish content in the Folder by adding Resources to Components in the Folder. They can do this without review or approval by the Folder owners. In a Closed Folder, only Folder owners may add Resources.

In a Moderated Folder, any user who can access the Folder may submit Resources to be published, but a Folder owner must approve all Resources before they are made visible to nonowners. Resources that have been submitted and are awaiting approval are placed in a special child Folder, which exists in every Moderated Folder, called the *Pending Items Folder*.

Note that only a Folder owner can add and remove Components in that Folder. Nonowners can publish a Resource of a given type only if a Folder owner has added a Component that handles that particular type of Resource.

When a Resource is published in a Folder, that Resource assumes the access control settings of the Folder in which it is published. Folder owners can override the access control settings of individual Resources so the access control settings of the Resource are different from the access control settings of the Folder.

THE WEBRIDGE EXTRANET APPLICATION SUITE
The Webridge Extranet Application Suite includes a collection of applications that provide content, collaboration, and commerce functionality. Developers can extend these apps as needed to fit application requirements.

The nifty thing about these apps, besides their lengthy list of features, is the way they all integrate with each other, right out of the box. Just as Microsoft Office lets you put spreadsheets in your word processing documents and put database data in your spreadsheets, the Webridge Extranet Application Suite enables relevant business data to flow smoothly among the applications in the suite.

For example, in Webridge Extranet, the data that is used to keep track of user accounts is extended and used for activity tracking and contact management. The documents that constitute the unstructured data on the site are managed by the content management system and are leveraged by the product catalog to provide design documents, specifications, white papers, and brochures for the products. The threaded discussion forums also store posted messages as documents in the repository so they can be easily searched based on their contents.

Content Management   In the previous chapters, you learned the how to use .NET to build the basics of a content access control system. In Webridge Extranet, the ideas of content access control to which you were introduced have been fully implemented.

You will recall from Chapter 5 that the question of where to store and how to process uploaded documents was left unresolved. Webridge Extranet implements its document repository by storing the document files under a Corpus directory. The contents of the documents are indexed using the Indexing Service. For each document in the Corpus, there is a proxy object in the database, which enables developers to work with documents as if they were software objects.

An upcoming version of Webridge Extranet offers the ability to store documents in an instance of Microsoft's Share Point Portal Server (SPS) instead of the Corpus directory, thereby leveraging the workflow and document management that SPS offers.

Webridge Extranet supports files of virtually any type, including Microsoft Office documents, CAD drawings, graphic images, and binary files. In Webridge Extranet, all of these files are generally referred to as *documents*.

A simple browser-based form enables users to classify documents and add Meta data, such as the document's title, description, author, owner, activation date, and expiration date. Users submit Documents to a Webridge Extranet site by clicking the Add button on the Document Component in a Folder in which they have authority to submit and/or publish.

A revision history is kept for each document, so that whenever the document is modified, previous versions are stored on the server and are available for administrators and document owners to roll back to if needed.

When a document is submitted, it adopts the content access settings of the Folder in which it is published. Additional content access settings can be added easily to provide Document-level security.

Each document has an activation date and expiration date. This enables content managers to keep the documents on the site fresh and current easily. The activation date is the date on which the document will automatically become visible on the Webridge Extranet site. The expiration date is the date on which the document will automatically become invisible on the Webridge Extranet site (it is not deleted and may be reinstated if required).

Once a document is published in a Folder on Webridge Extranet, it can be referenced in additional Folders on the site. For example, hyperlinks to a Bill of Materials document might exist in an Engineering Folder and in a Sales Folder. To simplify content management, only one copy of the document is maintained on the site, even though there might be several references to it in different Folders. When multiple references to documents exist, individual references can be deleted without affecting the remaining references.

Webridge Extranet provides a check in/check out mechanism to prevent users from overwriting each other's changes to documents on the site. This capability is essential for effective content management and for collaboration as well.

Only authorized users on a Webridge Extranet site can edit documents. When a Folder owner wishes to edit a document, he or she uses a simple browser-based form to check out the document and make edits to it.

While a document is checked out, no one else can edit it. When the Folder owner is finished editing the document, he or she can use another browser-based form to upload the updated version of the document to the Webridge Extranet site. The previous version(s) of the document are archived and can be accessed using the History and Rollback link for that document that is available to Folder owners. Once the document has been updated, the user can check the document back in to enable other authorized users to edit it.

The content search capability in Webridge Extranet allows users with browsers to search content on the site for key words, phrases, and/or properties such as an author's name. The full-text search function includes the ability to use Boolean terms, keywords, and quoted phrases. An advanced search page is included to enable searches on an extensible set of fields, including author, date published, type of content, and so on.

Searches can be conducted in individual Folders or across the entire site. The search capabilities are integrated into the security infrastructure, so search results will include only information that the user is authorized to see. For example, a search for pricing by a Platinum-level reseller will return only Platinum pricing, not Gold pricing.

Collaboration   Collaboration in Webridge Extranet enables secure, asynchronous, one-to-many, and many-to-many communications. With the Webridge Extranet Notification Manager, the business manager can automate the sending of bulk e-mail messages to a large set of recipients. The business manager does the following:

1. Selects a message template or creates a new one using the browser-based message template editor.

2. Selects a set of recipients.

3. Specifies the mode of delivery and starts the job.

Note that the same template can be used at different times to create different jobs. At any time the submitter of the job can view its status. The Webridge Notification Manager uses Microsoft MSMQ to deliver the messages. By chance if the network gets disconnected during delivery, jobs are not lost. Upon reconnection, message delivery resumes.

Webridge Extranet provides workflow for users to propose content and for content managers to review the new content and decide whether to reject it, edit it, or publish it. Content publishing on Webridge Extranet follows a "propose, review, reject, or publish" workflow process.

In a Moderated Folder, any user who can access the Folder may submit Resources to be published, but a Folder owner must approve all Resources before they are made visible in the Folder to nonowners. Resources that have been submitted to a Moderated Folder are placed in a special child Folder, which exists in every Moderated Folder, called the *Pending Items Folder*.

The Pending Items Folder inside each Moderated Folder is accessible only to owners of that Folder. Folder owners can be notified via e-mail whenever new items are placed in the Pending Items Folder. Using a browser, Folder owners can review the content and approve, edit, or publish it using a simple Web-based form. Once approved, the content is removed from the Pending Items Folder and is made visible to users who can access the Folder.

Discussions are organized around *forums*. Discussion Forums in Webridge Extranet are similar to news groups on the Internet, but they have the added capability of security so that sensitive information can be discussed and shared in a secure environment.

Discussion Forums contain threads of conversation that can occur over extended periods of time among multiple users. Users can start their own conversation threads, or they can follow or respond to messages on existing threads.

Folder owners can add a Discussion Forum Component to their Folder to enable these threaded discussions. Discussion Forums can be moderated by Folder owners to avoid clutter.

Discussion Forums are integrated into the search engine, so their relevant content can be retrieved easily. Discussion Forums are integrated into the security infrastructure, so only authorized users can access the Forums and their contents. Discussion Forums are integrated with e-mail notifications to encourage people to use them.

Webridge Extranet gives every authorized user in the company a single, centralized view of customer activity. Employees in marketing, sales, customer service, and other areas of the company can collaborate on projects at each stage of the customer life cycle. From prospect capture and lead qualification to customer shipment and satisfaction surveys, users all get a uniform, centralized view of all customer activity.

Relationship Management provides a platform for recording and managing all interactions with customers and partners, including telephone calls, meetings, e-mail, and Web hits.

Webridge Extranet Relationship Manager enables a company to nurture its sales prospects and effectively manage long and complex sales cycles. It provides a mechanism for businesses to develop a knowledge base of their clients and leverage that information to create new market opportunities. Team members inside and outside the business get a centralized browser-based view of total customer activity and avoid the complexities of separate Customer Relationship Management (CRM) or Sales Force Automation (SFA) systems.

Users can immediately access up-to-the-moment data while customers are still on the phone. For example, employees can manipulate customer data alongside product and price data while viewing customer's technical and service history, discussion group feedback, and shared calendar. Webridge Extranet Relationship Manager can automatically share tasks and activities between users and accurately model a company's unique business processes.

Relationship Management within Webridge Extranet provides comprehensive relationship management capabilities in three important areas:

- Business process management
- Activity tracking
- Contact management

From a technical perspective, RM does the following:

- Defines the structure of a database in which to organize and store information about customers and prospects.
- Provides a set of tools that end-users use to create, access, and manipulate information in the database.
- Defines a set of workflow automation mechanisms, called Queues, that allow users to track and manage task assignments as they flow through a company.

Commerce   Commerce means buying and selling. To buy and sell, you usually have to have a catalog. The Webridge Extranet Catalog enables companies to do more than conduct simple transactions over the Internet. It lets them to do business more effectively over the Internet and enhance their continuing relationships with their customers.

Using Webridge Extranet catalogs, companies don't merely buy and sell commodity products based on price. Rather, they buy and sell complex products in ongoing business relationships.

With the Webridge Extranet catalog, users log into the Webridge Extranet site, and, based on their identity, employer, role, and so forth, they are allowed to see specific catalogs. These catalogs are tailored for them, with specially designed products and pricing.

Because of the collaboration and content features of Webridge Extranet, in addition to catalog information, users can safely view other types of information that relates to the products, such as schematics, bills of materials, contracts, FAQs, messages from Discussion Forums, Web page links, and so on.

The catalogs themselves are easy to create and manage. Product Managers, using only a Web browser and without help from developers or Web masters, can create products, SKUs, and Catalog layouts.

With the Delegated administration and ownership capabilities of Webridge Extranet, it is also possible for the company that owns the Webridge Extranet site to delegate the creation and ownership of catalogs on the site. As a result, companies other than the company that owns the Webridge Extranet site can safely maintain catalogs for their products on the site. This enables a large corporation to use Webridge Extranet to host catalogs from each of its divisions, which can be targeted to multiple and interrelated groups of customers.

Products and services are organized into catalogs, each of which contains Product Categories (which may be nested) that contain the Products. Security may be applied at any level of the catalog using the standard Webridge Extranet permission forms. The same products may be represented in many different catalogs with different product groupings and hierarchies.

These capabilities permit parallel catalog building, where one group of people may populate products into a site while the other group is creating the catalog hierarchy and grouping.

Another compelling thing about the Webridge Extranet Catalog is that properties can be added to product types in a very flexible way. For instance, you can define a product type of book, with properties for the book's title, author, publisher, price, length, and so on. Then you can create a variant of the book type for audio books. These audio books will have other properties, such as the media format, number of tapes or CDs, and so on. The length property can be shared between printed books and audio books: the length in pages for printed books and the length in minutes for audio books. The other really cool thing is that you can define all of these complex product types using only a Web browser.

MANAGEMENT AND ADMINISTRATION

An area of B2B that often occupies a significant portion of developers' time is creating pages and writing code to enable easy administration of B2B applications. I won't go into all the details of the built-in management and administration functions of Webridge Extranet. However, I will mention three functions that are particularly helpful.

The first is an online backup facility. Webridge provides scripts that enable a Webridge Extranet-based B2B Web site to be easily backed up. The execution of these scripts can be scheduled and automated so that backups happen at regular intervals.

The second administration function is the ability to run a single script that compresses an entire B2B Web site, pages, code, data, and all, into a single zip file. This zip file can then be burned onto a CD or sent over the Internet, and it can be imported on another machine to produce an exact copy of the original site. This facility is useful for deploying a site to a customer's machine and in support situations where you need a copy of the entire site, including code and data, for testing or troubleshooting purposes.

The third administration function is the complete library of Web browser-based administration pages. Virtually all administration of a Webridge Extranet-based B2B Web site and applications can be done with a Web browser. Making these administration pages user-friendly, feature-complete, and secure is a significant development task, and in Webridge Extranet, Webridge has taken care of this for you.

SUMMARY

B2B applications require a hefty software infrastructure. The long list of features that make B2B applications truly useful are not simple to write.

Webridge Extranet is a software framework that provides the infrastructure for B2B applications. Its purpose is to enable the features that customers want for their own deployments to be created for them quickly and then to empower business users to handle as much of the administrative work as possible in their own B2B applications.

PEOPLE, POLITICS, AND B2B PROJECTS

Part 2 deals with the *people* portion of *how* to build B2B applications. The exploration of the *people-how* B2B topics in Part 2 begins with a presentation of security issues in B2B applications. This is followed by words of warning on the traps that are present in B2B development efforts. Following this you will find advice on how to form a B2B development team. And finally, you will learn about a lightweight methodology for managing B2B projects.

This part of the book will be of the most interest to readers who are tasked with managing B2B development projects or are otherwise responsible for making them successful.

Note: The chapters in Part 2 contain no source code. Developers who read a book primarily for source code examples will be inclined to believe that these chapters are not relevant to them. Developers can skim over these chapters if they wish. I suggest, however, that even though these chapters contain no source code, developers should at least skim these chapters to make sure they are knowledgeable on these topics.

I have seen at least three major B2B development projects where the programmers did a beautiful job of writing the source code, but the software was never deployed and the application was never used. And the programmers who wrote the code never got any credit for the fine work they did.

The programmers' lack of knowledge on the topics in this part of the book put them in a situation where they had a three- or four-month blank space on their resumes where they had little to show for their efforts. Had these programmers been aware of the issues presented here, they could have perhaps helped their project to succeed, or at least they could have foreseen the problems and avoided the project in the first place.

Project managers and their bosses will find that this part of the book contains information that is particularly relevant to them. B2B development has its own set of challenges, and in these chapters I do my best to prepare you to overcome them.

Security in an Insecure World

To conduct B2B Internet commerce, companies have no choice but to connect their internal networks and information systems to the rest of the world. They must connect their internal information systems with those of their customers, suppliers, and partners. With those connections come new threats: crackers, criminals, and industrial spies. These attackers can steal trade secrets, cause system failures, destroy valuable information, deface Web sites, and scare customers.

Internet connectivity between businesses is indeed a two-edged sword. It presents a great commercial opportunity, but it also makes a company vulnerable to exploitation and attack. This chapter gives advice for managing the security risks that are ever-present in B2B Internet commerce.

It seems that most of the existing material on Internet security is filled with acronyms and instructions. With all of this detail, it can be difficult to see an overall picture of security dangers and get a good overview of the technologies and techniques used to combat them. In this chapter, I try to provide that overview. The bibliography lists additional resources that you can consult to get further detail on specific topics in security on the Internet.

The key points for this chapter are the following:

- A primary role of a B2B Web site is to secure the flow of information between businesses.

- The B2B server itself must be hardened against attack to be effective in that role.

- Security threats can come from inside and from outside an organization.

- There are a variety of technical and procedural remedies that can reduce the security risks a company faces when conducting B2B Internet commerce.

8.1   SECURITY, A PRIMARY ROLE OF B2B WEB SITES

A primary function of a B2B Web site is to secure the flow of information between businesses. The data that is needed for effective B2B commerce is always found inside a company's existing information systems. Therefore, to conduct B2B Internet commerce effectively, a company has to open its information systems to its partners, suppliers, and customers. However, prudence demands that companies grant access to their internal systems only in a very select and secure way. To repeat my oft-repeated, classic example, a company that is conducting business with its partners over the Web must ensure that Partner A cannot gain access to any of Partner B's data. The company must also ensure that potential attackers are granted no access at all.

Almost without fail, a company's internal information systems are built for use only inside the protected walls of the enterprise. Traditionally, no thought is given to the prospect of these systems being opened up for access by users outside the enterprise. External access, and the requisite security that it demands, is typically not considered when designing the security features of internal information systems.

B2B-type security, the collection of security mechanisms needed to ensure that external users access only what they are authorized to access, must be bolted onto the front of a company's internal information systems. Furnishing this security is a primary function of a B2B Web site.

8.2   PROTECTING THE B2B SITE

A B2B Web site, which furnishes security for internal information systems, would be ineffective in that role if it were vulnerable itself. For this reason, a B2B Web site must be hosted on a secure server, and this server machine itself must be "hardened" so that it is less vulnerable to attack. To understand how best to harden a B2B server, you must understand something of the security threats that exist on today's Internet.

Businesses that do B2B Internet commerce are vulnerable to the theft of trade secrets, fraud, embezzlement, and cleanup expenses after computer viruses and other damaging attacks. Another significant threat is the disruption of business through denial of service attack.

Stolen trade secrets, embezzlement, and financial fraud can result in huge dollar losses for companies doing business on the Web, while computer viruses can cause devastating damage to a company's information systems. And just think of what would happen to a group of companies totally reliant on a fully automated B2B commerce system for their business interaction if their systems were shut down by a denial of service attacks.

Often the single greatest catalyst for implementing effective security in Internet commerce applications is a major security breach. The fact that it takes a major breach to trigger security improvements illustrates the low priority that companies commonly give to security. Security is often viewed as an expensive precaution that does not directly contribute to the bottom line. Because of the time, effort, and money required to secure the barn door, many companies neglect to close it until after the horse has gotten out or has been stolen or injured.

Recent history has demonstrated that outside the walls of any business there are people who would like to break into its computer systems and steal valuable data or wreak havoc on the company and its customers. However, company insiders constitute perhaps an even more significant threat to the security of computer systems. Security threats from insiders come in two varieties: negligent and intentional.

8.3 INSIDER NEGLIGENCE

Brilliant technology to handle security will not work if people neglect to use it. Imagine a company spending thousands of dollars on new a security system, only to have their employees turn it off because the system makes too much noise.

Also imagine that one employee sees another employee doing something that could compromise their company's security. Consider the following questions to determine whether the company's management is the party that is actually being neglectful in that situation:

- Would either employee know if the thing they were doing was right or wrong?

- Would the employee who saw the security breach know that he or she should report it?

- Would the employee know how to report the security breach?

Vigilance is the price that companies must constantly pay to keep their assets secure, and it should be a vital part of the culture of the firm. This culture of vigilance must start at the top, with a company's executives, directors, and managers.

This vigilance must be manifest in the company's policies. Management must create a framework of policies for effective security inside the organization. Adhering to security policies requires extra work on everyone's part. Employees won't be motivated to put in that extra effort unless security goals are tied to the mission of the organization and to their own rewards. The key is to make security relevant to the employees. Management needs to convey the message that if someone is lax about security, it can impede the company's progress and harm the employees' prospects.

When talking to employees, management must spell out in very clear terms what inappropriate security is and how it can prevent them from getting their jobs done.

Management must make security part of the organization's culture. They must impress its importance on employees from day one. That means security training should be part of employees' early orientation. They must be trained in the procedures for identifying and reporting security violations. They need to know the rules of security in their organization and know the right people to call if they suspect violations.

Despite these precautions, it is almost impossible to eliminate entirely security breaches by employees. A cracker was able to roam through Microsoft's network for several days during October 2000 and view some of the company's top-secret source code. The cracker was able to gain access because a Microsoft employee forgot to create a password when configuring a server he was setting up for a customer. The attacker initially entered Microsoft's network through the computer of a Microsoft employee. Once inside, the intruder searched for a server with a blank password and was able to get in.

Next, the intruder searched the network for computers with no passwords or with passwords that would be easy to decipher. As the intruder probed for access to other machines, Microsoft's network monitoring team discovered the intrusion. This intrusion clearly wasn't a technology problem. The technology was available to prevent a break-in, but the break-in was enabled by less-than-prudent machine configurations by negligent employees.

Negligence on the part of developers can also open the door for online thieves. For instance, some shopping cart applications have been vulnerable to phony price alterations through the use of the page-editing feature in Web browsers. A thief can select a product from an online catalog and proceed to a checkout page, which shows the product's price. The thief can edit the page in the browser to reduce the price and then submit the page to the server. If the code at the server does not verify the price on the checkout page, the thief is literally able to name his or her own price. It is negligence on the part of a developer to trust the data that comes back from a client browser, and negligence like this opens the front door for online thieves.

8.4 DELIBERATE ATTACKS FROM THE INSIDE

Unfortunately, sometimes the most trusted individuals inside of an organization are the biggest security threat. You may recall a few instances where an FBI agent turned to the dark side and began selling classified information. These cases involving FBI agents are particularly telling because they are employees who possess intelligence and potential, are in a position of trust, and are granted privileged access to sensitive data. Despite their potential, they find that their career has faltered or is not as rewarding as they would like. Over time they become frustrated and contemptuous of their employer, and before the employer realizes the extent of their contempt, they have done irreparable harm.

Sadly, cases like this aren't limited to the FBI. Companies in the private sector are at risk from similar perpetrators. Employees with potential and intelligence are granted trusted access to valuable data, only later to turn on their employers to reap the rewards they feel they deserve but have not received. Surprisingly, system administrators, network security personnel, and senior executives are often the culprits.

The experiences of Recourse Technologies *(http://www.recoursetechnologies .com)* are instructive in this regard. Recourse Technologies produces "honey pots," which are phony servers populated with false data designed to attract internal thieves. These honey pots can catch perpetrators who would never be suspect otherwise. Once, during a demo of the Recourse's Mantrap honey pot software at a large manufacturing company, a member of the manufacturing company's own network security team attempted to hack the honey pot server.*

In another case, a large financial firm discovered discrepancies in its payroll system. It set up some honey pots and gave each server an interesting name, such as "payroll server." The next morning, the company's chief operating officer was caught trying to jury-rig another executive's payroll account. Internal threats like these are compounded by the many threats that lurk outside the walls of an enterprise.

8.5 ATTACKS FROM THE OUTSIDE

The external threats to a B2B Web site are numerous and varied. Before exploring these external threats, it is helpful to define a few terms.

Hacking is the unauthorized use of an information system or network by circumventing its security mechanisms. Depending on whom you ask, a hacker is either a good guy or a bad guy. Some people say that a hacker is a champion of freedom and individuality who enjoys harmlessly exploring the details of computer systems for his or her own educational purposes. They somehow believe that trespassing is not a crime as long as the trespasser does not break or steal anything. Other people define a hacker as a person who trespasses into computer systems and steals things.

A *cracker,* on the other hand, is universally held to be a bad guy, someone who attacks computer systems with harmful intent. Crackers might hack into a system to steal things or to do damage to the system, or they might conduct denial-of-service attacks on a system.

A *samurai* is an expert programmer who is hired to break into a company's computer system or Web site to test for security holes.

Script kiddies are people who aspire to be hackers/crackers but who have limited knowledge or skills. Usually this term refers to young teenagers who use malicious programs that they obtain from the Internet.

Sniffing is electronic eavesdropping to obtain information that is intended for other computers as data is transmitted over a network.

With these terms in mind, you can begin to examine the security threats that confront companies conducting B2B Internet commerce. These include the threats illustrated in Figure 8-1.

---

*Information contained herein referencing Recourse Technologies, Inc. is extracted from the Honeypot Effective Study published September 22, 2000, conducted for Recourse Technologies, Inc. by Predictive Systems' Global Integrity Managed Services practice in Reston, VA. It is provided with permission from Recourse Technologies and Predictive Systems. All rights reserved. Recourse Technologies and ManHunt are trademarks of Recourse Technologies. ManTrap is a registered trademark of Recourse Technologies. All other trademarks belong to their respective owners.

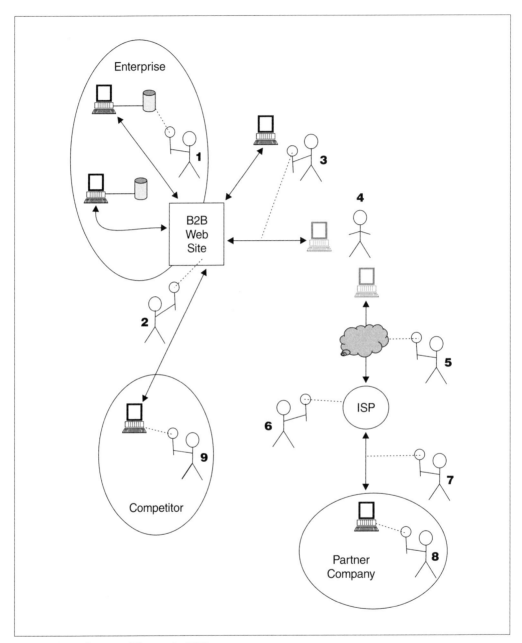

FIGURE 8-1   *Security Threats in B2B*

1. *Insider attack:* An employee of the organization, an insider, could access a server, application, or database to steal, alter, or damage valuable information.

2. *B2B Web site attack:* A cracker could break through the B2B Web site to access the internal information systems it protects to steal information or cause damage.

3. *Replay attack:* A cracker could tap the line to capture the communications between the B2B Web server and a client in order to carry out a replay attack, in which the attacker captures the session-based security credentials of a visitor and uses those credentials to execute counterfeit transactions.

4. *Man-in-the-middle attack:* A cracker could make a man-in-the-middle attack, in which the attacker intercepts all of the communications between two parties. The attacker makes each party think that it is communicating with the other, enabling the attacker to be in command of the communications.

5. *Sniff the Internet backbone:* A cracker could sniff the Internet backbone to listen for passwords or other valuable information being passed between computers over the Internet.

6. *Sniff the ISP:* A cracker could sniff the ISP to listen for passwords or other valuable information being passed between computers that use the ISP.

7. *Unauthorized access by a friend:* An employee of a partner company could conduct industrial espionage by viewing on the B2B Web site pages that contain information that he or she is not authorized to see.

8. *Unauthorized access by a foe:* A competitor steals trade secrets and conducts industrial espionage by viewing on the B2B Web site pages that contain information that he or she is not authorized to see.

8.6 BUILDING A HARDENED B2B SERVER

Hardening a B2B server will help prevent a hacking attack on the server, like the B2B Web site attack that is numbered "2" in Figure 8-1. The process of hardening B2B Web server varies with different operating systems and server software packages. The process involves configuring the server with appropriate user access accounts, setting permissions on files and resources, removing certain utilities and administration tools that could be used to facilitate an attack, ensuring that all passwords are adequate, and installing the latest security patches. It also involves setting up a network topology, including the use of firewalls, to minimize the risk of attack on the B2B server and the rest of the information systems in the enterprise.

The best place to find specifics on securing a server is technical security literature provided by your server software vendor. For example, you can consult *http://www.microsoft.com/security/default.asp* for advice and bulletins on security for Microsoft servers, and you can browse *http://www.oracle.com/ip/solve/security/* for information on security for Oracle servers.

It is important to note that the process of hardening a server against attack is an incremental one. New attacks are always being devised, and once they are developed, these attacks are published in various forums for all interested parties to see. These interested parties include both good guys and bad guys. Until server software vendors can build a defense for each new attack into a new security patch for their software, there is a window of exposure for the servers. Until an effective security patch is applied, a server is vulnerable and exposed to potential attack.

On a B2B server, whose job is to protect internal information systems, it is particularly important that the window of exposure to each attack be closed as quickly as possible. This means obtaining and installing all security patches as soon as they become available. In addition, active network monitoring can detect attacks and trigger an effective internal response to limit any potential damage.

8.7   SECURE COMMUNICATIONS IN INTERNET COMMERCE

Hardening the B2B Web server can make it difficult for attackers to hack into the B2B site or into the internal information systems that it protects. However, to guard against attacks that involve eavesdropping, like those numbered 3 through 6 in Figure 8-1, it is necessary to use encryption to transport data safely between computers.

Encryption provides four key functions that are vital to Internet commerce:

- *Confidentiality*, which is accomplished by scrambling the data that is sent between computers over the Internet so that eavesdroppers cannot decipher any of the information that they may obtain through sniffing of the communications lines

- *Authentication*, by which the people who receive a message can verify the identity of the person who sent the message to them

- *Integrity*, which ensures that a message has not been modified while in transit

- *Nonrepudiation*, which prevents an author of a message from being able to deny falsely sending the message

In practice, several encryption technologies are used in concert to supply these four essential functions for Internet commerce. Encryption on the Internet is used in several different forms to provide secure communications.

With encryption, you can take a message written in plain text that anyone could read and run it through a mathematical formula along with another number called a key. What you get out of the mathematical formula is a bunch of numbers that appear to be completely random and are not comprehensible.

In encryption terms, the original message that anyone can read is called the plaintext. The bunch of numbers that you get out of the formula is called the ciphertext. A message that is transformed from plaintext to ciphertext is called an encrypted message. The mathematical formula that is used to encrypt messages is called the encryption algorithm. The encryption process is illustrated in Figure 8-2.

The goal of encrypting a message is to make it impossible for anyone to reproduce the original plaintext message from the ciphertext without first obtaining the encryption algorithm and key.

If someone knows the encryption algorithm and key that were used to encrypt the message, he or she can run the ciphertext with the key through the encryption algorithm and derive the original plaintext. A message that is thus transformed from ciphertext back to the original plaintext is a *decrypted* message.

As mentioned earlier, the key is a number that is passed into the encryption algorithm along with the message to encrypt it or decrypt it. The larger the key, the more secure the encryption because it is more difficult to guess the key.

An encryption algorithm that uses the same key for encryption and decryption is called a symmetric key algorithm. Symmetric key algorithms are designed to be very fast and have a large number of possible keys. The problem, however, is that for two parties to be able to use a symmetric key algorithm to communicate securely, they must first securely exchange the encryption key that they will use to encrypt and decrypt their messages.

There is another type of encryption algorithm, sometimes called an asymmetric key algorithm, in which one key is used to encrypt the message and a different but

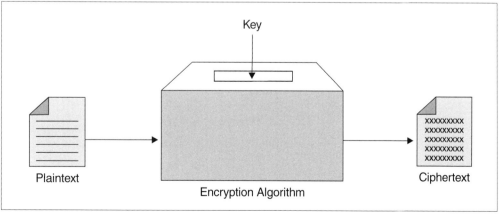

Key

Plaintext

Encryption Algorithm

Ciphertext

FIGURE 8-2 *The Encryption Process*

corresponding key is used to decrypt it. These algorithms are more commonly known as public key algorithms.

8.7.1   PUBLIC KEY ALGORITHMS

With public key algorithms, a pair of keys is used. One key is called the public key, and the other key is called the private key. The *public key* can be made publicly available without compromising the secrecy of the communications. For secrecy to be maintained, however, the private key must be kept private. Only the key holder should know it or have access to it.

The idea with public key algorithms is that I can create or obtain a pair of keys, one being my public key and the other being my private key. I can give my public key to you and lots of other people. I carefully guard my private key and give it to no one. I can then sign the messages I send to you using my private key, and you can read those messages using my public key.

The messages I encrypt with my private key are not secret because anyone who has my public key can decrypt them. However, if you are able to decrypt a message using my public key, you can be certain that Lyn Robison's private key was used to encrypt that message. If I have kept my private key private, then you can be assured that I am the person who wrote that message—not some imposter who simply claims to be me. In that way, you could say that the message is authenticated, which means that you have confidence that you know who the author is. The content of the message is not secret, but its source is authenticated.

Conversely, my *private key* is the only way to decrypt the contents of a message that you have encrypted using my public key. So you can be certain that the only person who can read a message that you encrypt using my public key is the person who has Lyn Robison's private key, and that would be me if I have kept my private key to myself. The idea is that my public key enables you to send secret messages that only I can decipher.

However, on my end of the communications, I cannot be certain about who actually wrote the message because just about anyone could have used my public key to encrypt the message. For all I know, it could be an imposter who claims to be you and is trying to deceive me. So the contents of a message encrypted with my public key would be secret but not authenticated.

In summary, if you hold a private key, you can do the following:

- Send messages that are authenticated but not secret
- Receive messages that are secret but not authenticated

If you hold a public key, you can do the following:

- Send messages that are secret but not authenticated
- Receive messages that are authenticated but not secret

However, in order for authentication to be reliable, I must guard my private key, and you must have some confidence that the public key you have is actually mine. How can you be certain that the public key you have is in fact mine?

For example, suppose that I have an evil twin named "Lex." Lex is identical to me in his appearance and mannerisms, but he is the opposite of me in that his thoughts, intents, and actions are evil instead of good. Suppose that Lex comes to you and says, "I am Lyn, and here is my public key. When you decrypt messages with this key, you will know for sure that I wrote them." Lex could then proceed with his devious plans, take advantage of the trust that you would naturally place in Lyn, do harm to you and others, and then pin the whole thing on me.

To prevent Lex from executing any of his dastardly schemes, I will obtain from a trusted third party a certificate that attests that a particular public key is in fact mine. Certification authorities are the trusted third parties that provide certifications such as these.

8.7.2 CERTIFICATION AUTHORITIES

Certification authorities issue certificates that attest that a particular public key belongs to a particular individual or organization. To obtain a certificate, a person or organization must acquire one from a certification authority. There are names of several certification authorities built in to the security dialogs of the Internet Explorer and Netscape Navigator browsers.

There are different classes of certificates available. In general, the lower-class certificates require less information from the user and are less expensive to obtain. The certification authority also makes less of an effort to verify that the user is not an imposter and places a lower liability cap on the certificates.

The higher classes of certificates require more information from a user, such as the person's name, address, driver's license number, social security number, and so forth, and they are more expensive. The certification authority also makes more of an effort to verify that the user is not an imposter. And anyone who receives a public key accompanied by one of these more stringent certificates can have more assurance that the public key does in fact belong to the user who claims to own it. So if I obtain a certificate, I can give you my public key and my certificate, and you can have some assurance that the public key I am giving you is in fact my own.

There is another way to use certificates and public key algorithms. You may recall that symmetric key algorithms are designed to be a very fast form of encryption. In fact, symmetric key algorithms are in general much faster then public key algorithms. However, the problem with symmetric key algorithms is that it is difficult to exchange securely the key that both parties will use for their communications. It is fascinating to realize that the secure exchange of the key for a symmetric key algorithm can be accomplished using a public key algorithm. In other words, the slower public key algorithm can be used to exchange securely the key that is needed for the faster symmetric key algorithms. A derivative of this idea is used in implementing the Secure Sockets Layer.

8.7.3 SECURE SOCKETS LAYER (SSL)

With SSL, two parties, such as a Web server and a Web browser, can establish an encrypted communications channel. The communications are confidential because they are encrypted, and the integrity of the communications is protected through the use of message authentication codes. Also, SSL is specifically designed to protect against man-in-the-middle attacks and replay attacks. Therefore SSL can guard against eavesdropping attacks like those numbered 3 through 6 in Figure 8-1.

When a communications session is initiated with the SSL protocol, a handshake occurs between the parties. During this handshake, a public key algorithm is used to share securely a number called a premaster secret. Then each party uses the premaster secret to derive a master secret, which is a key that both use with a symmetric key algorithm for the rest of their communications session.

Even though the protocol is sophisticated, SSL is surprisingly simple to use. It is designed to hide the complexities of cryptography from user and developers. Provided that the Web server and a Web browser are both SSL-enabled, using SSL from the browser is simply a matter of changing the protocol portion of the URL from "http://" to "https://."

On the Web server side, setting up SSL is a little more involved. You will need to obtain a server certificate from a certification authority, and you will probably need to perform some additional configuration of the server and its content. Consult your Web server documentation for detailed instructions on how to set up SSL on your Web server.

The fact that each of the messages must be encrypted and decrypted during the communications session makes the SSL protocol run slower than a nonencrypted protocol. However, in many B2B scenarios, the difference in the speed of the protocol has only a negligible effect on application performance. And the costs of a slightly slower communications protocol are far outweighed by the benefits of conducting communications that are confidential and resistant to tampering.

By enabling encryption of the communications between your B2B Web site and its users, you make attacks that involve eavesdropping, such as the attacks numbered 3 through 6 in Figure 8-1, much more difficult. Often, SSL is used to prevent a user's user ID and password from being stolen through eavesdropping on the communications line.

Of course, by using SSL you have not completely eliminated the possibility of such attacks. It is possible to hack through encryption algorithms. But the hope is that you have made those attacks so difficult and expensive to carry out that they would not be profitable for the attacker if he or she should want to try them.

As a complement to the hardening of the B2B server and to the encryption of the communications between the B2B server and users, the organization's information must be categorized according to its need for security and protected accordingly.

8.7.4 SECURING INFORMATION INSIDE AN ORGANIZATION

To guard valuable information from unauthorized access, as in the attacks numbered 1, 7, and 8 in Figure 8-1, it is necessary to decide which types of information in your organization need the most protection and then install security mechanisms to provide that protection.

CATEGORIZING INFORMATION

It is impossible to provide ironclad protection for all the data in an organization, so someone, preferably executive management instead of midlevel IT staff people, has to decide which protection to implement and where to place it. Because implementing security is costly and makes data more difficult for everyone to access, management must be deliberate when deciding which levels of security to apply to the various types of information inside an organization.

The first step in this process is to classify the data inside the organization according to its type. Management should define basic categories or classes of data, such as trade secrets, partner information, payroll data, contracts, customer correspondence, and so on.

The value of each class of data lies on a spectrum between data available to a few top executives and trivial data. In between these two extremes is a vast array of data types with different protection requirements.

Management should think further about how to subdivide the classes of data so that relevant information can be selectively exposed in the B2B environment. In your B2B applications, you will have people in partner businesses accessing the data inside your organization. In these B2B applications, you don't want Partner A to be able to access any of Partner B's data.

Simply creating a class of data called "Partner Data" and giving partners the ability to access it is not sufficient because within the partner data there will be information that is sensitive and that only certain partners should access. In particular, there will be confidential information that belongs to each partner; no other partner should be able to see. Management needs to think about how to categorize and subdivide the partner data so that these access controls can be implemented effectively.

To decide which security level is appropriate for a given class of data, management must ascertain how sensitive and valuable the information is. They must also decide who should have access to the data and who should not. Management must keep in mind that there are different types of access as well, such as read-only access, read-write access, and administrative- or ownership-type access.

Management must decide the relative importance of data inside the organization and specify which types of data really need to be secured. IT developers and security specialists can design various security mechanisms, but management must decide what data they must protect.

REDUCING RISKS

There is no way to eliminate completely the threats to valuable information systems. There is always some degree of security risk. Of course, this does not mean that the effort to secure valuable information systems is futile. Some risk is accepted as the cost of doing business, and a realistic objective is to reduce the security risks that the organization faces to an acceptable level.

Trying to prevent attacks can effectively reduce security risks. Preventive measures are implemented using technical and procedural means, some of which were explained earlier in this chapter. In addition, some security risk can be transferred through contracts and insurance.

In addition to reducing security risks by prevention and transference, you can further reduce risks with effective detection and response, which is done through active network monitoring. For many companies, using an Internet security service that provides detection and response is an effective way to install an Internet alarm system.

One company that provides detection and response services is Counterpane (*http://www.counterpane.com*). Counterpane also offers antihacking insurance from Lloyd's of London.

Detection identifies attacks and unauthorized actions as they are occurring or shortly thereafter, and it issues alerts to an accountable person to respond. Whether a company does detection themselves or hires specialists to do it for them, the detection process involves using network management and auditing tools. These include online scanning and monitoring, trend analysis, and attack forecasting.

After detection comes response. When possible security breaches are identified, security analysts and network administrators must determine the appropriate course of action. They need to apply the proper security remedies until the breach is rectified. By properly responding to security breaches in a timely manner, the risk of data loss or damage to the business is minimized.

The relationship between prevention, detection, and response is best illustrated with a simple example. If the owner of a warehouse wants to prevent burglars from entering the warehouse, a primary precaution the owner will take is to install good locks on the doors. Locks are preventive barriers that do in fact reduce the risk of intruders. However, a skillful burglar might know how to pick these particular locks and still gain entrance.

An effective alarm system coupled with a fast response system can repel the attacker before he has picked the locks. For a warehouse with an alarm system, a new lock-picking technique is not a critical security concern. Of course, the security manager should upgrade his locks to the new resistant technology, but until he can, he has his alarm system to fall back on. Even if an attacker successfully picked the lock, the attacker would still be detected and apprehended.

The same kind of thinking can apply to computer networks. Attackers can be detected inside corporate networks, regardless of which vulnerability they used to enter. Of course, alarms are not impregnable. Attackers will attempt to bypass the alarm system. This is always possible, but it is difficult because alarms provide defense in depth. It is not enough to bypass the door lock and the door alarm; an attacker has to bypass all internal alarms. On a computer network, alarms can be in every server, router, and network software package. Bypassing them can be a truly Herculean task.

A trusted employee might be able to steal from a company without setting off any alarms. That same employee could disable the alarm system. Still, an alarm system makes it much harder to penetrate a building undetected. And in any attack that takes time, an alarm system gives the police the time to respond and stop a crime. This is why banks have alarm systems in addition to blast-proof vaults.*

You can reduce the likelihood of the insider attacks and unauthorized access attacks, numbered 1, 7, and 8 in Figure 8-1, by securing information inside your organization. You can do this by assigning levels of protection to your information and by reducing your security risks through prevention, detection, and response.

You can also do this by encrypting the sensitive data stored in databases and in sensitive files on servers in the enterprise. Servers can be attacked and data can be stolen. If the data is not encrypted, the cracker will be able to read the information easily, but if it is encrypted, the cracker will have a difficult time reading the data.

SUMMARY

To conduct B2B Internet commerce, a company must open its information systems in a select and secure way. A B2B Web site can help accomplish that. Security threats come from inside and outside an organization. Vigilance, policies, and technology all play a role in reducing a company's risks online.

With a properly secured B2B Web site, a company can disclose relevant internal information to its business partners.

---

*Material from the Counterpane Internet Security, Inc. Web site <www.counterpane.com> reprinted by permission.

B2B Development Traps

This chapter will acquaint you with the risks and pitfalls of B2B development. After reading this chapter, you may wonder how any B2B projects are ever completed successfully. Perhaps you are already familiar with the six steps of B2B project management:

1. Wild enthusiasm

2. Confusion

3. Disillusionment

4. Search for the guilty

5. Punishment of the innocent

6. Promotion of the noncontributors

I present this chapter as nothing more or less than the list of common ailments that I have seen afflict B2B projects. These ailments stem from common mistakes and fits of bad judgment on the part of developers, project managers, and their bosses. To put it succinctly, these are the classic blunders of B2B development. This chapter tells you what doesn't work. By pointing out these blunders, I hope to help you recognize and avoid these traps in your own B2B projects.

9.1   COMPLEXITY OF B2B DEVELOPMENT

The sheer complexity of B2B systems is the cause for the large number of traps and difficulties in B2B development. Figure 9-1 shows the project management tasks, the software subsystems, and the individual technologies that are essential to B2B application development.

Documentation Performance tuning Change management Deployment Source code control Testing Managing expectations Risk management Development tools Team dynamics Scheduling Estimating Design Stovepipe problem Analysis Scope management Requirements gathering Project methodology	Browser	Information architecture, Site navigation, Web page design, Creative graphics, HTML, XSL, CSS, DHTML, HTML forms, Browser compatibility
	Web Server	
	B2B Application Framework	Content access, Personalization, N-tier, XML, User accounts, Authentication, OO programming, Scripting, Caching
	Component Services	State management, Integration with enterprise databases and applications
	Transaction Monitor	Distributing transactions, Resource pooling
	RDBMS	Stored procedures, Cursors, SQL, Transactions, Isolation, Concurrency, Schema design, Queries
	Server Operating System	Load balancing, Security, Scalability, Multi- threading, Clustering, Fault tolerance

FIGURE 9-1   *B2B Application Development*

The depth and complexity of the B2B-enabling technologies make B2B applications inherently complex and difficult to build. An understanding of the technological challenges is critical to your success.

9.1.1   B2B TECHNOLOGY

As you learned in Chapter 1, a B2B Web site is actually a three-tier business application with intrinsic requirements that are very difficult to fulfill. A B2B application requires a highly complex computing infrastructure. In the remaining chapters of this book, you will gain a greater understanding of the computing infrastructure requirements, but for now I will merely list the technologies that are required for even the most basic B2B applications.

- Web servers, browsers, HTML, XML, and script programming

- Security, authentication, and authorization

- N-tier application development

- Relational database servers and SQL

- OO and/or compiled programming languages

- Software component technology
- Object persistence
- Transactions
- Enterprise application integration

Each of these technologies performs valuable functions in B2B applications. In other words, you can't really get by without using most or all of these technologies in any real B2B application.

9.1.2 DIVERSE TECHNOLOGIES

The various B2B enabling technologies are distinct from each other. They each come from different branches of computer science. Unfortunately, it is far from obvious how best to use these technologies in concert with each other.

The various B2B enabling technologies were not created initially with the goal of integrating them into a single application. Each of these technologies was created to serve a particular purpose or to fulfill a particular need and was created independent of the other technologies.

Figuring out how to cobble these technologies together into a single, manageable application is no small undertaking. For instance, how do you best combine the strengths of a compiled OO programming language with a relational database server? How can OO and XML be used effectively in N-tier applications? And how do you use security, authentication, and authorization to control access to content stored on a B2B site? These are just a few of the questions you encounter when trying to integrate these diverse technologies into a seamless B2B application.

9.1.3 UNDERSTANDING THE TECHNOLOGY

Getting these technologies to mesh into a single application requires technical expertise on the part of both the developers and the site owners. In this chapter the *site owner* is the individual who is ultimately responsible for the success of the B2B application. This person is an employee of the company that is trying to create or deploy a B2B application, often an executive or department head who has sufficient authority to make the necessary things happen at the company to support all phases of the B2B project. This person is sometimes called the project's "sponsor." In the next chapter, which explains the B2B development team, I refer to the site owner as the "champion" of the project.

Executives need to realize that technology is now a driver of business strategy and no longer merely a tool to implement business strategy. Information technology has now advanced to where it is so powerful and influential that it influences and sometimes governs the creation of business strategy.

Executives who depend on their IT managers to relate technology to business strategy are on a dangerous path, one that may lead to their company's extinction. These executives are flying blind at a time when it is crucial that they understand modern information technologies and what they mean for their business.

Managers must have a strong e-Business strategy in place before considering specific B2B application investments. And a personal understanding of e-Business technologies is a prerequisite to being able to create an effective e-Business strategy.

B2B application developers also must, of course, understand the technologies so that they can use them to build B2B applications. They need to know how these technologies work and what their limitations are.

9.2 B2B DEVELOPERS

Developers with the requisite skills, knowledge, and experience to build successful B2B applications consistently are at a premium. "B2B" and "e-Business" are popular buzzwords, and many consulting firms and developers have embellished their promotional literature and resumes with these terms. Unfortunately, building a B2B application is not as easy as putting "B2B" on your resume. There are several common mistakes that inexperienced B2B developers can make.

9.2.1 UNDERESTIMATING DIFFICULTY

Developers who have built dynamic Web sites or client/server applications will often assume that building a B2B application is merely a matter of adding some new features to the existing code base. However, as you saw in Figure 1-3, a B2B application is not merely a dynamic Web site or client/server application. A B2B application uses the complex parts of both dynamic Web sites and client/server applications, and it includes some additional complexities that are unique to B2B applications.

When a developer begins building a B2B application, he or she must first be concerned with several architectural issues that arise on the middle tier. These issues include security, distributed transactions, multi-threading, synchronization, caching, connection pooling, object pooling, state management, and on and on.

A developer will need to build or buy an infrastructure that handles these middle-tier architectural issues before starting to build the B2B application itself. The .NET Framework can provide much of this infrastructure, while the rest of it will need to be provided by middle-tier software components. Generally, the middle tier of a B2B application has some low-level, infrastructure-type software components in addition to application-level business objects.

A client/server developer or a dynamic Web site developer may presume that they can build a sophisticated middle-tier infrastructure themselves from scratch. This is usually a mistake. People who have built B2B infrastructures know from experience that it is a huge undertaking and is not unlike building an operating system.

If you are a developer and are considering building your own B2B infrastructure from the ground up, try to imagine how your first project will go. After a couple of months your customer will ask about your progress on his application and what features you have implemented. You will tell your customer that you now have object persistence or caching or state management working and that you plan to start writing his app real soon now. The customer will likely not understand why you are working on features that he didn't ask for.

Smart developers will try to leverage the work of other capable programmers to complete their B2B projects in a timely fashion.

STOVEPIPE SYSTEM PROBLEM

There is another problem that confronts developers who try to create their own infrastructure. This problem stems from the fact that B2B applications usually consist of several software subsystems.

B2B applications are systems of complexity, and a system of subsystems is generally a good way of dealing with this complexity. However, if the designer does not do a good job of systems engineering, the system will be resistant to change. If the interfaces between the subsystems are not defined in an ideal manner, the system will be brittle and will require the wholesale replacement of interfaces and subsystems as the needs of the application change over time. This is called the "stovepipe systems problem."

Systems engineering is not easy. Proficiency in systems engineering is a skill that few developers possess. As a B2B developer, you would be wise not to use your first B2B project as an experiment to discover whether you have a flair for systems engineering.

9.2.2 LACK OF B2B DEVELOPMENT EXPERIENCE

Besides the problems of building an infrastructure, a developer will face many challenges in designing and building a B2B application. I will explain some of these challenges next.

LACK OF THREE-TIER WEB APPLICATIONS EXPERIENCE

Many new B2B developers come from a client/server application background. Client/server application developers often have difficulty making the jump to thin-client, three-tier application development. The ability to put application logic and state inside a fat client application is overwhelming. A client/server application can maintain constant connections to a database, and these connections can blast data between the app and the database like water through a fire hose.

It is difficult for client/server developers to realize that a thin client has only a very tenuous connection to the server. These developers must internalize the fact that a Web server is merely a black box that accepts URL strings from the client and sends HTML strings back. The only state information that the thin client can convey to the server is the state that can be placed inside a single string. This fact has profound implications for application design. A failure to grasp fully the way browsers work can lead to serious mistakes when building a B2B application.

A LACK OF HTML AND SCRIPTING EXPERIENCE

The fundamental concepts behind HTML are simple, but some of the details of HTML are difficult for client/server developers to grasp without some serious study. The different capabilities of the various browsers, the overlapping of HTML with cascading style sheets and inline styles, the need to understand how hyperlinks work, and the question of how to build an appropriate UI within a browser can be huge hurdles for client/server developers. These hurdles mean that no client/server developer can hope to build a B2B application successfully without first mastering HTML and its related technologies.

The concept of client side- and server side-scripts likewise can be troublesome to client/server developers. The syntax of scripting languages and the appropriate use of the browser's object model and the script language's object model are likewise difficult for many client/server developers. Client/server developers will need to climb the learning curve here as well.

LACK OF DATABASE AND/OR APPLICATION EXPERIENCE

Some new B2B developers have a Web development background but no real experience in building software applications. Web developers seem to sail through HTML, scripting, and browser questions, but they often have a hard time with databases, transactions, and queries. The concepts found in database servers are often baffling to Web site developers. A database schema design, a SQL Select statement, a join, an ADO.NET DataSet, a server-side cursor, a view, or even the concept of storing data in a relational database table with rows and columns can be mystifying for someone who has worked only with HTML and scripting languages.

The idea of transactions with atomicity, consistency, isolation, and durability is confusing and perhaps boring to many Web developers. Yet transactions are one of the central pillars on which B2B applications must stand. If a Web developer is to become a well-rounded B2B application developer, he or she must become proficient with these back-end, server-side, database-centric technologies.

9.2.3 BAD B2B IMPLEMENTATIONS

With the many new skills that developers must acquire to build their first B2B application, there is little wonder that bad implementations are somewhat common. These bad implementations can result in poor performance and a B2B application that is difficult to maintain and modify.

INEFFICIENT CODING TECHNIQUES

There are many places that a developer can put code in a B2B application. The developer can also write the B2B application code using many different programming languages.

Some programming languages produce fast executable code, and some don't. In addition, every programming language has within it some programming constructs and techniques that execute efficiently and other programming constructs and techniques that do not. Writing the right code in the right language and putting it in the right place in a B2B application are a huge challenge.

Some of the routines in a B2B app may get called a thousand times per second, while other routines may get called only occasionally. This means that a few judicious optimizations can go a long way toward improving the performance of the application.

PERFORMANCE TUNING

The complexities of B2B applications, the large number of subsystems, and their numerous interactions can make performance tuning a complicated process.

There are of course performance monitors and profilers available for the various subsystems in a typical B2B application. However, identifying the interactions between the subsystems can be intricate and time-consuming.

Frequently, the B2B app will run fine on the development machines, but it will run slowly on the production server. Performance tuning requires that you configure test machines so that they are functionally identical to the production servers that run the B2B application. Then you must load realistic data onto the test machines. And then you must test the app using genuine, real-world usage patterns. Performing all of these tasks can be a lengthy and difficult process.

After you have obtained valid data and usage patterns, you can begin your process of performance tuning in earnest. To be successful, you need to understand how each subsystem in your app works so that you can understand how to get them all working in concert with each other. A common mistake here is for developers and site owners to underestimate both the need for and the difficulty of the performance tuning process.

9.3 B2B SITE OWNERS

Sometimes the people who benefit the most from the completion of the B2B application, the owners of the B2B site, can unwittingly hinder its development. These problems typically result either when the site owner gives the project insufficient attention or when the site owner gives the project too much of the wrong kind of attention.

With a new application environment such as B2B, it is easy to get your expectations out of line with reality. These unrealistic expectations can manifest themselves in several different ways.

9.3.1 SCOPE CREEPS

A *scope creep* is my slightly too-cute term for a person who contributes to the process of scope creep in a B2B project. The classic example is a site owner. When site owners have their first B2B application built, they think it is a one-time thing, so they want this first version to do everything they will ever need. Or they may think that to get value out of the large sum of money that they are spending on B2B development, they need to pressure the developers to include lots and lots of features in the first version.

Unfortunately, demanding a boatload of features in the first version of a B2B application can put the whole project at risk More features do not add up to more value, but it can increase the risk of getting nothing that works.

Chapter 11 deals with this subject in more detail, but to maximize the chances of success, each B2B project should be scoped such that development is completed and the application is ready for testing and performance tuning within a 90-day development cycle. Compared to the other features of a B2B application, "up and running" is a crucial feature for the app to have.

9.3.2 UNFEASIBLE FEATURES

If a site owner is unfamiliar with software development in general and with Web development in particular, he or she may demand unrealistic features.

The Web is in many ways a constrained environment. The software that runs effectively on the Web must fit within the constraints of the Web. There are many features that are desirable in software applications that simply don't work in Web-based applications.

If site owners are unfamiliar with Web development, they need to convey their needs and wants clearly to the developers, but they also need to defer to their development team when it comes to feature implementations that may not work well on the Web. Site owners should never intractably demand features that are not workable in Web applications.

9.3.3 INCONSEQUENTIAL FEATURES

The features of a software application are each of varying importance. In other words, every feature is not a crucial feature. The site owner may demand features that are not pertinent and that are even trivial. To stick adamantly to unimportant features wastes valuable development time that could be spent on other important tasks in the project.

9.3.4 MUTUALLY EXCLUSIVE FEATURES

I have seen Web application development projects where the site owner steadfastly demands that each Web page contain several images that are time-consuming to download while also demanding that the site be fast and responsive for browsers with slow Internet connections.

Of course, the only way to satisfy both of these requirements would be for the developers to invent some new computer science that would enable the fast download of images over slow Internet connections. B2B application development is risky enough without trying to invent new computer science to satisfy conflicting requirements. The site owner needs to be sensitive to the limits of existing technology.

A B2B application always contains a series of feature tradeoffs. A wise site owner will not increase the risks on the project by insisting that the developers find ways to implement features that are mutually exclusive within the limits of existing technology.

9.3.5 INEXPERIENCED DEVELOPERS

A manager in an application development group of a large corporation once told me that company executives were going through his group and appointing people to be B2B Web developers. These developers had no qualifications in the field of B2B development, but the corporation needed to have a greater Web focus, and these random "knightings" were the way these executives hoped to achieve it.

As you learned earlier, successfully building B2B applications is decidedly more difficult than putting "B2B" on your resume. Site owners must use developers who know how to build B2B applications successfully, or the B2B applications will not get built.

9.3.6 MORE THAN A WEB SITE

You're just building a Web site. Web sites are not that hard to put up. What's the big deal with this one? As I mentioned in Chapter 1, a B2B Web site needs to perform the same functions that business applications must perform. The following are some of these functions:

- Share data with enterprise applications and enterprise databases
- Perform business processes in conjunction with enterprise applications

- Process data and transactions from other companies' B2B applications
- Implement complex logic, business rules, and business processes

This means that B2B application developers must write an application that does all of these things *and* works over the World Wide Web. The Web is a constrained software environment. It is much more difficult to build Web applications than it is to build client/server applications or Web sites. Site owners will add to the project's risk of failure if they try to measure a B2B project's progress against that of a traditional Web site.

9.3.7 FEATURES THAT DON'T ADD VALUE

I have seen site owners who, during requirements gathering and development, insisted that particular features are absolutely essential. However, late in the development phase we learned that some of these features were actually of secondary or cosmetic importance.

I am not sure what the motivation was for the site owner to claim that all of the features were mandatory, but the result was that the development team wasted valuable hours working on insignificant features, time that could have been better invested.

RENDERING IDENTICAL PAGES IN DIFFERENT BROWSERS

One common demand for an insignificant feature is that each page render identically in all of the various browsers. Any two Web browsers will render any given Web page differently. Internet Explorer and Netscape Navigator on Unix, Windows, and the Mac each have subtle and not-so-subtle differences that affect the way that they render HTML. Even the different versions of the same browser will display a Web page differently.

It is typically not productive to have B2B developers burn hours and days making pages look identical in every version of every browser. Not only is it not productive, but it is practically impossible.

It is probably not going to bother users of the site if a page looks a little different in Internet Explorer than it does in Netscape Navigator. How many people do you know whose work habits include comparing Web pages side-by-side in different browsers?

The important thing is that each page looks the best it can in each browser. The site owner must realize that some browsers are better than others at displaying Web pages, and they will have to settle for what each browser can realistically do.

CREATING A BAD PAGE DESIGN

Another demand for an unproductive feature is that the B2B Web site must use a page design that is flawed. It is easy to go beyond the mark with the creative graphics and UI design of Web pages. This sometimes happens in applications where the UI is designed by a committee or where the UI is designed to be all things to a diverse audience. The site owner can do the project significant harm by insisting that a faulty Web page design be replicated on every page of the site.

9.3.8 NOT ENOUGH ATTENTION TO THE PROJECT

As you will learn in Chapter 10, the site owner is a crucial member of the project team. If the site owner does not devote enough of his or her attention to the project, several problems can occur. A lack of sufficient attention by the site owner can be manifest in several ways.

FAILURE TO COMMIT DOMAIN EXPERTS

A crucial first step in any project is to determine what should be built. In other words, the project team must understand the problems that are to be solved by the application they are building.

This understanding comes from domain experts who usually manage and/or run the processes to which the new application will apply. They understand these processes better than anyone because they have firsthand knowledge of them.

These domain experts are often fully occupied with their existing work. It is therefore difficult to free them up for work on a new project. However, in order for the B2B project to succeed, the site owner must enable domain experts to spend significant time with the development team throughout the project. Failure to do so often leads to failure of the project.

SLOW IN MAKING CRUCIAL DECISIONS

The site owner is typically very busy running the existing business (or a portion of it) and may be occupied to the point that he or she is unable to devote time and attention to the B2B project.

Timeliness is paramount in B2B application development. Throughout a B2B project questions that only the site owner can answer often arise. Often these questions involve tasks that are on the critical path for the completion of the project. If the site owner does not answer these questions in a timely manner, the project is delayed, and every delay increases the risk that the project will derail.

SLOW IN GATHERING CONTENT

All B2B applications require business data that includes information such as the people who will log in to the application and their permissions, documents that will be published on the site, the product information that is relevant.

Gathering content and data for a B2B site can be a laborious process and usually can be done only by the site owner's company employees. The process requires the site owner to commit his or her people's time to collect and create information.

The application cannot be deployed until the data it uses is gathered in a usable form. In fact, the application cannot be tested for bugs and tuned for performance until after the data is gathered. Content and data gathering are often the critical path for the deployment of B2B applications. The site owner therefore needs to commit adequate resources early to this process.

DOES NOT COMMIT SUFFICIENT RESOURCES

As you perhaps have figured out already, creating B2B applications is a resource-intensive process. Site owners must commit to B2B projects developers who have sufficient knowledge and experience to build the applications successfully. Of course, every member of the team does not need to be an expert in every area of B2B technology. However, the development team as a whole must possess the necessary experience and knowledge.

As I mentioned previously, site owners must also commit nondevelopers to make B2B projects successful. These nondevelopers include domain experts and information gatherers. The B2B project team and the critical roles on the team are the topics of the next chapter.

DOES NOT BUILD THE BUSINESS INFRASTRUCTURE

Dr. Ravi Kalakota, in his popular book *e-Business: Roadmap for Success,* said, "The fundamental premise of an e-Business enterprise is that all information must be available in digital form. In other words, there's nothing available on paper that isn't also available electronically. This may sound obvious, but it's an essential concept. Digital information is more efficient to create and maintain. Rather than entering the same information multiple times, each item is entered only once. That's significant. Even more important is that words and numbers on paper are dead—you can't work with them. In digital form, information comes alive. It can be analyzed creatively, searched quickly, updated easily, and shared broadly."[1]

e-Business is the way a firm employs its computer systems to conduct business. It is the application of modern information technology to business processes.

A firm's front- and back-office applications comprise the engine of its business processes. The better these applications work, the more productively the company can do business. Front- and back-office applications are most effective in information-centric businesses, businesses that are structured to take advantage of the information their front- and back-office applications provide.

Truly to increase productivity and enable innovation, front- and back-office applications need to be integrated throughout the enterprise. Integrated applications

---

1. Ravi Kalakota and Marcia Robinson, *e-Business: Roadmap for Success* (Addison-Wesley, 1999), p. 77.

enable a company to address every facet and phase of its relationships with its customers, suppliers, resellers, and partners.

Most companies already implement e-Business to some degree, but companies typically have separate business applications that are based on functions and/or departments, such as accounting, manufacturing, and customer service. These function- or department-based applications typically are not built to integrate or share information with other applications across the enterprise.

An organization in which information flows properly is a prerequisite for B2B. The business processes must be integrated inside the enterprise before they can be integrated with other companies outside the enterprise.

Much of the functionality of B2B applications assumes that back-end processes are in place. If those back-end processes don't exist, the B2B application cannot operate. Therefore, before attempting to build any B2B applications, the site owner must build or buy and then successfully deploy the necessary e-Business applications.

9.4   PROJECT MANAGEMENT PROBLEMS

Figure 9-1 lists several tasks of B2B project management. Deficiencies in performing any of these tasks will result in problems for the project. Chapter 11 of this book provides more detail of B2B project management. In this chapter, I will discuss only the most troublesome of the B2B project management tasks. Building the right app with the right features is the most basic of prerequisites for a successful B2B project. Requirements gathering lets you be sure that you are building the right app with the right features to be successful. Do it perfectly, and things will fall into place throughout the project. Do it less than perfectly, and you will encounter problems throughout the project.

In the chapter on project management, I cover requirements gathering in more detail. Here, let it suffice to say that managing requirements requires a commitment from both developers and site owners. Developers must be committed to the requirements management process. They must realize that the onus for gathering and managing requirements rests with them, and the developers must take on the responsibility to do this effectively. Site owners must bend over backwards to cooperate with the developers on requirements issues. Site owners will ultimately end up with a better B2B application if they can bolster the requirements management process.

SUMMARY

The traps in B2B application development are many and varied. They can be avoided by making sure that you don't do the things that lead to these traps.

Developers should do the following:

- Know how to implement the B2B-enabling technologies
- Figure out how to mold these technologies into a single app
- Realize the difficulty of building their own B2B infrastructure
- Thoroughly understand three-tier, Web-based application development
- Implement the code for the app so that it is sufficiently fast
- Know how to do performance tuning on a three-tier, Web-based application
- Manage the requirements for the project

Site owners should do the following:

- Understand the relevance of the B2B-enabling technologies
- Not be a scope creep
- Ask only for features that work well in three-tier, Web-based applications
- Not ask for inconsequential features or conflicting features
- Not think that inexperienced developers can do the job
- Realize that they are building more than a Web site
- Not obsess about page rendering in different browsers
- Use a good page design
- Commit domain experts to the project
- Answer questions quickly when they are on the critical path for the project
- Gather content and data for the app in a timely manner
- Build the e-Business infrastructure first
- Help the developers manage the requirements for the project

The B2B Development Team

Acrucial early step in building a B2B application is assembling the team that will build the software. Issues of team dynamics are inseparably connected to issues of project management. However, before you can begin the project in earnest, you have to get the right people. This chapter deals with the issues of team dynamics. We will reserve the issues of project management for the next chapter.

An effective B2B team builds effective B2B applications. While there is a large body of existing literature on the topic of team dynamics, team issues are so fundamental to B2B development that I feel compelled to say what I can on the topic.

Much of the information in this chapter comes from personal experiences, anecdotes, and commonsense advice. This chapter does not get intense, and it is not rocket science. However, as simple as these ideas are, I have encountered many managers and developers who seem to be completely unacquainted with them.

The bibliography lists additional texts that drill down and provide more detail on the topic of team development. This chapter is Team Dynamics 101, and it will start you in the right direction.

The key points for this chapter are the following:

- The first thing to build when building a B2B application is the B2B development team.

- The environment has to be right in order for the team to materialize and function properly, and the team must be populated with individuals who fit the team and will contribute to its success.

- The software that the team produces is a barometer that clearly indicates the effectiveness of the team.

10.1   FORMING THE TEAM

There are several preconditions for forming an effective B2B development team. These preconditions constitute the environment in which the team is created and in which it operates. This section describes the environment that is needed for the team to function properly and also explains the necessary characteristics for the team to be successful.

The person who creates the team is usually the person who first envisions the B2B application and then assembles a team to implement that vision. I will refer to this person as the "champion." (I provide more details about the champion later in the chapter.) For now, you should just think of the champion as the person who has the vision of the B2B application, who has sufficient power and authority to make it happen, and who is working to make it a reality.

Building the team is one of the jobs that the champion must do to bring about his or her vision of the B2B application. The champion might delegate the details of forming the team to a subordinate, but that will require the champion to convey the vision of the B2B application effectively to the subordinate as well. Even with delegation, the ultimate responsibility for creating the team rests with the champion. The champion is also the person who must create, or perhaps clean up, the environment in which the team is to materialize and function. After the environment is established, the champion must make sure that his or her team has the right qualifications.

10.1.1   KNOWLEDGE IS POWER

Many years ago, I encountered a team leader who maintained his position of authority over the people on his team by withholding information from them. He withheld relevant information about the current situation and about the plans for the future. He understood that knowledge is power, and in order to maintain his power he deliberately kept his people ignorant about the team's circumstances.

Unfortunately, this meant that the people on his team were able to contribute only in the few areas he had shared his knowledge, which severely handicapped the team. The team was not greater than the sum of its parts. It was only as effective as this one person, and everyone else made minor contributions, and then only when they were assigned to do so.

Contrast this with a team where everyone knows everything about the current situation and circumstances. In that environment, every member of the team can see the problems clearly, and team members can apply their individual and collective expertise to solve them. In this way the team is not limited to the effectiveness of any one individual. And all of the team members (including the champion, the team leaders, and the team members) must feel that authority is derived from knowledge, not from position.

Legitimate authority comes from expertise, not from some official appointment. In an effective team, whoever has the most expertise in a given area works freely to solve problems in that area. Authority comes to them naturally by virtue of the fact that they know what to do in that area better than anyone else. Once that authority has been established naturally, then perhaps management can and should make that authority official, but the expertise has to be there before the title is bestowed. In an effective team, knowledge truly is power.

10.1.2 LEAD FROM THE FRONT

Because legitimate authority comes only from expertise, leaders will lead only where they have the ability to lead. That can be a difficult idea for insecure leaders to swallow, but it is a characteristic of an effective team.

Throughout my programming career, I have encountered managers who lack any technical knowledge. In fact, some managers seem deliberately to avoid technical topics and concentrate on trying to manage people and processes. In my opinion, this type of manager is slated for extinction. As the influence of technology continues to grow, it will eventually become impossible to manage anything without some knowledge and understanding of technology.

Leaders of B2B development teams need to be technical. The team will not be effective when its leaders do not understand the technology, since in B2B development, the technology drives the entire process. The technology determines what you can and cannot build. If the leaders do not understand the technology, they will not be able to lead the development process effectively.

Once the B2B team leaders have the necessary level of technical knowledge, the thing that really makes them leaders of the team is their unique knowledge of how to build the team and increase its effectiveness. The leaders' authority comes from their understanding of how to make the team reach its potential and work the way it should.

B2B team leadership, therefore, has a dual track: technical know-how and team dynamics know-how. The leaders must have progressed on both tracks to the point that they can function effectively using both sets of knowledge.

10.1.3 THE POLLUTED ENVIRONMENT

Several years ago, I was the Development Lead on a software project for a large corporation. Our team was tasked to build a piece of software that would be used by thousands of the corporation's customers. The corporation's competitors already provided software of this type to their customers, and now we had the opportunity to catch up with those competitors and beat them.

Our team had all of the characteristics it needed to be successful. We had a Project Manager who had sufficient technical depth and who possessed an excellent understanding of the problem domain. We had a capable (yet sufficiently humble) Development Lead. And we had a corral of eager developers who were anxious to prove themselves and be heroes inside the corporation.

Early on, we had some crucial team meetings where the Project Manager shared his vision of the software and helped us see that we could build a software package that would put our competition to shame. This made us a cohesive and driven team that would work in harmony for the good of the team and the project.

As we worked through the design and prototypes of the software, I remember thinking that the only thing that could stop us from beating our competition would be if our own corporate management told us to not write the software. Sadly, I turned out to be very right.

As we began work on the exception handling and error reporting mechanism of our software, we were told that another department in corporate IS was building standard error handling code. We were also told that the (nontechnical) head of IS had made an edict that everyone in the corporation must use that error handling code in his or her applications.

In investigating this error handling code, we learned that it would not handle exceptions but only expected error conditions—not the unexpected ones. In our minds, this made the error handling code inadequate for our application. The head of IS was unapproachable and unyielding (and untechnical). This irrational requirement that we use this inadequate code became a huge stumbling block for our team. Ultimately, this edict caused our team to lose confidence in corporate management.

We were a strong and effective team in a polluted and constrained environment. Most of us ended up leaving the corporation for greener pastures shortly thereafter, and we never did get to write the software we had envisioned and wanted to build. This is a case where the team was not sufficiently empowered to build the software. Before a team can be successful, environmental factors, such as empowerment, resource allocation, and enterprisewide policies, have to be right.

10.1.4 THE A-TEAM

People-related issues on the team have a more significant impact on development projects than any other factor, including processes or methodologies. An effective team will succeed despite inefficient process and cumbersome methodologies. However, no amount of process or methodology can save a project that has a dysfunctional team. B2B projects require a team effort. Therefore team dynamics are a huge contributor to the success or failure of the project.

To have a successful team, the champion must hire the right people for the team and must watch for and eliminate misfits.

Given the fact that knowledge is power, team members who don't have the necessary knowledge will be powerless to contribute to the effort. (Lists of specific technologies that team members will need to know to contribute to a B2B project are provided later in the chapter.) In addition to hiring people with the requisite knowledge, you must do all that you can to avoid hiring people who won't work well on the team—for example, the following:

- Are strongly opinionated

- Have religious software preferences

- Feel some need always to be right

- Think they are experts or authorities in certain areas

- Insist that they fulfill a particular role on the team

It is imperative that the team leadership select people who are right for the team, not just those who are available at the time. A person's performance on and contribution to the team should be the paramount consideration. The project will end up being completed earlier if you wait a few weeks or a couple of months to get the right people than if you go with subpar people right away.

Once the team is formed, it is vital that the team leader watch for team members who are hurting (or not helping) the team. There are several signs that indicate team members who are a drag on the team's progress:

- They might continue to repeat old arguments against decisions to which the rest of the team already agreed.

- They may be territorial and reluctant to share their work with other team members.

- They may feel that they are expert and don't need to listen to anyone else because they already know what to do.

- They might not agree to pitch in on duties that no one on the team enjoys but that other team members are willing to perform for the good of the project.

- Other team members might make wisecracks about them in their absence.

The common thread among all of these behaviors is that the person does not have the interests of the team and the project at heart. If any of these types of behaviors are manifest, it is incumbent on the team leader to take action quickly.

The leader should start by talking frankly and honestly with the person. However, if counseling doesn't produce results quickly, the leader should not be afraid to remove the person from the team. Even though the team will be losing a member, its progress will be improved by eliminating a member who is slowing down activities.

10.1.5 THE RIGHT MIX

An orchestra composed exclusively of tuba players would not be able to play a broad range of music. A B2B development team composed of people who all possess the same skill set would not be able to build the broad range of software that a B2B application requires.

An effective B2B team consists of a mix of people with specialized skills. The tasks that need to be accomplished are many and varied. A B2B development team needs to cover a broad patchwork of technical, creative, and managerial skill sets; and diversity and competence are crucial characteristics. It is generally good for the productivity of the team to let team members contribute in the areas in which they are most motivated to contribute. Note that this may or may not be the same areas the team members have worked in on past projects.

There are, of course, acts of drudgery that must be performed in every project, and everyone must be willing to do his or her fair share of these. However, in every project there are also areas of work that are creative and stimulating. The leader should not be too anxious to dictate the areas in which each particular team member will work. Rather, the leader should try to make it possible for each team member to gravitate naturally to his or her assignment or area of responsibility. This is helpful in getting the team members' heads in the game.

10.1.6 ONE PROJECT AT A TIME

It is also important to ensure that team members are free to concentrate on the project at hand. In other words, a B2B development team should not be expected to work on more than one B2B application at a time.

The exception would be part-time team members such as specialists, graphic artists, and copywriters who work only on a narrow slice of the project. For those working full-time, building an application is an all-consuming effort. The work performed by full-time members is on the critical path for the project. This means that these people cannot be delayed in their work without ultimately delaying the completion of the B2B application that they are building.

Full-time workers should not be expected to multitask. Asking them to work simultaneously on more than one B2B application or on other projects in addition to their lone B2B project will lead to productivity-draining context switches, which will cause delays. Delays in B2B projects always increase the risk of the project failing.

10.1.7 WHAT WE HAVE HERE IS A FAILURE TO COMMUNICATE

Building a successful B2B application requires the team members to work in concert with each other. Each member must know what the other team members are doing and the ultimate goal. Communications is vital in these circumstances. This includes team meetings, e-mail, project documentation, and informal conversations among team members.

The team leadership must ensure that there is always good communication in the team and that there are conditions conducive to effective communication. This most important mechanism I have seen for ensuring effective communication is to put the team in one place. Team members should be in the same city, in the same building, on the same floor; ideally, their workspaces should be adjacent to each other.

10.1.8 THE GEOGRAPHICALLY DISPERSED TEAM

So much of a successful B2B project involves a shared or mutual understanding of the work that must be done that it is difficult for a geographically separated team to be effective. Having the full-time members in different locations hampers their communications. In fact, their communications become so difficult that they are in reality unable to function as a team.

Certainly they can all read the project documentation and send and receive e-mail, but the countless informal conversations that must occur among the team members on a project cannot occur in a dispersed team. The frequency and the nuances of communications are lost when team members cannot go and talk face-to-face to their teammates whenever they want to.

Without these communications, the interface between the team members becomes narrow and inadequate for close work on a project. A dispersed team usually necessitates that the development work be divided among the team members so they can each work independently. This leads to artificial interfaces between software subsystems in the application and could contribute to a stovepipe system problem.

The interfaces between the software subsystems in your B2B application should be determined by technical concerns and not by the location of the team members. Getting the full-time members of the development team in one place where they can work together is precondition for building software that has no artificial interfaces or subsystems.

10.1.9 THE COHESIVE TEAM

An effective team has an identity and life of its own. The team itself becomes an entity. Knowing that you are part of a strong team is a powerful motivator. As part of a winning team, people are willing to make personal sacrifices for the team's success.

However, they must have confidence that the other members of the team are likewise committed to the team. This confidence is born of trust.

A team gels when the members of a team trust that their teammates will each place the interests of the team over his or her own interests. It helps when each of the team members knows something about the background as well as the goals and motivations of the teammates.

The process of building trust on the team starts when the team members see that the leaders of the team have the team's interests at heart. Interestingly, the leaders engender trust by demonstrating genuine concern for individuals on the team. Team leaders also help the team gel by painting a picture of what the team can or must accomplish and what the rewards will be.

10.1.10 VISION

Seeing the challenges and the rewards for conquering those challenges is what vision is all about. If a team has a vision of conquering difficult obstacles and being amply rewarded for it, the team will work to bring about that vision.

Team members will generally catch on to a vision when they see the following:

- A challenge that has an exciting and rewarding conclusion
- Team leadership that is on their side and wants the individuals on the team to enjoy the rewards of being successful
- Teammates who are capable individuals and are committed to the team's success

A good vision is one that can be articulated easily. You should be able to convey it in just a few sentences. It usually involves some healthy desire for conquest or beating one's competitors. It also involves an aspiration for some reward of fame and fortune.

The responsibility for stimulating the team's vision rests on the shoulders of the team leadership. Each member of the team must see the vision himself, and he or she must also see how clearly the team leadership sees the vision and how actively the leader is pursuing it.

10.1.11 TRAILBLAZING

B2B development is full of technical challenges. There will be no shortage of difficult technical tasks. Accomplishing these tasks will require the brains of everyone on the team.

The team leaders must lead from the front but should definitely not do all of the trailblazing themselves. If they did that, the team would be only as effective as its individual leaders. For a team to cover ground quickly, each of the team members must solve problems, find solutions, and create technology. In other words, everyone on the team needs to blaze trails occasionally.

Several years ago, I worked as a Development Lead on a team where, at first, whenever a developer on the team encountered something unknown or a problem, it stopped the team in its tracks. The developer would bring the problem to me and say something like "Let me know when you figure out what to do on this." The developer would then return to his workstation and wait for me to divine the solution to the problem.

Being a Development Lead who possesses an amazing grasp of the obvious, I saw that this pattern was not ideal. I was doing all of the thinking on the team and I was a bottleneck on the team's progress. The team was going to progress only as fast as I could find solutions to my developers' problems.

The Project Manager and I discussed this issue and then called a team meeting. I explained that the technical problems and questions that we encounter should be brought up at our regular team meetings. At that time, we would look for volunteers to solve the problems and find answers to the questions. The people who took on these challenges and found solutions and answers would present their findings at a subsequent team meeting. They would then be presented with a candy bar and would enjoy the respect and admiration of their peers.

This simple act fostered an environment in which all members of the team realized that they needed to find answers and solutions. They saw that they should not wait for me to solve every problem, and everyone should contribute wherever he or she felt the inclination and ability to do so. Each individual would blaze the trail when the team needed it.

As a complement to this strategy, the team needs to function in a collaborative environment where ideas are encouraged. Team members need to feel comfortable enough to be able to present their thoughts and ideas to the team. This means that team members must be willing to listen to their teammates. This gets back to the idea that you should beware of people who think of themselves as experts and are unwilling to incorporate input and feedback from their teammates.

I think that the best way to foster a collaborative environment is to use a workshop forum in team meetings where ideas, problems, and solutions are discussed. In a workshop, people present their proposed solutions and then ask for and expect feedback from the other team members. This simple act of asking for feedback disarms people's natural tendencies of defensiveness and aggressiveness that is harmful to the team psyche.

10.1.12   THE FEW, THE PROUD, THE TEAM

The best teams for B2B projects are small teams. Small teams possess several characteristics that make them more effective for B2B development than large teams. B2B projects need to be scoped carefully so that they can be completed in 60 to 120 days. This time frame optimizes the projects' chances for success. Sixty- to 120-day projects typically require only a small team of four to six full-time members and two to eight part-time members.

It is crucial for the team to develop a sense of identity, and it is usually easier for a small team than a large team to do so. The members of a small team can also gain a sense of being members of an elite group. This pride in the team can help increase the members' commitment to the team and enhance their willingness to sacrifice to make the team successful.

An ideal B2B team will, therefore, be small and specialized. Before I explain the specific roles that must be filled on a B2B team, let me provide for you a barometer that will measure and clearly indicate the health of any B2B development team.

10.1.13   PRODUCING THE SOFTWARE

The best way to measure the health of any B2B team is to look at the software that the team produces. If a team consistently produces the right software within the right time frame, the team is a healthy team. A strong team produces strong software. Conversely, weaknesses in the team are manifest in missed deadlines and unfinished software.

I once worked on a team that had problems that were manifest in missed milestones and slipped deadlines. The team leaders were ineffective in dealing with the problems on the team and were therefore ineffective in their efforts to complete an important piece of software.

On this team, when any individual member of the team was unable to fulfill his or her assignment within the deadline, the team leaders made no effort to bring the resources of the team to bear to identify the root of the problem and figure out a solution. The team leaders were nontechnical, so they were unable to delve into the code themselves to gain firsthand knowledge of the problem. The leaders simply tried to apply additional pressure on the developer to meet the next deadline.

Unfortunately, a lack of pressure was not the problem, and applying additional pressure did not solve it. The idea of examining problems as a team was suggested to the team leaders, but the idea was dismissed. The team leadership felt that each member of the team was already too busy working on his or her own assignment to look at anyone else's.

Eventually, the project failed because the root causes of a few crucial delays were never addressed. Ultimately, the solution that the team leaders tried to apply after the project had failed was to allow individual developers to fall on their swords, meaning that they either were publicly flogged during team meetings, had to leave the company, or were fired.

In this environment, individual developers were given assignments as something of a test. The team leadership felt that if the developer was able to complete the assignments, he or she was indeed a capable programmer. If the developer could not complete the assignment, he or she was not a capable programmer. As far as the team leadership was concerned, each project was an opportunity for each developer to prove himself or herself. (In practice, because the team leadership was nontechnical, the assignments were not evenly distributed, so some failures were inevitable.)

Software development projects that are used as a proving ground for individual developers do not produce very good software. The leadership of this particular team needed to stop testing developers and start concentrating on building software.

During a software development project, the team leaders need to keep their eyes on the progress of the software, the code that is being written, and the results of software testing. And they need to use the team to solve the problems when the software is not progressing as fast as it should. Having said that, it is now time to look at the roles that must be filled on a B2B development team.

10.2   THE ROLES

The roles on a B2B development team can be classified as either full time or part time. There are several specific full-time and part-time roles that must be filled for the team to be successful. There are also at least three crucial leadership roles that must be filled. These leadership roles must be clear for accountability purposes.

10.2.1   LEADERSHIP ROLES

CHAMPION

The single most important role on a B2B team is that of the champion. Without the champion, the B2B application will never come to fruition. The champion is the individual with the vision and the authority to make the B2B application a reality.

It is essential that the champion is an executive or senior manager of the organization that owns the B2B application. The champion must work for the company or organization that owns the app. In fact, the champion must be a senior-level manager inside that organization.

Champions must have a thorough knowledge of the problems that the B2B application will solve. They cannot simply manage from inside the corporate jet at 50,000 feet but must know exactly where the rubber meets the road in their business.

Champions must have sufficient authority to obtain the money to pay for the B2B hardware, software, and development. B2B applications are expensive, costing anywhere from a hundred thousand to several million dollars. The champion needs to have the authority to cut a check for that amount of money.

In addition, a B2B application will typically involve stakeholders from across the enterprise. These stakeholders will each have his or her own demands and agendas for B2B applications. The champion needs to have the muscle to pull these stakeholders in the right direction so that the B2B project can be properly scoped and supported to give it a reasonable chance of success.

The champion must envision the B2B application and then create the team and environment where it can be built. He or she must take a personal interest in building the team that will build the software. The champion must have the necessary power and authority to slay the dragons that are inside the organization and that might threaten the B2B team or its progress in developing the application.

The champion must also possess the clout and/or charisma to sell the implementation of the B2B application to the people who will use it inside and outside of the organization.

The users inside the organization have to be sold on the benefits of using this new B2B application, or they will not use it, and the app's potential will not be realized. For example, people inside the organization must be motivated to collect and maintain the content for the B2B Web site. A B2B Web site that contains no information is not very useful.

The users outside the organization—the other "B" in "B2B"—also have to be sold on the value that the application holds for them. It takes at least two B's to B2B. The champion has to sell the partner businesses on the value of the app; a B2B Web site that no one uses is a waste.

The champion will probably enlist a number of subchampions (for lack of a better term, I will call them "Squires")—managers and assistants who will help with the many tasks that the champion must accomplish. These Squires, if they grasp the vision of the B2B application, can be invaluable in the champion's efforts.

Champions must know the business, understand the technology, and be visionary about how B2B technology can strengthen their organization. They must sell that vision to people inside and outside their organization. And they must work tirelessly throughout the project to see that vision implemented.

Project Manager

The Project Manager is a full-time role on the B2B team. The Project Manager may or may not be an employee of the organization that owns the application. In other words, the Project Manager may work for the organization that owns the app, or he or she may work for a company that the organization hired to build the app for them.

The Project Manager must have a technical background. Because the technology drives every facet of the B2B development process, a nontechnical Project Manager will not be able to manage a B2B project effectively. A nontechnical Project

Manager will not understand what works and what does not work in a B2B environment. Ideally, the Project Manager will have worked as a developer in the past or would be capable of working as one now and understands the programming languages, databases, and server software that the application will use.

Nontechnical Project Manager is an oxymoron when it comes to B2B development. If you want to manage a B2B project, you must understand the technology, or you will be useless as a Project Manager.

The Project Manager takes the lead in scoping the project, writing the project documents, scheduling the milestones, allocating the resources, and managing the team. The Project Manager handles the business matters, such as contracts and licensing, as well as interfacing with the application owner.

The Project Manager needs to have a thorough understanding of the problems that the B2B application is supposed to solve. I will speak more about this when I cover project management and requirements gathering, but the Project Manager needs to understand the motivations behind the requirements for the application—the problem domain. The Project Manager then works with the Development Lead in the solution domain to design an app that will solve those problems.

The Project Manager should be located in the same place as the B2B development team because he or she must interact frequently with all the members of the team and, less frequently, with the owner of the application.

I have seen experienced B2B Project Managers who are able to manage multiple (two or three) projects simultaneously. A Project Manager's ability to handle multiple projects depends on the complexity of the projects and on the individual's level of experience. Certainly, the Project Manager must devote time exclusively to his or her first project.

The knowledge required by a Project Manager includes all the skills listed in this chapter. It is crucial that the Project Manager also be fluent with the technology that the developers will be using on the project.

DEVELOPMENT LEAD OR TECHNICAL LEAD

The Development Lead is a full-time role on the B2B team and may or may not be an employee of the organization that owns the application. The Development Lead is the most senior technical person on the team. He or she must know, better than anyone, the tools and software that are used to build B2B applications. The Development Lead is highly experienced in the solution domain, will have completed several projects as a developer, and will have vast expertise in B2B projects and software.

The Development Lead takes the lead in designing the application. Because of this, the Development Lead also must understand the problem domain or the set of problems that the app is supposed to solve. He or she must also be able to translate the requirements those problems generate into a software design that the team can implement in a reasonable amount of time.

The Development Lead works closely with the Project Manager throughout the project. This work includes designing the application, managing the developers and their work, and assessing the progress of the software. The Development Lead will often be the developer who codes the trickiest or most difficult portions of the application.

The Development Lead also functions as a mentor for the other developers on the team. The layers of technology in B2B development are nearly impenetrable for new developers without a mentor to speed their process of learning, and the Development Lead must be willing to fill that mentoring role.

The Development Lead must be located with the Project Manager and the rest of the team. Their interactions are too frequent for the Development Lead to be separated from the team.

The knowledge required by a Development Lead includes many of the skills listed in this chapter. In addition, the Development Lead must have an understanding of most of the skills listed under "N-Tier Application Development Skills," "Web Development Skills," "Component-Based Development Skills," "Object-Oriented Development Skills," "Relational Database Server Skills," "Network and Security Skills," and "Server Configuration and Maintenance Skills."

10.2.2   FULL-TIME ROLES

Full-time roles must be filled by people who are in the same location as the Project Manager, Development Lead, and the rest of the full-time team members. They must work on a single B2B project at a time and devote their full attention to it. They are also accountable to and managed by the Project Manager and Development Lead.

DEVELOPER

There will typically be one to five developers on a B2B project. These developers may or may not be employees of the organization that owns the app. A B2B application developer must possess a diverse set of computer science knowledge and application programming skills. B2B development requires expertise in three fundamental areas.

1. N-tier and Web site development

2. Object-oriented and component-based programming

3. Relational database servers

In most cases, a developer will need to be proficient in at least two out of these three areas to make a meaningful contribution to a B2B development effort. The developers' areas of expertise can be placed along a continuum, which has Web browser specialists at one end, business object specialists in the middle, and database server specialists at the other end. Developers tend to have their expertise concentrated in a particular region, and it is rare to find an individual who has a broad range of knowledge.

This is not necessarily bad as long as the B2B team has several developers whose knowledge covers all the necessary topics. For example, you don't want all of your developers to be database server specialists; you want a mix of talent and expertise. These are the specialist functions that the developers on a B2B team would fill. Each developer on the team is likely to function as more than one specialist.

Browser/HTML Specialists   A significant portion of the development time in a B2B project is occupied with getting the Web pages to look good in the many versions of browsers on the market. I have worked on projects where browser issues absorbed nearly half of the project's development man-hours.

A developer who possesses expertise in the area of HTML and browser compatibility can greatly reduce the number of hours the team burns on these types of issues. The knowledge required by Browser/HTML Specialists includes the skills listed under "Web Development Skills" in this chapter.

Page and Site Design Specialists   Designing Web usability, navigation, and information architecture is a discipline all its own. A developer who knows how to do this effectively for B2B applications will add polish and professionalism to the apps that the team produces. The knowledge required by Page and Site Design Specialists includes the skills listed under the "Web Development Skills" section of this chapter.

Business Object Specialists   A large portion of B2B applications involves the automating of business processes. The ability to transform business processes and business logic into programming source code inside of software objects is indispensable to a B2B team.

Creating business objects is central to creating B2B applications. The knowledge required by Business Object Specialists includes the skills listed under "Component-Based Development Skills" and "Object-Oriented Development Skills."

Network and Security Specialists   Knowledge of networks and network-based security is integral to any B2B application. This knowledge is integral to the B2B development team as well. The knowledge required by Network and Security Specialists includes the skills listed under "Network and Security Skills."

Enterprise Integration Specialists   As you know, e-Business is a prerequisite for B2B. e-Business means enterprise applications. And B2B applications will need to integrate with these enterprise applications. Enterprise Integration Specialists will need to know how to use whatever APIs and/or object models that the enterprise applications expose. They will also need to discern when it is best to integrate applications at the data level instead of at the API level, and they must know how to process application data from within relational database servers.

The knowledge required by Enterprise Integration Specialists includes the skills listed under "N-Tier Application Development Skills," "Component-Based Development Skills," and "Relational Database Server Skills."

Database Server Specialists   Relational database servers can be powerful tools. However, they are black holes to people who do not understand their mysteries. A developer or two with expertise in database servers are invaluable on a B2B team. The knowledge required by Database Server Specialists includes the skills listed under "Relational Database Server Skills."

TESTER
A good tester is worth his or her weight in gold to the B2B team leadership. The tester is in the best position of anyone on the team to determine reliably the progress of the software. The tester will often be an employee of the organization that owns the site because having knowledge of the problem domain can be very helpful in testing the application.

The knowledge required by Testers varies a bit, based on the type of testing they are called upon to do. The ideal tester would have as much knowledge about the software as the Development Lead, so the Tester could test the application at any level. It is probably overoptimistic, however, to think that you could recruit such a capable Tester. You will probably have to settle for someone with a little bit of programming in his or her background and who has lots of knowledge about the problem domain.

10.2.3   PART-TIME ROLES

The part-time people on a B2B team are those with very specialized skills and whose contribution does not require a full-time effort over the life of the project. These people typically are not managed by the Project Manager and Development Lead, and they are not really considered a permanent part of the team. These people can be considered consultants who take care of certain tasks that are too specialized for the full-time team members.

ACCOUNT MANAGER
The Account Manager is not an employee of the organization that owns the app but usually the salesperson who sold the organization on the idea that the organization should use his or her company to build the B2B app. The Account Manager often helps the Project Manager with contract and business tasks on the project.

CREATIVE ARTIST

The Creative Artists create the graphics artwork for the B2B Web site. Often they will help with the page layout as well. The Creative Artists may or may not be employees of the organization that owns the app. Sometimes an organization will have its own graphics department that does the artwork, and sometimes the organization will look to the company creating the B2B app to do the graphics work. In a typical B2B application, Creative Artists will perform at most a couple of weeks of work over the life of the project.

CONTENT MANAGER

The Content Managers create and maintain the information that is published by the B2B Web site. Content Managers are typically employees of the organization that owns the B2B application. The Champion or one of the Squires typically manages these Content Managers.

The importance of the work done by Content Managers cannot be overstated. As I mentioned before, a Web site with no information is not very useful. Often, the process of gathering the information for use in the B2B application is a huge job. I have seen several B2B applications where the software development work was completed and the application was ready to deploy, but the deployment was delayed because there was insufficient content to launch the site. The Content Managers must begin their work very early in the project in order to have the information ready when the app is ready.

10.3 B2B DISCIPLINES AND SKILL SETS

Here is a list of technical disciplines that are useful in B2B development. I have organized these disciplines by topic areas that you can find in technical books. You should be able to find a book or two on each of these disciplines and to obtain the knowledge you need to use that discipline in your B2B application development.

PROJECT MANAGEMENT SKILLS

- Expectation management
- Team dynamics
- Project methodologies
- Requirements gathering
- Project documentation
- Analysis
- Design
- Scope management
- Estimating
- Scheduling
- Change management
- Testing
- Deployment

N-TIER APPLICATION DEVELOPMENT SKILLS   WEB DEVELOPMENT SKILLS

- Scalability
- Performance tuning
- Load balancing
- Clustering
- Failure recovery
- Client/server development
- Two-tier vs. three-tier
- Fat vs. thin clients
- Middle-tier objects
- Database servers
- Stateful and stateless objects
- Contexts and interception/ interposition
- Just-in-time activation and object pooling
- Object request brokers
- Transaction monitors
- Transactional programming
- Distributed transactions
- Transactional object models
- Concurrency control
- Data access techniques
- Object persistence
- Isolation levels
- Security
- Role-based security
- Distributed security

- HTTP
- Browsers
- URLs
- HTML
- Push and pull concepts
- Page layout
- Forms
- Frames
- Images
- Image maps
- Links
- Lists
- Tables
- Style sheets
- Web navigation models
- Information architecture
- Page design
- Creative graphics
- Javascript
- Microsoft JScript
- DHTML
- Remote scripting
- Browser capabilities
- Browser-side caching
- Client-side programming
- Cookies
- Authentication

- ActiveX
- Plug-ins
- Java applets
- Wireless devices
- Sessions
- KeepAlive connections
- Web servers
- DNS
- Content indexing for full text search
- Server-side programming
- Application servers
- CGI
- ISAPI
- XML and XSL
- Database connections
- ADO.NET
- Server-side caching
- MIME types
- Streaming media
- FTP
- SMTP
- Analyzing performance data
- Maintenance
- Logging
- Certificates
- Digital signatures

COMPONENT-BASED DEVELOPMENT SKILLS

- References
- Proxies and stubs
- Processes and remote activation
- Multithreading
- Reentrancy
- Method invocations
- Events
- Object definitions
- Object models
- Patterns
- Interface-based programming
- Interface design
- Interface definition language
- Data types
- Inheritance

OBJECT-ORIENTED DEVELOPMENT SKILLS

- OO language programming
- Classes
- Types
- Namespaces
- Abstraction
- Aggregation
- Encapsulation
- Inheritance
- Polymorphism
- Virtual functions

- Data hiding
- Static functions
- Static data
- Pointers and references
- Threads
- Constructors
- Initialization
- Allocating and freeing memory
- Garbage collection
- Naming conventions
- Class libraries
- OO analysis
- OO coding
- OO design
- OO modeling
- OO patterns
- State
- Reusability
- Exception handling
- Catch and throw
- Persistence
- Class normalization
- OID's in RDBMS's
- OODBMS features
- Proxies
- RDBMS issues
- Relationships

RELATIONAL DATABASE SERVER SKILLS

- SQL
- SQL Queries
- Select
- Aggregates
- Joins
- Sorting
- Subqueries
- Unions
- Result sets
- Cursors
- Views
- Insert
- Update
- SQL functions
- Batches
- Stored procedures
- Query optimizer
- Query plans
- DDL
- Triggers
- Replication
- APIs
- ODBC
- OLEDB
- ADO.NET
- Data dictionary
- Integration approaches
- Schema design

- Data modeling
- Logical vs. physical design
- Normalization and denormalization
- Normal forms
- Indexes
- Referential integrity
- Cascades
- Keys
- Locking
- Concurrency
- Isolation
- Deadlocks
- Transactions
- Recoverability
- Performance bottlenecks
- Roles
- DBA
- System administrator

NETWORK AND SECURITY SKILLS

- DHCP configuration
- DNS configuration
- TCP/IP model
- IP addressing
- Classes A-E
- Public and private addresses
- Routing
- Algorithms
- Protocols

- The routing process
- Subnetting
- TCP/IP suite
- Ports
- Protocols
- Services
- Sockets
- WINS configuration
- IPv6
- IP utilities
- Troubleshooting
- Connectivity problems
- Name resolution
- Statistical monitoring
- Troubleshooting tools
- IP security
- Securing the Web server
- Attacks
- Defenses
- Firewalls
- Security policies
- Certificates
- Securing the information in transit
- SSL
- Securing the user's computer
- ActiveX
- Java
- Scripts
- Digital signatures

- Security holes
- Risk management

SERVER CONFIGURATION AND
MAINTENANCE SKILLS

- Windows 2000 operating system
- Windows XP operating system
- File systems
- Directory services
- Replication and fault tolerance
- Backup
- Disaster recovery
- Clustering
- File ownership
- Managing system resources
- Managing disk space usage
- Monitoring system load and memory
- Optimization

- Process control
- Shell or script programming
- Start-up scripts
- Shutdown
- Security and ACLs
- Network security
- Passwords
- TCP/IP networking
- DNS resolution and routing
- Firewalls
- Host files
- Troubleshooting
- User accounts
- Adding and removing users
- Groups
- User profiles
- LDAP
- Authorization
- Authentication

SUMMARY

A crucial ingredient when building a B2B application is the B2B development team. The environment must be right for the team to materialize and function properly. The team itself must have certain characteristics to make it successful, and it must be populated with individuals who fit the team and will contribute to its success.

The individuals on a B2B development team must have the right skills and the right personalities to be able to work together productively. The team leadership must create the team and then must manage it carefully. The software that the team produces is a barometer that clearly indicates the effectiveness of the team. Therefore the team leaders should always watch the software that the team produces to learn how the team is doing.

An effective B2B team builds effective B2B applications. This chapter provides a list of roles and areas of expertise for you to use in creating an effective B2B development team.

B2B Projects

Building a B2B application is a complicated endeavor, both from the technology and business standpoints. The inherent complexity of a B2B project breeds risk. This chapter outlines a lightweight and efficient method that will help you manage the risks that are ever-present in a B2B project.

The key points for this chapter are the following:

- The inherent complexity of B2B applications makes them risky to build.

- Reducing the complexity of a B2B development project can reduce risk and increase the project's chances for success.

- Scope management helps reduce complexity and risk in B2B projects.

- Provided that you have a proper software infrastructure in place, B2B apps are best built in a series of phases, each scoped to 90–120 days.

- Effective requirements management enables the analysis, design, development, and testing phases to be effective and the application to be deployed on time.

11.1   PREACH TO THE CHOIR

Before a company can begin to undertake a project that has the scope and expense of a typical B2B Web application, the business requirements that the app will fulfill must be articulated in a very clear and understandable way; the documentation that outlines why the B2B app is a good idea must be written in very plain terms.

There is a group of interested people who will need to be convinced that the B2B app is a good thing. This group includes people who will use the app as well as people who will approve the spending for its development. The group often includes those who will benefit from the B2B application but who will need to be convinced that any sacrifices they are called upon to make for the sake of the app will be worthwhile.

The best way to convince people that a B2B application is a good idea is to define the problems that exist because of the lack of a B2B app and then explain how the app will provide solutions to those problems. This means documenting both the needs of the users and the features of the app. The place to document the needs for and the features of a B2B app is in a Vision document.

11.1.1   VISION DOCUMENT

The Vision document captures the needs of the user, the features of the system, and other common requirements for the project. It defines, at a high level of abstraction, both the problem and the solution. The Vision document also serves as the basis for discussion and agreement among the primary stakeholders of the project.

The Vision document is powerful because it represents the gestalt of the application from all significant perspectives in a short, abstract, readable, and manageable form. As such, the Vision document is the primary focus in the early phases of the project, and any investment made in the process of gathering the information will pay handsome returns in later phases.

The Vision document is a concise description of everything you consider to be most important about the application. It is written at a level of detail and in plain language, so it is readily reviewable and understandable by the primary stakeholders of the project.[1]

Chapters 12, 13, and 14 are Vision documents for the three primary types of B2B applications: private exchanges, selling-chain management, and supply-chain management. You can use these documents as a point of departure as you begin work on the Vision document for your own B2B project.

11.1.2   UNDERSTANDING THE PROBLEMS

In developing the Vision document for your B2B project, you must identify the problems that create the need for the B2B application. It is important that you understand the root causes or the problems behind the problems. This insures that you do more than merely treat the symptoms and that you reach effective solutions.

The problem of <state the problem> affects <identify the stakeholders affected by the problem>. The results of which are <describe the impact of this problem on stakeholders and business activity>. The benefits of a B2B application to address this problem include <list the key benefits>.[2]

---

1. Dean Leffingwell and Don Widrig, *Managing Software Requirements* (Addison-Wesley, 2000), p. 170. © 2000 by Addison-Wesley. Reprinted by permission of Pearson Education, Inc.
2. Ibid., 39.

11.1.3 AGREEING ON THE PROBLEM DEFINITION

One of the simplest ways to gain agreement is simply to write down the problem and see whether everyone agrees. One function of the Vision document is providing a vision of the problem and the solution. It serves as a lightning rod for input from the stakeholders and then acts as an ensign that the proponents of the app can rally around.

The process of creating the Vision document is in fact the process of gaining agreement on the problem definition. The "champion" (described in Chapter 10) is the person who usually authors the Vision document. The champion confers with the stakeholders to gain consensus on the problem definition and writes the gestalt of that problem definition into the Vision document.

11.1.4 IDENTIFYING THE STAKEHOLDERS

Addressing the needs of the stakeholders is crucial to the success of any B2B application. The stakeholders include anyone who is materially affected by the implementation of the B2B app. The list of stakeholders certainly includes the users of the application. In addition, there are many people who are not users of a B2B app who have a stake in its implementation, including the following:

- The IT department that will likely be called upon to support users of the app and perhaps to manage or host the software and hardware for the application

- Managers inside and outside of the enterprise who will approve the use of the app

- Managers and process specialists whose work processes will be automated and perhaps modified by the app

The needs of all of these stakeholders must be addressed effectively if the B2B application is to be successful.

11.1.5 DEFINING THE SOLUTION BOUNDARY

After the stakeholders have been identified, and once they agree on the definition of the problem, it is time to consider potential solutions. In essence, the solution consists of a system made up of software applications and hardware that can be deployed to address the problem.

The initial topics to consider regarding the solution system are the types of things the system should do and where it should fit in relation to the other systems that already exist in the enterprise. This means thinking about the boundaries of the solution system. By defining the boundaries of the system, you define the system's size and shape. From this you get an idea of what niche the system fills and the roles it will play in the enterprise.

As you think about the system's boundaries, you also need to consider what and who will interact with the system. Certainly, there will be human users involved. There are people who will use the system and other people who will perform administrative and maintenance tasks. In addition, a B2B system will no doubt need to interact with other applications in the enterprise.

This may seem obvious, but defining the system boundary and identifying the elements that interact with the system are crucial steps in the analysis process. Once the boundary and actors are defined, you can draw a simple block diagram that illustrates the system, its users, and the other applications with which the solution system interacts. A diagram like Figure 11-1 is very helpful in explaining to stakeholders what the proposed system will and will not do.

11.1.6 IDENTIFYING THE CONSTRAINTS

After defining the system boundary, you need to identify the constraints on the system. A constraint is a restriction on the degree of freedom you have in designing and implementing a solution. Each constraint has the potential to impact your design and implementation severely. Some constraints may even cause you to rework your whole design. Therefore you must carefully consider each constraint during the planning process.

Here are some potential sources of constraints and questions you can use to elicit the constraints.

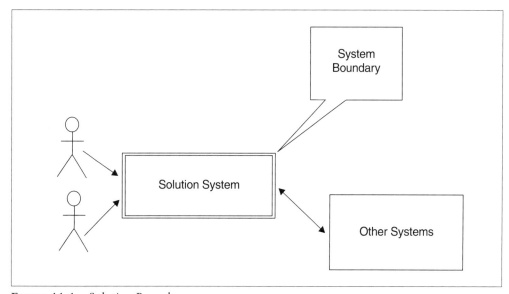

FIGURE 11-1   *Solution Boundary*

ECONOMIC

- What financial or budgetary constraints are applicable?
- Are there licensing issues?

POLITICAL

- Are there internal or external political issues that affect potential solutions?
- Are there interdepartmental problems or issues?

TECHNICAL

- Are you restricted in you choice of technologies?
- Are you constrained to work within existing platforms or technologies?
- Are you required to use any commercial off-the-shelf software packages?

SYSTEM

- With what existing systems must the solution be compatible?
- What types of programming interfaces must be supported?

ENVIRONMENTAL

- Are there any constraints from a legality perspective?
- What are the security requirements?

SCHEDULE AND RESOURCES

- Is the schedule defined?
- Are you restricted to existing resources?
- Can you use outside labor?
- Can you expand resources? Temporary? Permanent?
- Are you severely limited in finding certain technology skills?

Once identified, some of the constraints will become requirements for the new system. Others will affect resources, implementation plans, and project plans. It is the problem solver's responsibility to understand the potential sources of constraints for each specific application environment and to determine the impact of each constraint on the potential solution spaces.[3]

11.1.7 COMPLETING THE VISION DOCUMENT

After you define the problem, identify the stakeholders, and define the solution boundary and the constraints on the solution, you have enough information to complete the Vision document. This Vision document should articulate the problems that the B2B app addresses, categorize the stakeholders and users, and list the features of the application.

There must be agreement among the stakeholders on the contents of the Vision document before the project can move forward. Once completed and agreed upon, the Vision document can be used as the basis for the Statement of Work if a consulting firm is building the app. The champion, project team, and stakeholders also use the Vision document as they begin to consider the scope of the first version of the application.

11.2 SCOPE

Before developing more detailed specifications, you need to establish the scope of the first version of the B2B application. The scope of a software development project consists of three things:

- The functionality of the application
- The resources available for the project
- The time available for the project

The level of functionality of the application is dependent on the resources and the time available for the project. Figure 11-2 shows the functionality that can be implemented in a software project as the area that is dimensioned by Resources on the y-axis and Time on the x-axis. If either of these dimensions changes in magnitude, then it materially affects the functionality that can be implemented during the project.

11.2.1 MANAGING COMPLEXITY

B2B applications are inherently complex in terms of the combination of client/server and Web technology that they require. They are complex in the business processes they must automate and in the enterprise applications with which they must interop-

---

3. Ibid., pp. 44–45.

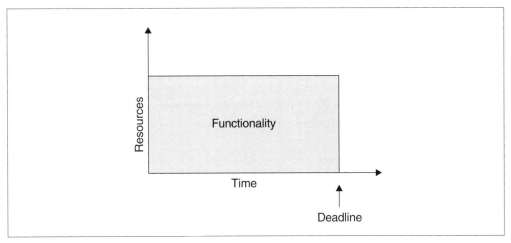

FIGURE 11-2 *Project Scope*

erate. And they are complex in their diverse audience of users and stakeholders who work in different departments inside and outside the enterprise.

A software project's complexity will increase if either the resources or time allotted to the project increases. The more functionality you try to implement, the more complex the project becomes. As complexity increases, so do the risks that the project could get off-track during development. Therefore managing complexity is one of the primary enablers of B2B project success.

Managing complexity always involves overhead. To stay on top of a highly complex project, you have to create procedures and processes and follow a strict methodology. Methodologies that effectively manage a high degree of complexity have the undesirable effect of adding inefficiency to a project. In my experience, the most efficient way to manage complexity in a software project is to reduce it.

The best way to reduce the complexity of a B2B project is to limit the time allocated to the project. This has the effect of limiting the functionality of the application and thereby limiting the project's complexity.

Based on the 30 or so B2B projects that I have seen, a 90-day maximum for the development phase seems to be the magic time frame. Ninety days is long enough to develop a significant application but not so long that the complexity gets out of hand.

Theoretically, given a 90-day time frame, you can increase the resources allocated to a project and achieve any level of functionality you desire. In practice, however, B2B projects are always resource-constrained because of the high degree of technical knowledge required on the part of the developers. It is so hard to find developers who possess the requisite skills that development resources always limit the amount of functionality you can implement in a B2B app.

Because the shortage of developers puts a practical ceiling on the resources that are available for a B2B project, limiting the time allotted for development to 90 days has the effect of limiting the functionality of the application. Limiting the functionality of the app reduces the project's complexity.

Let me sound a loud note of caution here: There is a significant danger that these short, 90-day projects will lead to a brittle application that ultimately has to be completely rebuilt (refactored) after two or three projects for the application to remain viable.

The way to make sure that you do not have to rebuild the entire application after just a few iterative projects to add features is to have a robust infrastructure in place before you start the projects. In other words, before you can do a series of short projects to build out the features of a B2B application, you must have in place an infrastructure that can accommodate the present and future features of the application. That infrastructure typically cannot be built in a 90-day time frame.

11.2.2 "Up and Running"

Managing the scope of a B2B project can be tricky because managing the scope means limiting the functionality of the application. Each stakeholder will have his or her own particular needs and wants for the B2B application. Stakeholders may not be enthusiastic about seeing their particular feature requests go unimplemented in the project. In addition, the people who are in charge of paying for the application will sometimes be averse to seeing stringent limits on the feature set for the project.

Reducing the project scope has the potential to create an adversarial relationship between the project team and the stakeholders of the application. Fortunately, it does not have to be that way.

The project team must realize that the application does not belong to them but to the stakeholders. The development team needs the stakeholders' input to make key decisions, and only the stakeholders can really determine how to manage scope and achieve a useful deliverable.

The stakeholders must realize that it is in their best interests for the application development effort to be successful. Getting a few of the features they want in the first version of the app and waiting for future versions to get additional features are preferable to getting no features at all because the development effort failed under the weight of too much complexity.

Among the list of features that a stakeholder might request in a B2B application, "up and running" must be listed as a high priority. Once the stakeholders buy into the fact that "up and running" is a vital feature, scope management becomes easier.

11.2.3 PHASED APPROACH

The best way to approach the problem of limiting the feature list to a 90-day scope is to build the application in phases. Then it becomes not a matter of "if" a particular feature will be implemented but rather "when" it will be implemented.

Taking a phased approach enables the champion and the project team to build their credibility among the stakeholders. In the first phase, the team takes on a project with limited scope, so they have a high probability of success. When the first phase is completed successfully, the team earns valuable credibility. A very perceptive person once told me, "After you have a little bit of success and show that you can deliver, you're the man!" (Or woman, as the case may be.)

Once the team has established its credibility, it becomes a little easier to manage the subsequent phases of the project effectively because the stakeholders will have faith in the team's ability to deliver what they say they can deliver. The project team can then tackle the second phase of the project with another 90-day development effort. After that is complete, they can tackle the third phase, and so on.

The team should limit the scope of each phase to a 90-day development cycle. The complexity of B2B apps never really goes away. Even in the later phases of a B2B project, the complexity is always there, and the way to manage the risks that that complexity brings is to manage the scope of each phase diligently.

11.2.4 EXPERIENCE

Knowing what can be delivered in 90 days of development takes experience. The Project Manager and the Technical Lead on the project team need to draw on their experience with previous B2B or similar projects in order to know how to manage scope effectively. A B2B team with inexperience at the Project Manager or Technical Lead positions is a team that faces great risk.

11.3 REQUIREMENTS MANAGEMENT

After you have obtained buy-in from the stakeholders on the Vision document and have nailed down the scope of the first phase of the application, you need to go into requirement-gathering mode. Before I talk about requirements gathering, let me first go over some principles of requirements management.

11.3.1 SOFTWARE REQUIREMENT SPECIFICATION, OR SRS

A software requirement specification, or SRS, is a collection of documents that describes the external behavior of an application. The SRS is derived from the Vision document. It explains what the application has to do to deliver the features that the Vision document describes.

The SRS package is not a frozen tome, produced to ensure ISO 9000 compliance and then buried in a corner and ignored as the project continues. Instead, it is an active, living package, playing a number of crucial roles as the developers embark on their implementation effort.

- It serves as a basis of communication among all parties: the developers themselves and the developers and the external groups, users, and other stakeholders with whom they must communicate.

- Formally or informally, it represents an agreement among the various parties: If it's *not* in the package, the developers shouldn't be working on it. And if it *is* in the package, they are accountable to deliver that functionality.

- It serves as the project manager's reference standard. The project manager is unlikely to have the time to read the code being generated by the developers and to compare that directly to the Vision document. The project manager must use the package as the standard reference for discussions with the project team.

- As noted earlier, it serves as input to the design and implementation groups. Depending on how the project is organized, the implementers may have been involved in the earlier problem-solving and feature-definition activities that ultimately produced the Vision document. But it's the SRS package they need to focus on for deciding what their code must do.

- It serves as input to the software testing and quality assurance groups. These groups should also have been involved in some of the earlier discussions, and it's obviously helpful for them to have a good understanding of the vision laid out in the Vision document. But their charter is to create test cases and QA procedures to ensure that the developed system does indeed fulfill the requirements laid out in the SRS package, which also serves as the standard reference for their planning and testing activities.

- It controls the evolution of the system throughout the development phase of the project. As new features are added or modified in the Vision document, they are elaborated within the package.[4]

11.3.2 SRS Package Ownership

The project manager typically manages the documents in the SRS package. This enables the project manager to document their communications with the stakeholders and exercise more control over the scope of the project.

4. Ibid., pp. 262–264.

11.3.3 SRS PACKAGE ORGANIZATION

Remember that the SRS package is not read from cover to cover like a novel but is primarily a reference. Each developer will use it to find specific instructions on what the portion of the software they are assigned to write is supposed do. The documents should be organized such that they are easy to navigate.

11.3.4 SRS PACKAGE CONTENT

The Vision document cites the application's features in the users' language and describes the system at a high level of abstraction. However, it would probably be difficult to write code based on the Vision document. The Vision document is written at too high a level of abstraction for this purpose. The requirements document, therefore, should be written with enough detail that a developer could write code based on the information it contains.

LEVEL OF DETAIL

The answer to "What level of specificity must the requirements provide?" is "It depends on the context of your application and how capable those doing the implementation are to make the right decisions or at least to be certain to ask questions where there is ambiguity."

The goal is to find the "sweet spot," or the balance point wherein the investment in requirements provides "just the right amount" of specificity and leaves just the right amount of ambiguity for others to resolve further downstream. Figure 11-3 illustrates this.

As you move to the left of the sweet spot on the curve in Figure 11-3, you lower both the ambiguity and understandability. As you move to the right of the sweet spot, ambiguity goes up but understandability again goes down. Finding the sweet spot is a learned skill. It will depend on the abilities of the team members, the context of the application, and the level of surety that you must provide so that your application works as intended.[5]

REQUIREMENTS

Specifically, the requirements document should define the following:

- Inputs to the system
- Outputs from the system
- Functions of the system

5. Ibid., pp. 273–274.

- Attributes of the system
- Attributes of the system environment

You can evaluate whether a "thing" is a software requirement by testing it against this list.

There is also information that the requirements should not contain:

- Project information
- Budgets
- Schedules
- Testing plans
- Design information

Having said this, it might be acceptable to include some *hints* on testing in the requirements documents. After all, the requirement writer had a specific behavior in mind for the requirement, and it's reasonable to give only as much help as possible. The topic of design information in the requirements documents deserves additional attention.

EXCLUDING DESIGN INFORMATION

The requirements should not include information about the system design or architecture. Otherwise, you may accidentally have restricted your team from pursuing whatever design options make the most sense for your application. ("Hey, we have to design it that way; it's in the requirements.")

Whereas the elimination of project management and testing details from the list of requirements is fairly straightforward, the elimination of design/implementation

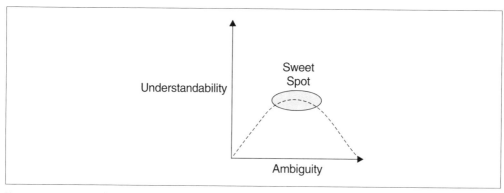

FIGURE 11-3   *Ambiguity versus Specificity*

details is usually much more difficult and much more subtle. Suppose, for example, that a requirement is worded something like this: "SR63.1 Trending information will be provided in a histogram report written in Visual Basic, showing major contributing causes on the x-axis and the number of defects found on the y-axis." Although the reference to Visual Basic appears to be a fairly blatant violation of the recommended guidelines (because it doesn't represent any input, output, function, or behavioral attribute), it's useful to ask "Who decided to impose the requirement that the histogram be implemented in Visual Basic, and why was that decision made?" Possible answers to that question might be the following:

- One of the technically oriented members of the group defining the Vision document decided that Visual Basic should be specified because it is the "best" solution for the problem.

- The user may have specified it. Knowing just enough about technology to be dangerous, the user worried that the technical people may adopt another technology, one that's more expensive or less readily available, knows that VB is readily available and relatively cheap, and wants that technology to be used.

- A political decision within the development organization may have mandated that all applications will be developed with Visual Basic. In an effort to ensure compliance and to prevent its policies from being ignored, management insists that references to Visual Basic be inserted into the requirements documents whenever possible.

If a technical developer decides to insert a reference to Visual Basic because of an arbitrary preference for the language, it obviously has no legitimate place in the list of requirements. If the user provided the requirement, things get a little stickier. If the customer refuses to pay for a system unless it's written in Visual Basic, the best course of action is to treat it like a requirement, *although you should place it in a special class, called design constraints, so it is separated from the normal requirements, which influence only the external behavior*. Nevertheless, it's an implementation constraint that has been imposed on the development team. (By the way, if you think that this example is unrealistic, consider the common requirement imposed by the U.S. Defense Department on its software contractors until the late 1990s to build systems using Ada.)

Meanwhile, the discussion of Visual Basic in this example may have obscured a more subtle and perhaps more important requirement analysis: Why does the trending information have to be shown in a histogram report? Why not use a bar chart, a pie chart, or another representation of the information? Furthermore, does the word "report" imply a hard-copy printed document, or does it also imply that the information can be displayed on a computer screen? Is it necessary to capture the information so that it can be imported into other programs or uploaded to the corporate intranet? The feature described in the Vision document can almost certainly be fulfilled in various ways, some of which have definite implementation consequences.

In many cases, the description of a problem from which a requirement can be formulated is influenced by the user's perception of the potential solutions that are available to solve the problem. The same is true of the developers who participate with the user to formulate the features that make up the Vision document and the requirements. As the old adage says, "If your only tool is a hammer, all your problems look like a nail." But you need to be vigilant about unnecessary and unconscious implementation constraints creeping into the requirements, and you need to remove such constraints whenever you can.

REQUIREMENTS VERSUS DESIGN

Requirements gathering should precede design. Users should make requirements decisions. Technologists should make design and implementation decisions. These rules sound straightforward, but in real-world projects, there is a feedback loop between requirements and design. Current requirements cause you to consider selecting certain design options, and selecting design options may initiate new requirements.

Occasionally, discovering a new technology may convince you to throw out a host of assumptions about what the requirements were supposed to be. You have discovered an entirely new approach that obviates the old strategy. ("Let's throw out the entire client/data access/GUI module and substitute a browser-based interface.") This is a prime, and legitimate, source of requirements change.

This process is as it should be; to attempt to do otherwise would be folly. On the other hand, there is grave danger in all of this, for if you do not truly understand the customer's needs *and* the customer is not engaged actively in the requirements process—and, yes, in some cases, even understanding our *design-related activities*—the *wrong* decision might be made. When properly managed, this "continual reconsideration of requirements and design" is a truly fantastic process, since technology drives our continually improving ability to meet our customer's real needs. *That's the essence of what effective and iterative requirements management is all about.* But when it is improperly managed, you continually "chase your technology tail," and disaster results.[6]

TYPES OF REQUIREMENTS

There are three types of requirements.

6. Ibid., pp. 230–236.

- Functional software requirements, which express how the system behaves. Functional requirements can be stated in simple, one- or two-sentence statements and perhaps correspond and make reference to specific wire frame page mockups.

- Nonfunctional software requirements, which focus on things such as usability, reliability, performance, and ease of modification and maintenance.

- Design constraints, which are restrictions on the design of a system, or the process by which a system is developed, that do not affect the external behavior of the system but that must be fulfilled to meet technical, business, or contractual obligations.

Generally, the best way to handle design constraints is to follow these guidelines:

- Include all design constraints in a special section of your SRS package. That way, you can easily find them and review them when the factors that influenced them change.

- Identify the source of each design constraint. That way, you can go to the source later to question or to revise the requirement.

- Document the rationale for each design constraint to remind you later as to what the motive was for the design constraint.

It is important that you don't get too hung up on defining whether each and every requirement is a functional requirement, nonfunctional requirement, or design constraint. Use these classifications to serve you, and don't delay your project while you try to decide what to do with a few hard-to-classify requirements.

11.4 REQUIREMENTS GATHERING

Having explored requirements management, the context has been set to delve into the requirements-gathering process.

This process starts when representatives from the development team meet with the stakeholders in what is typically called a "kickoff meeting." I derived much of this information on kickoff meetings from my friend Ahklaq Kahn, a long-time Project Manager with several successful B2B projects to his credit.

11.4.1 KICKOFF

The kickoff meeting is where the Project Manager and Technical Lead meet the primary stakeholders in person. In this meeting, the Project Manager and Technical

Lead gather the requirements for the current phase of the application. They also set the expectations of the stakeholders and manage the scope of the project.

The kickoff meeting is the ideal time for the Project Manager and Technical Lead to set the agenda for the lifetime of the project and have that agenda effectively communicated to the entire population of stakeholders. It typically lasts for two to five days, depending on the complexity of the project. Kickoff meetings usually require many participants, so it is essential that they be planned carefully in advance.

The Project Manager (PM) should start by making room in his or her own schedule. Kickoff meetings generate a lot of momentum, excitement, and enthusiasm on the stakeholder side. It is important that the PM maintain this excitement by providing a quick turnaround on action items that are to be delivered shortly after the meeting, such as the requirements and wire frame documents. All of this will require a considerable amount of the PM's time and attention. PMs should do the following:

- Before scheduling the kickoff meeting, make sure their own schedule is free from previous engagements so they can devote most or all of their time to the new project.

- Allow plenty of time for the stakeholders to inform and gather all relevant people for the kickoff meeting, taking into account that some of them may be traveling from remote locations.

ATTENDEES

Although it is the stakeholders' prerogative to choose whom to invite to the kickoff meeting, the PM can help them by suggesting some roles that will help the success of the project, such as the following:

- Managers and process specialists who have firsthand knowledge of the processes that the application will automate

- IT staff who will support the use of the application and who may host the application on servers they maintain

- Managers or executives who approved the money for the development and deployment of the application

KICKOFF MEETING WORK

The goal of the meeting is to do the majority of the requirements gathering. To do this effectively, over the course of the meeting the Project Manager and Technical Lead must come to understand fully the stakeholders' needs and expectations. They do this through a series of conversations and group discussions with the stakeholders throughout the kickoff meeting. During these discussions, stakeholders will often explain their needs in ways that are vague and ambiguous. The stakeholder might say, "I need easier ways to understand the status of my inventory" or "I'd like to see a big increase in the productivity of sales order entry."

In their excellent book, *Managing Software Requirements,* Dean Leffingwell and Don Widrig note that when interviewed about their needs or requirements for a new system, stakeholders typically describe neither their needs nor their requirements. That is, stakeholders often tell you neither their real need—"If I don't increase productivity in this department, I won't get my bonus this year"—nor the actual requirement for the system—"I must reduce sales order entry transaction processing time by 50 percent." Instead, they describe an abstraction.

These high-level expressions of desired system behavior are actually the features of the application that they have thought of. These features are often not well defined and may even be in conflict with one another. "I want increased order processing rates," and "I want to provide a far more user-friendly interface to help our new employees learn the system"—are but a representation of real needs nevertheless.

What is happening in this discussion? The stakeholder has already translated his or her real need into a system behavior that the stakeholder has reason to believe will solve that real need. In so doing, the *what* ("I need") has subtly shifted to the *how* ("what I think the system should do to address this need"). This is not a bad thing, since the stakeholder oftentimes has real expertise in the domain and real insight into the value of the feature. Also, because it is easy to discuss these features in natural language and to document and communicate them to others, they add tremendous richness to the requirements schema.

However, there is a caveat to this discussion: If the Project Manager and Technical Lead leave the kickoff meeting without an understanding of the need behind the feature, then there is a real risk. If the feature does not solve the real need for any reason, then the system may fail to meet the stakeholders' objectives even though the implementation delivered the requested feature.

In any case, this high level of abstraction—these *features*—are very useful in that they are a convenient way to describe the functionality of a new system without getting bogged down in too much detail. The Project Manager and Technical Lead can later translate these features into requirements to define the application.[7]

BARRIERS TO EFFECTIVE REQUIREMENTS GATHERING
In trying to elicit the requirements from the stakeholders during the kickoff meeting, people exhibit some natural tendencies that can make the process of requirements gathering difficult. Leffingwell and Widrig identify three barriers to requirements elicitation, each of which I have encountered myself.

---

7. Ibid., pp. 87–89.

The "Yes, But" Syndrome   One of the most frustrating, pervasive, and seemingly downright sinister problems in all of application development is what has come to be called the "Yes, But" syndrome. This is named for the user's reaction to a new piece of software. *For whatever reason, there are two immediate, distinct, and separate reactions when the users see the system implementation for the first time.*

- "Wow, this is so cool. We can really use this. What a neat job—good job."

- "Yes, but, hmmmm, now that I see it, what about this . . . ? Wouldn't it be nice if . . . ? Whatever happened to . . . ?"

The roots of the "Yes, But" syndrome appear to lie deep in the nature of software as an intangible intellectual process. To make matters worse, development teams typically compound the problem by rarely providing anything earlier than production code for users to interact with and to evaluate.

The users' reaction is simply human nature, and it occurs in various other day-to-day circumstances. The users haven't seen your new system or anything like it before. They didn't understand what you meant when you described it earlier, and now that it's in front of them—after months of waiting—they have an opportunity to interact with the system. And guess what? It's not exactly what they expected!

The "Undiscovered Ruins" Syndrome   Leffingwell and Widrig tell of a friend of theirs who was once on a tour bus in the Four Corners area, an area defined by the common borders of Colorado, New Mexico, Utah, and Arizona. The tour bus route included the majestic peaks of the La Plata mountain range and the sprawling ancient Anasazi ruins of the Mesa Verde and the surrounding area. On this trip, a tourist reportedly asked, "So, ummm, how many undiscovered ruins are there?"

In many ways, the search for requirements is like a search for undiscovered ruins: The more that are found, the more you know remain. You never really feel as though you have found them all, and perhaps you never will. Indeed, software development teams everywhere continually struggle to determine when they are done with requirements elicitation—that is, when have they found all of the requirements that are material, or when have they at least found enough.

Taking the time during problem analysis to identify all of the stakeholders of the system is of tremendous value because many nonuser stakeholders are often holders of otherwise undiscovered requirements. As with finding all of the undiscovered ruins, you must acknowledge that you are on a mission that can never be completed. The goal is to make sure that you have discovered enough.

The "User and Developer" Syndrome   The third syndrome arises from the communications gap between the user and the developer. Users and developers are typically from different worlds, speaking different languages and having different backgrounds, motivations, and objectives.[8]

The onus is on the Project Manager and Technical Lead to bridge this communications gap during the kickoff meeting. They may need to use multiple elicitation techniques during their conversations with the stakeholders to be successful.

TOPICS FOR THE KICKOFF MEETING

There are some crucial issues of which the Project Manager and Technical Lead must gain an understanding of the stakeholders' needs during the kickoff meeting.

Application Functionality   What is this application going to do? What business processes will it automate? As you can imagine, the questions are short, and the answers are necessarily long when it comes to discussing the application's functionality.

Look and Feel   The "look and feel" of the application refers to its user interface (UI), which in B2B applications is usually a Web browser. The look and feel discussions during the kickoff meeting consist of ideas for Web pages and the information elements that will appear on them. There won't be any time for graphic design at the kickoff meeting. Rather, the participants discuss and define the information architecture and a rough site map.

There should also be discussions and decisions on browser issues, such as whether to use frames, drop-down menus, ActiveX controls, Java applets, and so on. While it is true that these are design and implementation issues and not really requirements issues, discussion of them leads into a crucial discussion of what versions of browsers the application needs to support.

Some Web browsers are more capable than others, and the more capable browsers can provide a more powerful and easier to use UI than the less capable browsers. However, supporting only the most capable browsers means that the users of the app will be limited to using only those particular browsers. And trying to build a Web application that can take advantage of powerful browsers and then gracefully degrade for less capable browsers is a significant development effort. So, as you can tell, there is a lot to discuss and decide on this topic.

Security and Content Access Control   One of the crucial features of a B2B application is its security. By definition, a B2B app crosses enterprise boundaries. The only

8. Ibid., pp. 82–84.

way to do this safely is within a secure application environment that ensures users see only the information that they are allowed to see.

The Project Manager and Technical Lead must come away from the kickoff meeting with a clear understanding of what types of content access are permitted for what types of users.

Enterprise Application Integration   B2B applications are typically built to integrate business processes across enterprise boundaries. Forward-thinking companies have already automated the business processes inside their enterprise by implementing enterprisewide applications. B2B applications need to integrate with these enterprise applications in order to extend them across the enterprise boundaries. The Project Manager and Technical Lead must gain a thorough understanding of requirements for this enterprise application integration.

Data Migration   B2B applications often have their own data that they process, manage, or provide access to. This data may already exist in some form inside the existing enterprise applications and databases.

The Project Manager and Technical Lead must get a handle on what data will be required for the B2B application and where that data needs to come from. They need to think about how that data will be migrated into the B2B app effectively.

Hosting   The hosting of the B2B app is of paramount importance. It could be hosted by the company that owns the application or servers in their facility. Or the app could be hosted at another company's facility, one that specializes in application hosting.

The Project Manager and Technical Lead must find out what the requirements are for the server environment that will host the B2B application and begin to help the primary stakeholders make that decision.

Documentation and Training   Documentation and training are often afterthoughts in software projects. However, the owners of a B2B application can ill afford to have a system that is undocumented or that the necessary people do not know how to use.

The Project Manager and Technical Lead must carefully assess the needs for training and documentation to make the application a success.

What's the Scope?   Throughout the discussion of these topics, the Project Manager and Technical Lead need to think constantly about and manage the project's scope. They must point out to the stakeholders which features they think can reasonably be completed in the first phase of the application. They will probably be called upon to make snap judgments about what features can and cannot be done in a 90-day development time frame. They should be conservative. It is always good to underpromise and overdeliver.

OUTPUTS OF THE KICKOFF MEETING

A successful kickoff meeting will produce several documents which contain the essential information for the design of the application. These documents are primarily two types: wire frame diagrams and lists of user requirements.

The wire frame diagrams will probably be pretty rough. They will likely consist of text and boxes drawn on pieces of paper, with one paper page per Web page in the B2B app. The purpose of these wire frame diagrams is to illustrate the basic contents of each Web page on the site.

The user requirements will probably be rough, too, in that the requirements won't be organized or categorized. But all of the requirements that the Project Manager and Technical Lead elicited from the stakeholders need to be written down.

DELIVERABLES AFTER THE KICKOFF MEETING

Within a few days after the kickoff meeting, there are some important documents that the development team must complete. There will be documents that stakeholders must produce also.

The Project Manager and Technical Lead must produce the official Requirements document, based on the list of user needs they elicited at the kickoff meeting. This document must be formal enough for the stakeholders to review, understand, and sign off.

The PM, or perhaps a graphics artist on the team, needs to formalize the wire frame diagrams. These wire frame diagrams will be simple, consisting of just text and lines and boxes printed on pages of paper, but they need to be drawn on a computer and be consistent and clear enough for the stakeholders to review and sign off.

As a result of the discussions during the kickoff meeting, there will likely be some work that stakeholders must do. Stakeholders will need to define the taxonomies for the various types of information that will be used in the application. Taxonomies for classifying users and their access levels will also need to be defined.

Immediately following the kickoff meeting, the Technical Lead should begin working on the technical architecture for the application. This is probably where the critical path is for the development of the application, so this technical architecture work should not be delayed. However, before any development work can begin, the stakeholders need to sign off on the requirements and the wire frame documents.

SIGNING OFF

As soon as the Project Manager has completed the Requirements document and has obtained the formalized wire frames, he or she needs to send them to the relevant stakeholders for approval.

Having the stakeholders sign off on the requirements and wire frames is a crucial milestone in the project. The act of having the stakeholders formally agree that these are the correct requirements is what enables the design and development work to begin in earnest.

The Project Manager needs to be very deliberate about this step. If the stakeholders don't sign off on the requirements and wire frames, development work should not begin on the project, and the Project Manager and Development Lead will have to try to elicit the requirements again. This is generally not a good thing. They need to get the requirements right the first time, or the project will languish.

Once the stakeholders sign off on the requirements and the wire frames, the development team and the stakeholders have a firm foundation on which to build their B2B application.

11.5   ANALYSIS AND DESIGN

After the requirements gathering phase is complete, signaled by the stakeholders' sign-off on the requirements document and wire frame diagrams, the analysis and design work can commence. From the outset, the analysis and design work is branched into two parallel efforts: the creative work and the technical work.

11.5.1   CREATIVE WORK

The creative side of the team takes the wire frames and begins the process of designing the browser-based user interface. This process involves both art and engineering. The art part is the process of making pages that are aesthetically pleasing. The engineering part involves making a user interface the helps the user perform the functions of the application.

In this creative process, there are macro issues, such as the information architecture and the navigation model. And there are micro issues, such as the selection and placement of appropriate fonts, colors, and graphics on the pages.

The deliverable from this process is a page design template that can be applied to the wire frame pages that were defined during the kickoff meeting. This page design template needs to be shown to the relevant stakeholders for their sign-off.

11.5.2   TECHNICAL WORK

At the same time the creative work begins, the technical side of the team takes the wire frames and the requirements document and begins the process of designing the software and hardware architecture of the system. This is a highly involved engineering process, and the Technical Lead performs the bulk of this work. It is a combination of top-down and bottom-up design work.

The top-down work typically involves doing design work in four areas. Based on the requirements, the Tech Lead must define the following:

- Entity relationships, which involve defining the logical entities that exist in the application and their relationships to each other. These entities and their relationships are later implemented as a physical schema in a database system.

- System outputs, which are implemented as Web pages that show information from the application. These system outputs are later implemented as HTML that is sent to the browser-based user interface.

- Roles, which define the different types of users and what they can do and see in the application. These roles define the security and content access structure for the app and are later implemented as security mechanisms on the Web server, in the application source code and in the database.

- Business rules, which perform the functions of the application. These business rules are later implemented in source code that is embedded in script programs, executable binaries, object methods, software components, and/or database stored procedures.

The bottom-up technical design work involves looking at the current computer hardware, operating system, server software, and programming technology, and figuring out how best to implement such an application using these technologies.

Another way of expressing this would be to say that the top-down work is the analysis, and the bottom-up work is the design. The analysis is logical, and the design is physical. The design is the physical implementation of the analysis.

Of course, the design must work within any design constraints that were identified during the kickoff meeting. The following are the deliverables from this process:

- An entity relationship diagram and a decision on what type of database to use to implement it.

- A list and brief description of a set of browser-based forms that enable administrators to add, edit, and delete data in the app. These administrative forms will be based largely on the entities defined earlier.

- Further definition of the wire frame documents where appropriate, showing the information content in greater detail.

- A list of the roles in the application and a delineation of what parts of the app they can use and what data they can access, based on the information taxonomy that the stakeholders have specified.

- A list of the functions or methods that must be written in programming source code, including the most appropriate programming languages or environments to use.

11.6 PROJECT PLAN AND SCHEDULE

With the deliverables from the Analysis and Design work, the Project Manager can create a project plan. In its simplest terms, the project plan is a list of distinct tasks that must be accomplished in order to build the application. The list must include estimates of the time it will take to complete each of the tasks. The Project Manager and the Technical Lead may need to work together to create this list of tasks. The list should also include tasks associated with testing the application, providing training, loading data, deploying the application, and anything else that was agreed to at the kickoff meeting.

Completing the project plan is a matter of figuring out the dependencies among the tasks and identifying the critical path for the project. The PM can then look at the resources that are available to him or her on the development team and verify whether the project is scoped correctly for a 90-day development time frame.

11.7 DEVELOPMENT

There are a few things that must get done right at the beginning of the development process. There has to be a transfer of knowledge about the problem domain from the Project Manager and Technical Lead to the developers. The development infrastructure has to be set up. And assignments for housekeeping-type tasks and for general areas of responsibility among the developers must be made.

The period right after the kickoff meeting is a very busy time for the Project Manager and Technical Lead. However, in between all the demands on their time, they need to find time to train their developers about the problems that the application is supposed to solve.

If the developers have an adequate understanding of the problem domain, they will better understand the requirements, and they will produce better code with fewer bugs. Taking time to train the developers in the problem domain will pay big dividends later in the project.

11.7.1 DEVELOPMENT INFRASTRUCTURE

There are two main components to the "development infrastructure": the version control system and the bug-tracking system that the development team uses on the project.

The version control system enables the Project Manager and the Technical Lead to control the changes to the source code. Early in the project, the source code control can be fairly lax because the team is primarily working on new features. As the development work proceeds, the focus will shift to a bug-fix phase and a code freeze, and the Project Manager and the Technical Lead must monitor code changes more carefully. As the development work nears completion, code changes must be done only with the approval of the Project Manager and/or Technical Lead. A version control system enables you to do this.

In addition to tracking bugs, a good bug-tracking system enables developers to make to-do lists and reminders for themselves. This is better than developers using individual notebooks and sticky notes because the information in the bug-tracking system is accessible to the rest of the team should a developer leave the project for whatever reason.

By looking at the information from the version control system and from the bug-tracking system, the Project Manager and the Technical Lead can get a very clear picture of the volume of code churn and how close the software is to being complete.

11.7.2   ASSIGNMENT OF TASKS

The assignment of tasks among developers can be some combination of volunteering and being "volunteered." Every software development project has tasks that are unpleasant to some degree. Everyone on the team needs to be willing to handle his or her share of those tasks. There will also be a long list of development tasks that must be completed. Each developer will be better able or more willing to tackle certain tasks. To a certain degree, the Project Manager and the Technical Lead should let this division of labor happen naturally. However, invariably there will be some tasks that will require an assignment of a developer by the Project Manager or the Technical Lead.

11.8   TESTING AND DEPLOYMENT

As in the topic of team dynamics, there is probably little new material that I can add to the body of existing literature on testing. However, I feel compelled to say what I can about it here.

Testing can be conducted in earnest during development. When the testers say the application is ready, the app can be deployed. Functional testing can and should, of course, be conducted throughout the project. It is feasible for the developers and testers to test much of the functionality of the app against the requirements during development. However, when it comes to real-world performance testing, things get a little trickier.

The biggest challenge in performance testing a B2B app is duplicating the environment in which it will run so that you can test the app under real-world conditions. To do this, you have to have two things: lifelike data and lifelike usage patterns.

The quantity of data in B2B applications can be very large. In addition, the relationships between the data elements can be complex. It is often difficult to create test data in the proper volume and with the proper relationships. Therefore it is often difficult to test a B2B app with lifelike data.

The number of users of a B2B app can be large also. It can be difficult to predict which parts of the app will be used the most and what the usage patterns will be. Therefore it is likewise difficult to write automated test scripts that simulate real-world usage of the application.

In my experience, you are forced to do the best you can in performance testing the app and then count on a period of tuning and tweaking after the app is deployed. The Project Manager and Technical Lead should set the stakeholders' expectations accordingly so they are not unpleasantly surprised when the app needs some tuning after it is deployed.

11.9 ACCEPTANCE AND SIGN-OFF

Once the app has been deployed and demonstrates its fit and function, it is time for the relevant stakeholders to sign off on their acceptance of the application.

After a brief celebration and a short breather, it is time to start thinking about the next phase of the app, and this process starts over again. The application described in the Vision document was likely not completely implemented in this first phase. There may have been some business or technological changes that are relevant to the application as well. Therefore it probably makes sense to create a "delta Vision document," which talks about the changes from the original Vision document and perhaps discusses what features were implemented in the first version and what features will likely be implemented in the next version of the app.

11.10 PROJECT TIMELINE

With the lightweight methodology that I have outlined, the project timeline does not have to be lengthy. The maximum time between the kickoff meeting and stakeholder acceptance of the app should probably not exceed 120 days. This lightweight methodology would be inadequate for projects that are longer than three or four months.

Here are the time frames for the various phases of a B2B project that uses this project methodology.

KICKOFF MEETING—2 TO 5 DAYS
This is where the project starts in earnest. This is also where the bulk of the requirements are identified. At the kickoff meeting, the Project Manager and Technical Lead must also manage scope and set the stakeholders expectations.

ANALYSIS AND DESIGN—2 TO 3 WEEKS
This is a particularly busy time for the Project Manager and Technical Lead. They must produce wire frame diagrams and the requirements document for sign-off very

soon after the kickoff meeting so the stakeholder enthusiasm that was generated at the kickoff meeting does not wane. They must also design the application and build a project plan and schedule in short order.

DEVELOPMENT—90 DAYS
The development phase contains the following important milestones:

LIVE ALPHA VERSION—30 DAYS AFTER KICKOFF MEETING
A live Alpha site is vitally important, and it is something that most development teams are not accustomed to doing. Thirty days after the kickoff meeting, certain primary stakeholders must be given the IP address of a Web server where they can browse their application as it is being developed. The machine that they browse should be the server machine that the team is using as their development server, and it should contain a daily build of the application. In other words, the stakeholders should be able to browse the server anytime they want after the 30-day mark and see the current build of their app.

At this 30-day mark, the app should be 50 to 70 percent functionally complete. There will still be lots of unfinished work on the app. The pages will not have graphics or colors, and they will look like the wire frames that were defined during the kickoff meeting. There may also be bugs in the functionality that has been implemented. And there will be 30 to 50 percent of the functionality that is as yet unimplemented. In addition, there may be incompatibility problems with some of the versions of browsers that are to be supported.

This idea of a live Alpha site is an unorthodox idea, and I have seen development teams who were unwilling to do it. They were concerned that in opening up the app this early, the stakeholders would be more upset about what wasn't finished than happy about what was finished. However, my experience has been that the good far outweighs the bad in this approach.

There are several reasons why this live Alpha site is important. It tends to engender trust in the development team and excitement about the app among the stakeholders. There are several action items that the stakeholders need to complete for the B2B application to be deployed. They must do things such as gather the data for the app, begin a marketing plan for the launch of the site among its external users, and arrange for the app to be included in the enterprise's IT backup and maintenance processes. Having an up-and-running Alpha version of the site that the stakeholders can see is a great motivator for them to get their tasks done so that the app can launch on time.

With the live Alpha version, the development team does not need to worry about reporting the status of their work to the stakeholders. The Alpha site lets the stakeholders see the status of the development effort firsthand, whenever they want.

Status reporting is a patently inefficient act, of dubious value to developers and stakeholders alike. Developers hate doing it, and stakeholders sometimes don't believe the status reports anyway. Exposing a live Alpha site eliminates the need for it altogether.

A live Alpha site does something else that is very important. It addresses the "Yes, But" Syndrome. The users can see the app and get their "Yes, Buts" out early in the development phase. This pays big dividends later in the project.

FEATURE FREEZE—45 DAYS AFTER KICKOFF MEETING

There needs to be a period right after the Alpha site goes live when the stakeholders can give feedback and request changes in the application. The two weeks after the Alpha site goes live is when the stakeholders are given this opportunity. Of course, the Project Manager needs to manage the scope of these changes. However, allowing a few changes at this stage of the project goes a long way toward ensuring that the stakeholders are satisfied with the application at the conclusion of the project.

At 45 days after the kickoff meeting, the features of the application need to be frozen so that the project team can concentrate on implementing the specifications by the deadline.

BETA TEST—60 DAYS AFTER KICKOFF MEETING

At the 60-day mark, the site should be opened up to a select group of users for Beta testing. By this time, the developers should have completed all of the functionality and have incorporated the page design template from the creative people. Colors and graphics should be on the pages, and the site should look much as it will look in its final form.

The thrust of the development effort from here should be devoted to browser compatibility issues. I have worked on B2B projects where browser issues, getting all of the pages to look right in all of the supported browsers, occupied nearly 50 percent of the development time. The development team needs to allow significant time to browser issues early in the project if the application is going to deploy on time.

FINAL TESTING AND DEPLOYMENT—90 DAYS

Oftentimes the application does not go live immediately after it is deployed. Given the difficulty of creating a lifelike test environment for a B2B app during the development phase, it is often necessary to set up the app and test it in a near real-world environment. This is best done just before the app is to go live. The idea is to root out as many problems and perform as much tuning as possible before real users start to exercise the application.

SUMMARY

B2B projects can be risky, which means that there are lots of ways a B2B project can fail. Most of the risk can be traced back to the fact that B2B applications and projects are complex.

If you can reduce the complexity of a software project, you can increase the chances that it will succeed. Having in place a software infrastructure on which you can build the B2B applications enables you to add application features in a series of relatively simple 90-day projects (see Chapters 7 and 12 for information on infrastructures for B2B applications).

After the infrastructure is in place, a lightweight project methodology, combined with effective scope and requirements management, can help greatly in reducing a project's complexity and increasing its chances for success.

VISION DOCUMENTS FOR TYPICAL B2B APPLICATIONS

A modern Software Requirements Specification (SRS) is a collection of documents that describes what an application does. The SRS consists of several documents, including wire frame page mockups and specification documents. Often the SRS documents are organized hierarchically, with a set of parent documents at the top that describes the overall application and a set of child documents beneath for each of the subsystems. Figure P-3 shows a hierarchy of SRS documents.

As you can see in Figure P-3, the wire frame and specification documents are derived from a document called the Vision document. The Vision document describes the application in general terms. It describes the users of the application, their needs, and the features of the app, as well as both the problem that the application is to solve and the solution it provides. It describes the users' needs and the features of the application.

The chapters in Part 3 provide Vision documents for the most frequently used B2B applications. Chapter 12 provides the overall Vision document for B2B applications. It describes the user needs and application features that are common to all B2B applications. Specifically, Chapter 12 explains how a server called a Private Exchange encapsulates many of the features that are common to all B2B applications. In this way, Chapter 12 is the parent Vision document for B2B applications, and Chapters 13 and 14 are the child Vision documents.

Chapters 13 and 14 are Vision documents for selling-chain management and supply-chain management applications. These chapters describe the user needs and application features that are unique to those particular applications. These Vision documents should provide a starting point for you as you begin to define your own B2B applications.

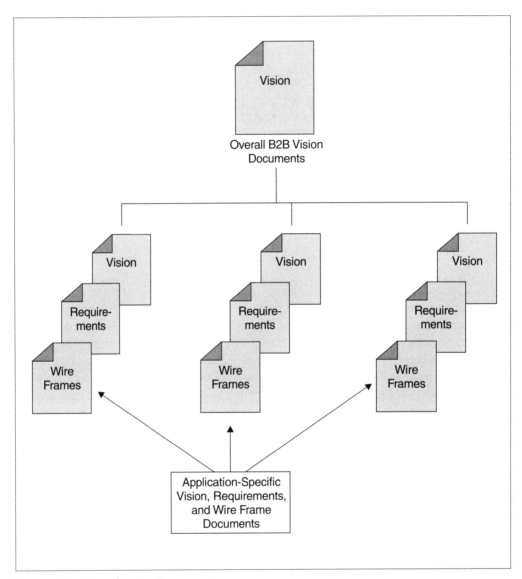

FIGURE P-3 *Specification Documents*

Extranets and B2B Web Sites

B2B Internet commerce is more than automated transactions between businesses. It is more than buying, selling, paying, and shipping. And it is more than shopping for the best prices on commodities in online Public Exchanges and Marketplaces.

Businesses that fully leverage B2B Internet commerce use their B2B apps to manage and enhance their relationships with their customers. They use their B2B applications to provide secure content, collaboration, and commerce with their customers and with their allies.

This chapter describes extranets and B2B Web sites, which provide secure content, collaboration, and commerce and enable companies to move their businesses to the Web.

12.1 INTRODUCTION TO EXTRANETS AND B2B WEB SITES

As explained in Chapter 2, an *extranet* is a Web site that can be used to expose a company's internal information systems in a secure way to a preferred customer. Typically, a company will use one extranet site to do business with one particular customer. Because of the hardwired nature of traditional extranet sites, to do business with many customers, a business would likely need to deploy many extranet sites, one for each customer. Because of the difficulty of building extranet sites, their use has been somewhat limited until recently.

A *B2B Web site* is an exceptionally robust Web site that aggregates several extranets into one site. Now with the advent of B2B Web sites that provide in a single site the functionality of many extranet sites, extranets can be built and deployed more readily. A B2B Web site can provide value to a company in three ways:

1. A security context in which B2B applications can safely transfer information across company boundaries

2. A portal in which to integrate the data and the functionality of the various applications and information systems inside the company

3. An infrastructure on which company-specific B2B applications can be built

First, let's talk about the security context for B2B applications. As explained in Chapter 2, a B2B Web site provides the security context in which B2B applications operate. This is illustrated in Figure 12-1. A B2B Web site provides a security context in which information is exchanged and transactions are conducted with trading partners.

The second way in which a B2B Web site is valuable is that it provides a vehicle for integrating applications inside a company. A B2B Web site enables users inside and outside of an organization to view multiple information systems and applications through a single user interface, usually a Web browser.

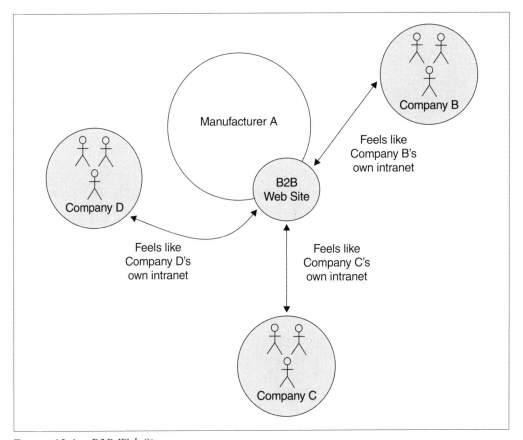

FIGURE 12-1   *B2B Web Sites*

A B2B Web site provides a practical platform on which a company can integrate its back-end legacy systems. It does this by extending the user interface of each system to a single, aggregated user interface inside a browser.

A B2B Web site provides a portal into a company's legacy information systems and its disparate, department-based applications. Using a B2B Web site, a company can "Web-ify" its existing systems without having to rebuild them.

Finally, a B2B Web site provides a software infrastructure for building specific B2B applications. A B2B Web site provides the computing infrastructure, the secure Web site and everything that goes with it, that B2B applications require to enable secure content, collaboration, and commerce.

12.1.1 THE PURPOSE OF B2B APPLICATIONS

Modern business relationships require a healthy diet of fresh information. In many ways, the quality of the information that is shared between businesses determines the quality of their relationship.

A business's customers, employees, and partners are the vital parties in its business-to-business relationships. A B2B application that only provides for online buying and selling does little to share business information and therefore does little to enhance business relationships. To realize the highest lifetime value from its relationships, a company needs B2B applications that do more than buying and selling.

To enhance business-to-business relationships truly, a business needs to have its own B2B applications that enable its employees, partners, and customers to come together to obtain information, collaborate, work, enhance their relationships, and conduct complex business transactions in a secure, personalized, information-rich, online environment. The Bodacious Boogey Boards example later in this chapter explains this more.

Enhancing a company's business-to-business relationships means integrating the appropriate internal business processes with the internal processes of its partner companies. A company that integrates its business processes with its partners' processes enhances the symbiotic relationships it has with its partners. B2B applications provide a safe, secure forum in which companies and their customers can conduct business cheek-to-cheek instead of at arm's length.

Unlike traditional forms of doing business with partner companies, in which information passes slowly across enterprise boundaries and requires significant management oversight, worker-hours, and lead times, B2B applications enable interenterprise processes to be accomplished without undue overhead, and revenue is realized using smaller inventories, fewer worker-hours, and smaller lead times.

If a company can safely integrate the right business processes with its partner businesses, both companies benefit. Each company is able to concentrate on its core competencies and satisfy its customers and reduce costs in ways that it could not without its B2B applications.

12.2 OVERVIEW OF B2B WEB SITES

Let's take a closer look at B2B Web sites and the role they play in B2B Internet commerce.

12.2.1 A BROAD DESCRIPTION OF B2B WEB SITES

A B2B Web site is the computing platform—that is, the server hardware and software—on which B2B applications are built and hosted. A B2B Web site is a server that is both open and secure, where users can obtain information that is relevant and for their eyes only, where partners and customers can collaborate on one project and compete on another, and where buying and selling can take place in the context of relevant and secure information.

A B2B Web site is private. It is not like a Public Exchange or online Marketplace, in which the servers are owned by a company that is trying to create an online marketplace for specialized commodities. Rather, a company that owns a B2B Web site typically owns its own Web server and uses its B2B Web site to work more effectively with its customers and partner businesses.

The B2B Web site multiplexes information from multiple organizations, multiple applications, and multiple processes. With a B2B Web site, a business can create B2B applications that offer unique products, services, and incentives tailored to each of its partners and each of its customers. A B2B Web site also enables a company to integrate the appropriate internal process with the internal processes of its partners so it can form an e-Business cluster. In addition, with the real-time feedback and analysis that a B2B Web site can provide, a B2B Web site enables managers to improve continuously their company's offerings.

12.2.2 A PRECISE DESCRIPTION OF B2B WEB SITES

A B2B Web site is a server for building and hosting secure B2B Web applications. In short, a B2B Web site is a secure Web site with a set of integrated programming tools. Chapters 1 through 6 of this book illustrate how to begin building a B2B Web site using the .NET Framework. Chapter 7 describes a commercial software package named Webridge Extranet, which provides a fairly complete implementation of a B2B Web site right out of the box.

Both the do-it-yourself .NET Framework-based B2B Web sites and the Webridge Extranet-based B2B Web sites run on Windows 2000 Advanced Server (and its future successors). These B2B Web sites use Internet Information Server for the Web server, SQL Server for the database, objects derived from the .NET Framework Class Library for middle-tier Business Objects, and XML Web services and BizTalk Server for application integration and the development of automated business processes.

As explained in Chapter 1, a B2B Web site is in fact a three-tier business application that has a database back-end, a Web server and Business Objects on the middle-tier, and Web browsers as clients. The structure of a B2B Web site is illustrated in Figure 12-2 (see also Figure 1-3).

As I said, a Windows-based B2B Web site uses IIS for the Web server, SQL Server for the database, the .NET Framework for middle-tier Business Objects, and

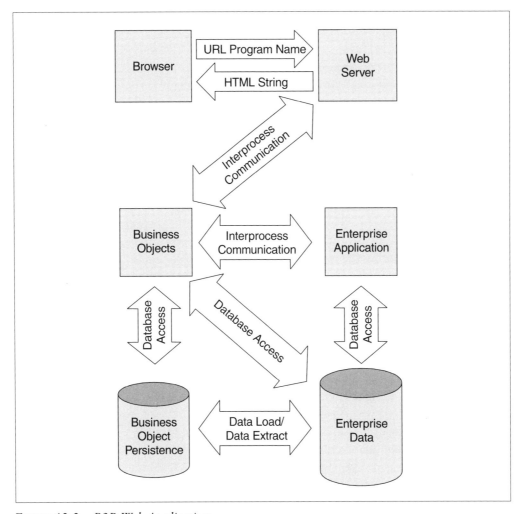

FIGURE 12-2   *B2B Web Application*

XML Web services and BizTalk Server for application integration and automated business processes.

As you can see in Figure 12-2, a B2B Web site consists of several subsystems, including a Web server, Business Objects, and a database. As requests come in from users with Web browsers, the Web server calls the Business Objects to perform the requested tasks. The Business Objects report the results of these tasks back to the Web server, which sends the results to the browser as a string of HTML. There might be information among the results of these tasks, which the Business Objects performed, that needs to be saved (or persisted). This information is saved in the database.

To put this another way: A user with a browser sends a request to the Web server for a task to be performed; the Web server tells the Business Objects to perform the task; the Business Objects perform the task and send the results to the Web server, which sends these results to the browser as HTML. And if the Business Objects need to save some of those results, the information is saved in the database. Additional requests can come into the B2B Web site through XML Web service method calls or through business documents submitted to BizTalk Server.

As you can also see in Figure 12-2, for the Business Objects to perform their tasks, they might need to obtain information from some enterprise application or enterprise database. Further, there may be times when it is necessary for data to be loaded or extracted between enterprise databases and the B2B Web site database.

Perhaps this whole process is best illustrated with an example. Let's say that Bodacious Boogey Boards, Inc. is a manufacturer of boogey boards. Bodacious Boogey Boards, Inc. has a B2B application that they and their suppliers use for supply chain management. Let's say that one of their suppliers logs into the Bodacious B2B site with a browser and requests Bodacious's forecast for the upcoming quarter's demand for one of the materials that this supplier supplies to Bodacious. The supplier's browser sends this request in the form of a URL to the Bodacious B2B Web server. The Bodacious Web server fires up the appropriate Business Objects, which retrieve this information from Bodacious's Enterprise Resource Planning (ERP) application. The results are sent as HTML back to the browser, and the fact that this information was sent to this supplier is saved in the database. Eventually, this data in the database is extracted into another enterprise database and used by an enterprise application to generate reports on the effectiveness of the supply chain process. What could be simpler, right?

Of course, actually building all of this software could be a large undertaking. To build this supply chain management application, Bodacious would first need to have implemented their own Enterprise Resource Planning (ERP) system, and then they would need to have built or bought a robust B2B infrastructure.

This B2B infrastructure is what a B2B Web site provides. A B2B Web site consists of a server machine or set of server machines that runs a B2B Web server, a set of

Business Objects, and a database server. These hardware and software systems constitute the infrastructure that B2B applications require.

Mind you, the real power of a B2B Web site is found in its Business Objects. In Chapter 9 we saw that the middle tier of a B2B application typically has some low-level, infrastructure-type software components in addition to application-level Business Objects. In the Bodacious example, the application-level Business Objects would be the supply chain management Business Objects that communicate with the ERP system to discover the forecast for the upcoming quarter. There would also need to be many low-level, infrastructure-type Business Objects that would handle tasks such as these:

- Provide low-level, application-specific interfaces with the company's enterprise applications and enterprise databases

- Generate the HTML that is sent to the browsers, based on who the user is, what the user does, and what company the user works for

- Implement effective security and content access controls

- Cache each user's content access settings appropriately so that repeated authorization checks do not become a drag on the system's performance

- Save the appropriate data from Business Objects in the database and handle the object-to-relational mapping

- Save documents to and retrieve documents from a robust and secure document repository

- Make method calls that invoke application logic and that transfer data over networks and across the Internet

- Perform all of these tasks inside of transactions so that all of the participating information systems remains consistent with each other

These are the operations that are common to all B2B applications, and these are the functions that the B2B Web site performs. Having a B2B Web site in place enables B2B application developers to concentrate on implementing the B2B application logic and enables developers to build out the features of B2B applications in a series of short 90-day projects without having to refactor the entire application after each project or two.

The .NET Framework provides a portion of the necessary infrastructure for a B2B Web site right out of the box. It provides objects that generate the HTML that is sent to the browsers. The .NET Framework's XML Web services enable method calls across the Internet, and the .NET Framework, COM+ Services, and BizTalk Server provide a robust transaction infrastructure.

In addition, the .NET Framework provides partial implementations of the code to interface with specific applications and databases: The event system needed to implement the content access controls, and the hooks needed to cache each user's content access settings, some of the code for object-to-relational mapping, and at least three possibilities for building a robust repository in which to store documents. Chapters 2 through 6 of this book show you how to get started writing your own code to perform these functions.

The infrastructure code that performs these functions is the foundation of a B2B Web site. In addition to infrastructure-level functionality, there are many application-level features that must be part of a B2B Web site. Later in this chapter, there is a list of the operations that a B2B Web site must perform.

12.2.3   B2B WEB SITE AS A PLATFORM FOR B2B APPLICATIONS

If you are going to build B2B applications, you will need a B2B Web site. In other words, you are going to need a server platform that provides the infrastructure that your B2B applications will use.

SEPARATING B2B INFRASTRUCTURE FROM B2B APPLICATIONS
Anytime you have software that is as complex as B2B applications, you will find that it is vital to separate the things that change in the software from things that stay the same or from things that change at a different rate or for different reasons. You will want to segment the subsystems in such a way that you can upgrade the infrastructure and the applications separately.

What this means is that a B2B Web site must be separate and distinct from the B2B applications that are implemented on the site. This concept is best illustrated with a couple of examples.

SAP   SAP is a large, international software company that produces a highly successful suite of ERP software packages. SAP software supports functions such as accounting, finance, production planning, materials management, human resources, sales, and distribution. You can run an entire enterprise on SAP software. In fact, many Fortune 2000 companies do run their businesses on SAP. SAP is a dominant ERP software company.

As good as SAP software is (and it is very good), it suffers from a flaw in certain modules that makes the software somewhat inflexible. If your business processes do not happen to match the processes that are codified into the SAP software . . . well, there is good news and there is bad news.

The good news is that it is entirely possible to modify the SAP software so that it matches your own business processes. SAP even provides software tools to help you do this. The bad news, however, is that when you receive the next software update from SAP and go to install it, the installation program might pause and say something like "You have modified certain objects in this module. Would you like to apply the update?" This innocuous-sounding question is really asking, "Do you want to upgrade to the latest version of the SAP software and lose your changes, or would you rather hang on to your changes and not upgrade your SAP software?"

In certain modules of the SAP software, modifications that users make to the software become a branch that gets cut off with every update from SAP. This is because in certain SAP modules, there is not an adequate separation between the infrastructure and the application. This concept can be illustrated further with another example.

Amazon.com   Amazon.com launched their popular B2C Web site as a book-selling site. The server infrastructure for the site is complex because it has to support high traffic, accommodate huge amounts of data, provide security for commerce, and generate much of the information that is published on the site dynamically from databases.

When Amazon expanded their offering from books and added music, they did not build all of that infrastructure software again from scratch. When you look at the Amazon site, you can see in the features of the site many similarities between the book section and the music section. Books and music both enable customers to post reviews. Books and music both show an Amazon sales ranking, and the procedure for ordering books and music is the same.

Amazon reused their infrastructure for multiple applications. Before they went public with a book-selling site, they first built an infrastructure that could support high traffic, accommodate huge amounts of data, provide security for commerce, and generate information dynamically from databases. Then they used that infrastructure to build a book-selling Web application. After that, they used their infrastructure again to build a music-selling Web application, and they have subsequently reused their infrastructure to build many more applications to sell all kinds of things.

Amazon was careful to separate infrastructure from application, and it has paid off for them. We already see the relative ease with which they can build new applications. In addition, if some new, faster database technology were to come along, do you think that Amazon would have to rebuild all of their applications to take advantage of it? The answer is no because the database is part of their infrastructure. They can upgrade their infrastructure without breaking their applications. Each time their infrastructure is upgraded, all of their applications will simply run faster.

B2B WEB SITE AS REQUIRED FOR B2B APPLICATIONS
The complexity of the software for B2B applications is comparable to the complexity of the software for SAP and Amazon.com. This level of complexity requires a clear distinction between the B2B infrastructure and the B2B applications that run on it.

So before a company can build any B2B applications, it will first need to build or buy its own B2B Web site, which provides the needed infrastructure for building and hosting B2B applications.

There are several B2B Web site platforms on the market. They are produced by B2B software vendors such as Webridge on the Microsoft platform and Vignette and BroadVision on Unix. In addition, several other companies, such as Commerce One, Ariba, Microsoft, Oracle, IBM, and SAP, offer B2B infrastructure and B2B application software packages. Not all of these vendors refer to their products as a B2B Web site, and each of the platforms varies in terms of what it does and how well it does it.

Evaluating these platforms and deciding which one is best for you is a painstaking process. Later in this chapter, there is a list of the features a B2B Web site must have to support the building and hosting of B2B applications adequately.

To understand the context in which the B2B Web site features are used or to understand why these particular B2B Web site features are required, it is requisite that you first understand the users of B2B Web sites, who they are, and what they do.

12.3   USERS OF B2B WEB SITES

Users of a B2B Web site, who are typically company employees and workers in partner companies, will want to do the following:

- Access content that is relevant and fresh and for-their-eyes-only. This enables them to find the information they need to do their jobs quickly, with fewer worker-hours.

- Collaborate and perform work in workflows for business processes that are integrated with partner companies' processes. This enables companies to work seamlessly in concert with their partner companies to create new value for their customers.

- Perform secure commercial transactions for buying, selling, shipping, and paying. This enables companies to transact business with fewer mistakes, using fewer worker-hours.

12.3.1   USER PROFILES

Now we'll look at users of B2B Web sites. However, in subsequent chapters we discuss users from the perspective of particular B2B applications. In this chapter, we discuss users from the perspective of their interaction with the B2B Web site as a generic computer system.

From this computer system perspective, there are four distinct categories of users of B2B Web sites:

- Anonymous users: people from the general public who have not logged in to the site and who can only access the public content

- Authenticated users: people who have user accounts on the site and who are authorized for selected content, collaboration, and commerce

- Content managers: people who have authority to publish and/or approve the content that is published on the site

- Administrators: people who have authority to change the structure and organization of the site itself

The following sections of this chapter provide the detailed profiles of each of these classes of users.

ANONYMOUS USERS

These are people who visit the public portions of the B2B Web site and who may or may not log in to see the secure portions of the site. Anonymous users vary greatly in their level of sophistication. They may never have used a Web browser until now, they may be experienced Web surfers, or they might be so experienced that they are hackers who are trying to gain illegal access to the site.

Anonymous users are often those who are having their first contact with the company that owns the site and are seeking information. They might be trying to do the following:

- Learn about a product that the company makes or sells, or a service that the company provides

- Find a local reseller or an integrator with a particular area of expertise

- Obtain technical support or customer service to get their questions answered

- Find specialized information that they think the company might possess

- Get enough information about this B2B Web site to decide whether it might be useful to them

It can be difficult for people outside of an enterprise to find information they need. They might be looking for information that is specific and that would be easy for the right person inside the enterprise to provide if only they knew whom to contact. When people outside the enterprise are trying to do a detailed product evaluation or trying to find a reseller who can work with them effectively, a lack of information is always the primary problem. The following problems can interfere with the anonymous user's success:

- Telephone and regular mail inquiries are often ineffective because the person does not know whom to contact at the enterprise, and even if he or she finds that person, the contact is sometimes unresponsive.

- An enterprise's public Web site often consists only of brochure-ware, and it does not provide the kind of interaction that the person may need.

- It is difficult to obtain, through traditional means such as printed pages sent through regular mail or faxes, information that is current, complete, and up-to-date.

The companies that can readily provide this information are the companies that will be successful in establishing relationships with them.

AUTHENTICATED USERS

These are people who already have an existing relationship with the company that owns the B2B Web site. Authenticated users usually access the B2B Web site using a Web browser, and that browser could be running on a standard PC or on a portable wireless device. Authenticated users can vary greatly in their level of sophistication. They may be someone who has never used a Web browser until now or who may be an experienced Web surfer.

Authenticated users are looking for content, collaboration, and/or commerce that is relevant to them and are trying to do the following:

- Find information that is specific to their role in the relationship with the owner of the site or in their relationship with the other users of the site. Examples of the information they are seeking would be "insider" technical information or for-their-eyes-only pricing data or the status of collaboration and/or commerce that is currently in process.

- Collaborate with the people with whom they have relationships. This collaboration might take the form of posting and reading messages in a threaded discussion forum, or it might consist of processing documents or forms or drawings that are ready for their attention and posting completed ones for the subsequent people in the workflow.

- Perform commercial transactions such as buying, selling, or paying. These transactions will usually interface with ERP applications that run inside the enterprise. Examples of this would be placing orders for products from a manufacturer or requesting raw materials from a supplier.

It is crucial that each authenticated user see information that is individually tailored for him or her when logging into the B2B Web site. Each user should be presented with Web pages that are highly personalized and targeted. This type of secure access to content, collaboration, and commerce is what enables B2B applications to be effective. Without secure access to individualized content, collaboration, and commerce, B2B Internet commerce is not possible.

Within the next few years, the companies that do business with other businesses (which includes nearly all companies) will be expected to have B2B capabilities. Once one company in a value chain implements B2B Internet commerce, the other companies in the chain that do not have secure B2B capabilities will be at risk of being replaced by competing companies that do.

The following problems can interfere with this type of user's success:

- The traditional channels of communication are inadequate to support the tight and secure information flow that is required for B2B. Printed communication ages too quickly and is too hard to keep current. E-mail is not formal enough for typical business transactions. Faxes are often cumbersome and not secure, and phone calls are hit and miss.

- B2B communications must be asynchronous yet fast, formal enough to carry out transactions yet informal and flexible enough to convey unstructured information, current and up-to-date yet not flood the channel every time there is an update.

A B2B Web site is the only forum that is suitable for the secure integration of business process. On a B2B Web site, an authenticated user can safely locate sensitive information, post work that only they are authorized to perform, and conduct transactions in a way that enables the linkage of business processes across enterprises.

CONTENT MANAGERS

These are people who have authority over particular content, collaboration, and commerce on the B2B Web site. Content managers tend to be experienced users of Web browsers. In addition, they have relevant domain expertise, have particular responsibilities on the site, and have been granted certain administrative rights on the site.

Examples of content managers could include those people in the Marketing Department of the company that owns the site and who are charged with producing documents about a company's products or services. An engineer who produces product specifications might also function as a content manager so other engineers at the company that owns the site or at partner companies could collaborate on those specifications using the B2B Web site. Content managers may also be called upon to review and/or approve the content that is submitted for publication on the site by other users. Content managers can be employees of the company that owns the B2B Web site, or they may be managers of a partner business that uses the site.

If they are employees of the company that owns the site, they could be specialists on particular areas of content, collaboration, or commerce on the site. They would have administrative rights over that content, collaboration, or commerce. Or they might be account managers who are responsible for the relationships that their company has with particular companies on the site. In other words, they use the site to maintain the relationships with the companies whose accounts they manage.

If the content manager works for a partner business that uses the site, he or she would have administrative rights over the people from that company who use the site. In other words, they would specify which people from their company have the authority to access particular content, collaboration, and commerce but, of course, could grant access only to that which they have been given access.

On the site, content managers' responsibilities are the following:

- Produce content that will appear on the site. This requires them to be domain experts in relevant content areas.

- Post that content onto the site and specify which users or groups of users have the authority to view and/or modify that content.

- Manage and administer the accounts of particular users (typically people from their company) on the site.

- Review content, moderate collaboration, and/or approve commerce that occurs on the site among the group of people for which they are responsible.

In traditional Web sites, it is often the Web master who actually places the content on the site. The Web master is a developer who knows HTML and the other relevant Web technologies and is charged with building and maintaining the Web site.

In this Web master scenario, the people who produce the documents and/or HTML pages that go on the site will hand off their finished materials to the Web master for publication on the Web site.

The problem with this process is that the Web master is a bottleneck in the process of getting content onto the Web site. In a B2B Web site, the volume of information that is published and the frequency with which it is updated would quickly outpace a Web master's capacity to place new and updated content on the Web site.

It is crucial, therefore, that the people who produce the content be able to place the content directly on the Web site, without the intervention of a Web master. The task of administering the content on the Web site must be distributed to those people who actually create and maintain the information.

Content managers must be able to manage content on the B2B Web site using only their Web browser. A content manager should not have to use a fat client application to do content management on the B2B Web site. There could be many content managers, and they could be in widely distributed locations, so it may be difficult to provide all of the content managers with a fat client application for publishing content on the site. Providing the ability for content managers to add documents and review content on the site using only their Web browser would enable them to do their job whenever and wherever they can find access to the Web. Enabling content managers to do their job with only a Web browser would also avert the need for keeping a fat client application updated on their computers.

ADMINISTRATORS

Administrators are people who have authority to change the structure and organization of the site itself. They are employees of the company that owns the site. They determine who can and who cannot use the site and in what way. They grant access and administrative permissions to users on the site. They manage the system data that the site uses. They also can change the organization and structure of the content, collaboration, and commerce on the site.

Administrators are experienced Web browser users. In addition, the administrator(s) of a site must have a solid overall understanding of the site and the business functions that it fulfills. The administrators' key responsibilities are the following:

- Administer the database of users of the site, and assign appropriate levels of access and responsibility to them.

- Manage the various types of system data that the site uses. This could include such diverse types of data as the list of topics that are used to organize content, the list of countries that are valid for users' addresses, the maximum age of business documents that appear on the site, and so on.

- Perform configuration, maintenance, and backup of the site.

- Ensure that the site runs smoothly and fulfills the business functions for which it was built.

In traditional Web sites, it is typically the Web master who performs administrative functions on the Web site. The problem is the fact that the process of administering a B2B Web site could easily overwhelm a Web master.

B2B Web sites are highly complex, using technology from several different branches of computer science and potentially being composed of several servers running in a distributed configuration. Administering them requires that the infrastructure on which the B2B Web site is built provide easy-to-use administrative interfaces.

Administrators are a select group and could potentially use a fat client application to perform their administrative tasks. A Web browser interface would be nice, but realistically, the depth and complexity of the administrative tasks needed to administer a B2B Web site could be impossible to implement in a browser-based administration tool and may require the robustness of fat client applications.

12.4 FEATURES OF B2B WEB SITES

The B2B Web site features discussed here are the base functionality required for typical B2B applications. To produce this list of required features for a B2B Web site, I took the top-down approach of looking at the required features of B2B applications first and then worked my way down to figure out what features a B2B Web site would need to support those B2B application features.

To obtain the list of B2B application features, I looked at the best-of-breed B2B applications that several companies have implemented and about which a few books and articles have been written. I used the information on B2B application features as the basis for the subsequent chapters in this part of the book.

To produce the list of required features for a B2B Web site, I also looked at the best-of-breed features of the existing B2B Web site platforms on the market. This helped round out the list by catching those B2B Web site features that perhaps have not yet been used by B2B applications.

To manage complexity, the capabilities listed here are abstracted to a high enough level to result in a relatively small number of features. The list of features in this section provides the fundamental basis for product definition, scope management, and project management for building or buying a B2B Web site.

1. The site is implemented on an application server that can handle secure access from Web browsers, fat client applications, and enterprise servers.

2. The site is an infrastructure for B2B applications and is not a B2B application itself. There must be a clear distinction between infrastructure and application. An infrastructure that supports only one application is not an infrastructure. The infrastructure must be able to host multiple applications. The infrastructure must also be upgradeable without breaking any of the applications.

3. The site enables server-to-server integration between the B2B Web server and enterprise servers, such that either server can access data in databases on other servers and can fire off processes on the other server.

4. Transactions (two-phase commit transactions and long-running transactions) encapsulate all database access and function execution on the site and between the site and other servers, so that when data modifications are made on multiple servers and applications, they are kept consistent with each other.

5. Security and access control is an integral part of the site, with all content, collaboration, and commerce guarded by access controls, with

each client or user on the site being authenticated, and with each access of content, collaboration, and commerce being authorized.

6. The site provides a secure login facility, which requires users to specify a user ID and a password for authentication any time they try to access secure portions of the site. For Web browser-based users, this would be implemented as a login page. A successful login could deposit on the browser's machine a cookie that the server can use to manage the secure session for that user. The user ID identifies the user and provides the security context for determining which content the user is authorized to access on the site.

7. Certain users can be specified as administrators and/or content managers on the site and given authority over particular content, collaboration, and commerce.

8. Administration and content management are flexible and distributed, so there are no Web masters or developer bottlenecks on the site.

9. The site uses flexible security model(s), including group-based security, where people belong to groups and where administrators and content managers assign each section of content, collaboration, and commerce to be accessible only to certain groups, and permission list-based security, where administrators and content managers assign each section or piece of content, collaboration, and commerce a set of permissions, and users who fit the attributes of those permissions are granted access.

10. On the site every user can personalize his or her own home page, which will contain the particular content, collaboration, and commerce that each user is authorized to see and that interests him or her. Each user is able to choose, from among the information that he or she can access, which information he wishes to see on the site.

11. The information on the site is uniquely targeted for each user. Based on personalization data and on the user's particular relationships on the site, users are automatically presented with information that is highly relevant to their work on the site.

12. Content management tools on the site are sufficiently robust to handle structured data, such as product catalogs, and unstructured data, such as free-form text and file-based documents.

13. Structured data, such as product catalogs, is searchable by whatever attributes (or fields) are appropriate for the application.

14. Structured data can include simple data types such as numbers, text, and dates and can also include references to graphics and image files.

15. Structured data can be edited by administrators and content managers using Web browsers and can also be bulk loaded to and from enterprise databases.

16. Security applies to individual rows of structured data, so users can see only the data they are supposed to see.

17. Unstructured data, such as free-form text and file-based documents, is indexed and searchable on the site by users with Web browsers.

18. Unstructured data can include free-form text, such as messages that users post to newsgroup-type discussion forums on the site.

19. Unstructured data can include document files that are created by application software, such as spreadsheets, word processors, and drawing programs.

20. Document files can have corresponding structured metadata, such as the creation date or author, which users of the site can use when searching for documents.

21. Users, content managers, and administrators on the site using Web browsers can submit document files for publication on the site.

22. Content managers and administrators can process (review, reject, edit, and/or approve) the documents that users submit before the documents are actually published on the site.

23. Unstructured data can be edited by administrators and content managers using Web browsers and can also be bulk loaded to and from enterprise databases.

24. Security applies to unstructured data, so users can see only the messages and documents they are supposed to see.

25. Collaboration in the form of workflow is supported on the site and can use a combination of structured data and unstructured data.

26. Workflows on the site can be implemented by simple means, such as a status field that indicates in which stage in the workflow the artifact is currently located, and by robust means, such as a complete workflow engine that manages the routing of artifacts among individuals and the tracking of their progress.

27. As artifacts move through workflows, whether they consist of structured or unstructured data, security and access controls remain in effect to prevent unauthorized access to the information.

28. Collaboration is also supported on the site through newsgroup-type threaded discussion forums.

29. Messages posted on the threaded discussions are indexed and searchable so users on the site can find the relevant postings easily.

30. The threaded discussion forums on the site are accessible only to the people who have the proper security credentials

31. The site is capable of producing HTML that is compatible with whatever browsers are specified for the applications. For instance, the site does not dictate that only those browsers that support HTML frames can be used on the site.

32. The site supports programming languages that make it relatively easy to find developers to build B2B applications. The site does not require a new, unique programming language and/or a low-level programming language for which it is difficult to find developers.

33. The site provides for localization and support of foreign language versions of its pages. In addition, instead of merely having identically formated pages in different languages, each localized section of the site could sport a fundamentally different look and feel. Also, users are brought to their appropriate localized sections of the site automatically, based on their personalization settings.

34. The site provides sufficient throughput and scalability so that the system remains responsive at times of peak usage. The site may take advantage of caching, such as the database server cache, an in-memory object cache, static HTML caches, application-level caches, and the Web browser client cache, to enhance its performance, but ensures that the data in the caches remains consistent throughout the system.

35. The site includes applications that are usable and adequate to enable administrators to configure and maintain the site to keep it running smoothly.

36. The software for the site is optimized for a particular operating system to provide maximum power on that platform. Typically, a multiplatform, least common denominator approach does not yield highly effective server software.

37. The licensing of the server software that runs the site is not cumbersome or onerous to the company that owns the site, so limits are not imposed on the usefulness of the site. For instance, license agreements that require a fee be paid to the software vendor for each transaction performed on the site might cause an artificial ceiling to be placed on the throughput of the site.

SUMMARY

A B2B Web site enables a company to provide secure content, collaboration, and commerce for its employees and business partners. The ability to provide them, however, is well beyond the capabilities of a typical Web site and requires the robust power of B2B applications.

A B2B Web site provides the basis, the infrastructure for building and hosting B2B applications. A B2B Web site consists of a secure Web server, a set of Business Objects, and a Business Object persistence database, all implemented on an open and easily accessible application server.

A B2B Web site enables a clear distinction between a B2B infrastructure and the B2B applications it supports, thus enabling the infrastructure and the applications to be updated separately.

Building a B2B Web site from scratch is not a trivial undertaking. The .NET Framework gets you part of the way there and provides development tools for building the rest of it yourself. In addition, there are several companies that offer full-blown B2B Web site implementations.

The features of a B2B Web site can be distilled down to a relatively small list. You can use the list of features presented in this chapter as you evaluate the various B2B Web site platforms on the market and decide which one is right for you.

Selling-Chain Management

The key points for this chapter are the following:

- Selling-chain management applications help businesses boost sales.

- These applications streamline the sales process and make it more effective.

- Effective selling-chain management is a strong competitive advantage.

- Selling-chain applications are used by employees, partners, and customers.

- Selling-chain applications require several features to be effective.

13.1   INTRODUCTION TO SELLING-CHAIN MANAGEMENT

Dr. Ravi Kalakota's book, *e-Business: Roadmap for Success,*[1] includes an excellent chapter on selling-chain management. This chapter echoes much of what Dr. Kalakota says on the topic. In fact, his explanation of selling-chain management is so helpful as an introduction to the topic that I quote directly from his book in places.

In this chapter, I also go beyond what Dr. Kalakota defines for selling-chain management and provide a description of users and a list of concrete features that a selling-chain management application must have to do its job and fulfill its vital functions.

1. Ravi Kalakota and Marcia Robinson, *e-Business: Roadmap for Success* (Addison-Wesley, 1999), pp. 138–150 © 1999 by Addison-Wesley. Reprinted by permission of Pearson Education, Inc.

13.1.1 THE PURPOSE OF SELLING-CHAIN MANAGEMENT APPLICATIONS

The business of business is selling. However, companies are facing a wide range of problems with existing sales processes.

- It is difficult for customers and resellers to find up-to-date product information from manufacturers because marketing information is not consistent, printed marketing material is old, and pricing information is out-of-date.

- Sales people are inundated with non-value-added tasks, spending 30 to 50 percent of their time on administrative tasks.

- Manufacturers find that they must compete with each other for mindshare among resellers. This is because resellers tend to concentrate on selling those products for which the sales process is the least cumbersome. VARs, integrators, and dealers are swamped from manufacturers with printed product information that is out-of-date and ineffective. Manufacturers must find a way to simplify their sales process in order to attract resellers.

- Fragmented order support is a problem after the order is placed. This forces customers to deal with multiple company contacts who have difficulty accessing order status information.

- Current sales applications are not responsive or flexible because the IS staff is backed up with requests for new functionality.

- Current systems are not integrated, which means orders are rekeyed multiple times.

The purpose of selling-chain management is to create new real-time links between previously disconnected sales functions and to build a complete sales cycle from initial customer contact and product introduction to billing transactions and sale completion.

13.2 OVERVIEW OF SELLING-CHAIN MANAGEMENT

Selling-chain management is the application of technology to the activities in the whole life cycle of an order—from inquiry to order. Companies need to move away from automating discrete tasks, such as lead management, configuration, and pricing, and move toward an integrated infostructure that views order acquisition holistically, as an end-to-end process involving every department, from marketing to logistics (see Figure 13-1).

By approaching sales or "order acquisition" as a process rather than as a function, companies will begin to see things from their customers' point of view, arguably the best vantage point from which to win their loyalty, respect, and purchasing dollars. In other words, look at selling-chain applications as tools to streamline the integrated set of activities businesses perform to acquire and fulfill orders. To support this view, you need a new application framework to enable the integration of information that's fragmented across the organization.

13.2.1 PURPOSE OF SELLING-CHAIN MANAGEMENT

The strategy of selling-chain management is to move beyond the simple automation of sales functions and to manage the entire order acquisition process. These are the purposes of selling-chain management applications:

- **Make it easier for the customer.** This means making the entire order process seamless. For example, consider Haworth, a manufacturer of office furniture. Traditionally, if you needed an office system, you'd go to an architect to have it designed for you, but it could take a couple of months to figure out just what you want. So Haworth put in a computer system that lets the customer to do more of the work. The customer and dealer sit in front of a screen and design the office system in real time. Instead of taking weeks, it takes only an hour. Then, when it's delivered, you don't send it back because it's exactly what you expected.

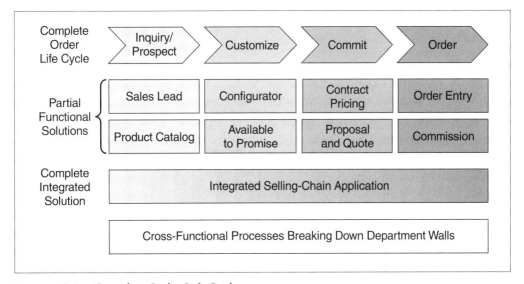

FIGURE 13-1 *Complete Order Life Cycle*

- **Add value for the customer.** This means thinking about the order process as something that adds value for the customer. Just being an order taker isn't going to cut it. Companies really have to be involved in a collaborative effort with the customer to identify the requirements, configure a solution to meet their needs, and then deliver it.

- **Make it easy to order custom products.** This means matching what customers want and what companies sell. This reduces unsold inventory and increases sales. Companies are beginning to explore the possibility of integrating the front-end sales configuration system with the back-end planning engine that bases deliver-date promises on material availability in the supply chain. The goal is to increase overall sales revenue by meeting customers' orders quickly, accurately, and, of course, profitably.

- **Increase sales force effectiveness.** Despite the tactical productivity advances represented by technology, little has been done to improve the strategic effectiveness of salespeople or to increase sales volume, trim sales cycle times, or lower costs per sale. The focus on sales effectiveness is increasing as companies look for ways to increase revenues while reducing the cost of operations.

- **Coordinate team selling.** As more companies become multinational organizations and service customers in many different countries, there is a much greater need to store customer information in a central location and to coordinate sales activities. The need to coordinate activities and share information is an especially critical process in complex, team-selling environments in which various members of the team work concurrently to close a deal.

Clearly, the order acquisition environment today is very different from the way it was five to ten years ago, and the pace of change is only getting faster. Many of these changes—regulatory changes, shifts in reseller channels, and product line expansion—are increasing the pressure on sales organizations.

The selling environment is getting tougher and tougher. Shorter product life cycles, intensified competition, and, above all, more sophisticated and demanding customers are making the salesperson's life ever more difficult. Increasingly, customers are demanding solutions designed and configured to meet their needs. These challenges are exacerbated by difficulties in the management of pricing, promotions, and commissions, in addition to other sales parameters. Sales organizations must add more value for the customer, operate with greater speed and accuracy, and cut their own costs—all at the same time.

Consider the following scenario: A sales representative meets with a customer. Despite being armed with volumes of product information, the salesperson cannot answer the customer's questions: "Can you deliver the product with these modifications by this date? How much will it cost with these modifications? When can I have it?" The salesperson cannot answer these questions because the company's product and service offerings have intricate structures and seemingly endless variations, with associated pricing combinations and discount structures.

So the salesperson tells the customer, "I'll get back to you in a couple of days." She has to go back to the office and begin the time-consuming process of configuring the order, developing and submitting a price quote, and negotiating with manufacturing and shipping for an acceptable delivery date. Several days or weeks later, the customer finally receives the answers to his questions. In the meantime, a competitor with the ability to answer the customer's questions with the most timely, accurate, and actionable information has walked away with the business.

On hearing that the order is lost, the salesperson complains to the manager, "Give me the ability to configure orders in real time and to deliver a price quote and related product availability on the spot. Also give me software that will seamlessly integrate with the back-office process (manufacturing and distribution) so that we can track orders and provide customers with accurate commitment dates." Now ask yourself. Does this scenario sound familiar? How are your salespeople spending their time? How effective are their tools? What obstacles do they face before closing a sale? Does your organization have the necessary selling tools to facilitate order acquisition?

Salespeople have a difficult enough time getting the prospect's attention, coordinating schedules, and keeping the prospective client on the telephone. But maintaining the prospect's attention is even harder, especially if he or she has questions or objections that the salesperson can't respond to quickly. That is why the sales force must have close at hand integrated applications that provide real-time access to all current product, price, and availability information so that they can answer customer questions completely, handle objections skillfully, and, ideally, close the sale on the spot.

Traditionally this process has not been easy. During a typical conversation with a customer, a salesperson may need to confer with manufacturing to ensure that a product can be configured with certain features, contact engineering to verify that a solution meets the customer's needs, or check with distribution to confirm that a product is in stock or is ready to ship. Obtaining all this information can be an arduous, time-consuming task that slows down the sales cycle. But without this information the risk of order errors (which can cause delays, annoy the customer, and, ultimately, result in lost revenue) is huge.

The bottom line is that the order acquisition process, in most enterprises, has undergone little or no automation to date. However, recent technological advances now make selling-chain automation solutions feasible. Clearly, in the networked economy, the sales organization has a profound impact on downstream decisions made across the enterprise, as well as decisions that relate to outside suppliers. Unfortunately, there's widespread confusion in management ranks as to what should be included in the selling-chain life cycle and how to support it using software applications. Exacerbating the confusion are the fluid scope of software capabilities, the dynamic nature of the market and vendors, and ever-changing tools and technology. This chapter sheds some light on this complex and dynamic topic. But before going any further, let's look at the business trends driving the corporate adoption of selling-chain solutions.

13.2.2 BUSINESS FORCES DRIVING THE NEED FOR SELLING-CHAIN MANAGEMENT

Several fundamental market issues are driving the interest in selling-chain applications: the rise of self-service, the excessive cost of presales support, the increasing cost of order errors, changing sales channels, increasing product complexity, and the rise of mergers and acquisitions. Companies can cope with these issues by implementing selling-chain management systems. To achieve successful implementation, companies must integrate their sales systems with other enterprise systems in order to bring enterprise information to bear at the point of sale (such as kiosks, salespeople's laptops, Web sites, and call-center representatives' PCs).

To reduce selling costs, companies need to integrate isolated sales and order acquisition applications with their other core front- and back-office enterprise systems. They then will be better positioned to increase sales throughput, lower costs, reduce order errors, and increase customer satisfaction.

THE RISE OF THE SELF-SERVICE ORDER

The sales process is getting increasingly complex, as customers demand higher levels of service, faster turnaround times, and more customization. The early 1990s brought the concept of mass customization to the marketplace, which has evolved to serve a "market of one." Consumers want what they want and when they want it, and they want it packaged uniquely to meet their individual needs. In this new market, companies need to reexamine their sales procedures for ease of use. For years, Citibank captured a significant share of the college student market for credit cards simply by making it easy for students to obtain credit, while competitors made it difficult.

One aspect of selling that has been significantly influenced by self-service is the selection process. Today, after a consumer has narrowed the possibilities, he or she looks for a final selection process that is more comfortable and convenient and less irritating. An example of this dynamic can be found in the online used car business. For many potential customers, the experience of choosing a used car is an ordeal. But new methods for selecting used cars are transforming the industry. Companies such as Auto-By-Tel, Microsoft CarPoint, CarMax Auto Superstore, and AutoNation USA have targeted the selection experience as their competitive focus. At a CarMax show-room, customers sit in front of a computer and specify what features they want in an automobile. They can scroll through detailed descriptions of cars that might meet their needs. The final, no-haggle price for each vehicle is listed. A sales assistant then lets the customers inspect the autos that interest them and handles all the paperwork if they decide to buy. The "selling" is done not by the salespeople but by the customers themselves.

THE EXCESSIVE COST OF PRESALES TECHNICAL SUPPORT

Companies that fail to address systematically the quality and turnaround time associated with preparing sales quotes and proposals are likely to lose sales and market share to more responsive competitors.

The effective translation of prospect needs into product specifications results in the increased use of technical sales specialists during the presale phase of a sales process. Generally, technical sales specialists have a superior grasp of the capabilities of the entire product line and a better understanding of how these capabilities may meet a prospective customer's needs.

While effective, using technical support drives up the cost of selling and shifts the burden of expertise from the salesperson to the technical sales specialist. The result: excessive time consumed preparing complex sales quotes and proposals. As the pace of business accelerates and consumers expect shorter response times, it's imperative that companies deliver accurate and thorough sales proposals in record time.

The increasing trend toward the "market of one" makes it more difficult to create standardized proposals because each document is as unique as the product it proposes to sell. The cost of preparing high-quality, accurate quotes and proposals rises relative to the level of complexity and customization per product.

THE INCREASING COST OF ORDER ERRORS

The increased sophistication of custom products, services, and systems has resulted in an overall increase in the cost and frequency of order errors, which occur throughout the sales-and-deliver cycle. At the point of sale, an error can be made by simply proposing a product configuration that does not actually meet a customer's technical requirements or by offering a product that can't be manufactured.

Errors occur in order entry because incompatible options are not rejected or ancillary equipment has not been included in the order. In manufacturing, an invalid configuration can shut down the production line. If a miscalculated, multivendor product configuration is actually shipped to a customer, the cost of correcting the mistake in the field can be excessive, if not irrecoverable.

Human errors often account for order mistakes: insufficient access; noncurrent, inaccurate back-office information; misinterpretation of what's valid; misunderstanding the product line or how a product will perform; and simple typographic errors when processing an order. Companies that do not automate these processes and integrate their selling functions with their back-office systems will continue to be plagued with order errors. No matter what the cause or where the errors occur in the sales cycle, increased costs will result.

THE INCREASING CHANNEL PROLIFERATION PROBLEM

Selling is not as simple as it used to be, due to the rapid proliferation of channels. The channel applications that serve the order acquisition side are manifold.

- Field sales and in-store/branch sales: assisted in-person selling

- Telesales: assisted call-center selling

- Self-service: unassisted selling via the Web

- Third-party resellers or channel selling

The relative success of direct-to-the-end-user and build-to-order models are beginning to put pressure on companies to improve the information flow through various sales channels in order to improve time to market, reduce costs, and compete more effectively.

In addition, to achieve global expansion and/or market penetration more quickly, many organizations are attempting to implement integrated multichannel sales strategies. These require the efficient passing of leads and the even tougher challenge of keeping all parties informed on the status of the sales process.

THE INCREASING COMPLEXITY OF PRODUCTS

The increasing complexity of products and the rise in customers' demands for time-efficient ordering processes have put pressure on companies to increase the productivity and responsiveness of their sales force. Furthermore, the pace of introducing new products has accelerated dramatically, causing shorter product life cycles, which makes the salesperson's job of staying current even more difficult.

Sales efficiency and productivity remain major issues in many industries that are experiencing tight labor markets for seasoned sales professionals. The sales force must become adept at dealing with an ever-growing, ever-changing set of products (and/or services) as companies seek to broaden their product portfolios to sustain or accelerate growth rates.

All this makes it difficult for sales representatives and end users to keep up with changing product and compatibility information. These difficulties underscore the need for tools and a central repository of up-to-date product information to increase the productivity and accuracy of sales representatives and to enable end users to select, configure, and order products independently.

THE RISE OF DEREGULATION, MERGERS, AND ACQUISITIONS
While some organizations may face new sales and marketing challenges due to new channels and product line expansions, others face dramatic changes within their industries, such as the impact of deregulation on both the telecommunications and utility industries. Until now, companies in these industries haven't had to worry about having efficient and effective sales and marketing departments because they've enjoyed a monopoly. Now that they must compete, many of these companies are rapidly adopting selling-chain applications, not only to improve service but to survive.

In addition to deregulation, mergers and acquisitions have created corporations with diverse product lines, often sold by a consolidated sales force with little experience in selling the entire range of products.

13.2.3 TECHNOLOGY FORCES DRIVING THE NEED FOR SELLING-CHAIN MANAGEMENT

Business drivers highlight the importance of watching customer preferences and trends in selling-chain management. Just as important are the technology issues and trends that steer a company in a direction that will position it either for the future or for failure.

Managers should not make application investment decisions without a clear understanding of technology limitations. Many of the sales automation applications have mixed reputations in corporations due to vendors who made promises that didn't come to fruition. The reasons for these failures are varied.

- Integration was not a factor considered in the selection and implementation of applications.

- Many of the then-current software solutions were unwieldy or difficult to implement.

- The breadth of product functionality did not meet business requirements.

- Sales and marketing staff refused to use the products because they didn't increase sales effectiveness.

Let's examine application issues and look at recent technology advances that have helped overcome some of the problems in the mid-1990s.

THE SELLING-CHAIN APPLICATION CONTINUUM
The driving business forces and limitations of existing applications, coupled with the emergence of necessary enabling technologies, have companies scrambling to invest in sales automation solutions so they aren't left behind by more technically advanced

competitors. In order to understand where we're going, however, we need to understand the application continuum (see Figure 13-2).

The current business environment requires offering the right product or service to the right customer for the right price via the right channel at the right time. This requires more customer-centric sales functionality. Yet effective *sales* require a broad range of capabilities for integrating, automating, and managing sales interactions throughout an enterprise. This requires relationship-oriented order acquisitions (see Figure 13-2), which leading companies are implementing. Where is your organization in the selling-chain continuum?

The selling-chain continuum allows us to see where most companies are focusing their energies today and in which direction we need to move. Integration has become a hot topic at many corporations, but few understand why it's so critical. People are concentrating current integration efforts via functionally isolated efforts or line-of-business organizational structures. Both are insufficient for moving toward an enterprisewide order acquisition environment.

PROBLEMS WITH EXISTING SALES FORCE AUTOMATION
The first generation of selling-chain solutions burst onto the marketplace in the form of sales force automation (SFA) software, which is used to manage the entire sales process by capturing data at every step, from lead generation to contract closing.

The first generation of SFA software included stand-alone, task-oriented tools, such as personal organizers (appointment calendars and address/telephone directo-

	Traditional Sales Force Automation	Evolving Sale Force Automation	Customer-Centric Sales	Relationship-Oriented Order Acquisition
Integration	Task-oriented	Functionally isolated	Lines of business and select integration	Enterprisewide and highly integrated
Sales/Service Approach	Account-centric	Account-centric	Customer-centric	Relationship-centric
Application Emphasis	Productivity	Productivity	Effectiveness = closing the order	Effectiveness = revenue growth

FIGURE 13-2 *The Selling-Chain Application Continuum*

ries). The focus of these products was to coordinate and manage the diverse activities of a direct sales force throughout the entire sales cycle.

Second-generation SFA software focuses on improving the administrative productivity of salespeople by automating functions such as contact management, opportunity management, sales forecasting, and commission tracking. Another aspect of second-generation SFA is telesales. Telesales automation increases the productivity and efficiency of call centers, with the goal of increasing sales closure rates. Many companies spend bushels of money implementing second-generation SFA, yet success has been limited. The reason for the lack of success is that SFA tools suffer from the following problems:

- **Limited, task-oriented functionality.** These systems have archaic interfaces that are inflexible, have limited capabilities, and often require different sessions to access various core programs.

- **Functional isolation.** These products have limited back-office integration to perform such activities as inventory availability checks, fulfillment functions, real-time pricing, and account management, all of which emanate from sales-initiated customer contact.

- **Organizational resistance.** No enterprise wants to buy an off-the-shelf sales automation solution. Almost every company views its sales processes as a unique, key part of its competitive differentiation. Although most companies realize the inefficiency of building and maintaining a custom application, they won't accept a cookie-cutter approach either.

- **Limited view of the customer.** Salespeople don't sit at desks, so it's difficult to tie them directly to the enterprise applications and provide a 360-degree view of the customer. Also, sales activities are organized by product or account for operational efficiency. Thus incomplete understanding of the total customer situation propagates throughout the entire customer interaction and destroys sales opportunities.

Sales professionals often find the current crop of applications to be more administrative burdens than productive tools and eventually stop using them. Clearly, new sales applications that closely mimic the sales and order acquisition process need to be developed.

LIMITED PROCESS FUNCTIONALITY
Many sales applications are built for some limited subset of product and functionality, which results in narrow process capabilities. For example, a banking sales application may serve only credit card, mutual fund, or insurance products. The ability to take a customer view—an integral part of CRM—is thus severely restricted. This

results in lower productivity from the sales force, more customer call-backs when needs can't be met in one phone call, and an increased possibility of error when data has to be entered more than once.

Sales professionals are typically mobile users operating in "frequently disconnected mode." Users require applications that allow them to operate offline generally and to connect occasionally to a network to synchronize their local data store with a central database. *Selling-chain applications, by definition, must automate processes across multiple user types and functional areas. These issues add a significant degree of complexity to the selling-chain application.*

Selling-chain vendors today are just now bringing to market first-generation solutions that address the issues of variations in customer requirements, mobile computing, and cross-functional process integration. The selling-chain market is poised for take-off, mainly because of the quality and sophistication of the products now available, the increasing integration of the technology into enterprise systems, and the increasing number of success stories. Businesses are also influenced by the current marketing hype surrounding this hot topic, fearing that if they don't take advantage of the technology, they may be left in their competitors' dust.

LIMITED SALES EFFECTIVENESS: THE NEED FOR MORE INTEGRATED APPLICATIONS
Salespeople can be only as effective as the systems in which they work. Companies are demanding more integrated applications to help improve sales efficiency. Why is sales effectiveness critical? The challenge for companies today lies in gaining market leadership by helping their global sales force effectively sell a variety of products, from the simplest items, such as office supplies, to the more complex, such as build-to-order systems like a Boeing 777 aircraft. Businesses that develop, manufacture, and market customizable products, services, and systems must meet their customers' unique needs, respond quickly, and offer high-quality, competitive cost, excellent service, innovation, and flexibility, while ensuring that orders are accurate.

How does integration facilitate effective selling? Salespeople are demanding the integration of sales applications into their enterprises' back-office systems. The implications for any company are far-reaching because all departments will be affected.

13.3   USERS OF SELLING-CHAIN APPLICATIONS

Now that you have some background in the business and technology forces that are driving selling-chain management, you are in a position to understand the features that selling-chain applications must have.

However, before you can fully appreciate the features of selling-chain applications, you must understand who uses these applications. Users of selling-chain applications consist of company employees, employees of resellers and dealers, and customers or end-users.

13.3.1 USER PROFILES

There are eight distinct categories of users of selling-chain management applications:

- Prospective resellers: Anonymous Users (see Chapter 5 for a description of Anonymous Users) who are employees or principals of companies that are potential resellers but have not yet established a relationship with the company that owns the selling-chain application.

- Prospective customers: Anonymous Users who are potential customers or end users of the products or services of the company that owns the selling-chain application. They might use the selling-chain application to locate a dealer or reseller who can help them.

- Customers: Authenticated Users (see Chapter 5 for a description of Authenticated Users) who are customers or end users of the products or services of the company that owns the selling-chain application. They could use the selling-chain application to obtain technical product information, customer service, or technical support.

- Employees of partners: Authenticated Users who are employees or managers of companies that are resellers for the products of the company that owns the selling-chain application. They could use the selling-chain application to obtain pricing information, current promotions, technical product information, customer service, or technical support.

- Partner Administrators: Content Managers (see Chapter 5 for a description of Content Managers) who are principals of resellers that have a relationship with company that owns the selling-chain application. Partner Administrators have administrative rights over the people from their company that use the selling-chain application. In other words, they specify which people from their company have the authority to access particular content, collaboration, and commerce within the selling-chain application.

- Content Contributors: Content Managers who are employees of the company that owns the selling-chain application. They could be specialists in particular areas of content, collaboration, or commerce on the exchange. They would have administrative rights over that content, collaboration, or commerce. Or they might be account managers who are responsible for the relationships that their company has with particular resellers or customers. They use the selling-chain application to maintain the relationships with the companies whose accounts they manage.

- Content Administrators: Content Managers who are employees and are perhaps principals of the company that owns the selling-chain application and who are specialists in particular areas of content, collaboration, or commerce. They are called upon to review and/or approve the content that is submitted for publication on the selling-chain application by other users.

- Site Administrators: Administrators (see Chapter 12 for a description of Administrators) have the authority to change the structure and organization of the selling-chain application itself.

13.4   FEATURES OF SELLING-CHAIN APPLICATIONS

The features of selling-chain applications are the base functionality required for typical selling-chain applications.

To obtain the list of selling-chain application features, I looked at the best-of-breed applications that several companies have implemented and about which a few books and articles have been written.

My hope is that you can use this list of selling-chain application features as a basis for building your own selling-chain application. There are several commercial off-the-shelf (COTS) selling-chain applications on the market. However, it is important to remember that every company has its own selling process, and a COTS package may not be flexible enough to fit the needs of your business. You will be further ahead if you build or buy a robust B2B application platform (such as a B2B Web site) and use it to build your own selling-chain management application. This list of features should help you do that.

To manage complexity, the capabilities listed here are abstracted to a high enough level to result in a relatively small number of features. The list of features in this section provides the basis for definition, scope management, and project management for building a selling-chain management application.

1. The selling-chain application includes a product catalog that provides customers and channel partners interactive access to all the company's product information. This product catalog includes pictures, pricing, and availability data, along with case studies, partner solutions, planning guides, deployment guides, slides, white papers, FAQs, QAs, and other collateral brochures. In other words, the whole encyclopedia of marketing information is now directly accessible from a standard browser.

2. Product managers can update the product catalog using browser-based administration forms. This enables product managers to update the information in the product catalog directly and to publish the changes on the Web site immediately without the help or intervention of a Web master or the IT department.

3. Pricing information is secure, and access is controlled by the security mechanisms in the application. The price related attributes are associated with business logic so that the appropriate discounts are automatically applied. This also provides a great starting point for implementing sophisticated pricing schemes based on tiered and volume discounts.

4. The selling-chain management Web site provides powerful navigation and searching capability. The information is organized for easy navigation and retrieval and invites browsing due to the attractive, professional, customizable page design. End-users can search for product alternatives using a full-text search engine or perform searches based on multiple product attributes such as price, SKU number, technical specifications, and so on.

5. Multiple custom views of the main company product catalog can be easily created for customer and partner needs. Sales representatives and customers that are interested only in certain products need not view the entire catalog. These subsets remain linked to the main catalog, ensuring that they will be updated when any changes are made to the product database or central catalog.

6. The selling-chain application readily integrates with enterprise applications. The application is built on an open architecture that allows easy integration with legacy data and applications, as well as with other networked commerce applications (for example, interactive product configuration, ordering, product promotions). This integration allows the catalog to act as the product selection interface for your sales applications, providing the customer with an intuitive application to search for products subsequently to be configured, quoted, priced, or ordered.

7. Channel managers can easily create and continuously maintain a repository of partner related information. Once new partners have been created in the database, they can be allowed to use the Web to serve themselves and maintain current contact information. This type of self-service simultaneously reduces the IT burden as well as promotes accuracy and currency of the partner database.

8. Channel managers can quickly create and maintain a variety of partner categories (for example, VAR, Enterprise Reseller, Federal, System Integrator, OEM, ISP) and track program memberships (Premier, Gold, Silver). Similarly, at the individual representative level, a variety of information can be tracked, including categories (sales, presales support engineer, postsales support engineer), certification levels, training course completions, special support status, and so forth.

9. The application allows for partner-initiated customer access, which allows partners to offer selectively some of the benefits of their privileged access to online services to their customers. Providing basic self-help support solutions frees staff to address more difficult questions and problems. Customer issues, in turn, are resolved more quickly. Partners may also provide customers with real-time access to the latest software releases. Partner-initiated customer access leverages the resources of partners and fosters higher levels of customer satisfaction and loyalty.

10. The selling-chain application, via the B2B Web site, provides the easy hosting of custom newsgroups and chat sessions to foster the sharing of information that promotes sales and support between the enterprise and the channel as well as among the channel partners themselves. The virtual community can facilitate team selling, the forging of dynamic new business relationships, and creative collaborations that directly benefit overall sales.

11. An online reseller locator allows prospects browsing the Web site to locate a reseller based on ZIP code or reseller specialization. It integrates with the reseller information and is typically available within the products catalog pages as a convenient hyperlink.

12. Easy to use browser-based administration forms enable product managers to alert sales representatives and customers instantly to a variety of cross-selling and up-selling promotions, complementary products, and bundled products and services.

13. The application enables partner-specific pricing, which allows the implementation of rich personalization of all information going to the channel partners. An example of this is partner-specific pricing and discounts.

14. Personalized delivery mechanisms enable partners who register themselves over the Web to sign up for regularly scheduled "push" deliveries of personalized content, using a variety of mechanisms such as Web push, e-mail, fax, and so on.

15. The application enables customers and partners to create and track orders electronically as well as to help direct customers and partners manage the entire ordering process. When integrated with the legacy software, customers and partners can obtain current information about their orders, reduce order errors, lower administrative costs, and shorten the deployment time for new networking solutions. Users have interactive access to all the company's product information databases, so pricing and ordering data will be correct before submission.

16. A catalog of standard Microsoft Office document templates containing high-level outlines for quotes and proposals allows sales representatives to build customized, professional sales quotations and proposals quickly and easily. Partners have immediate access to documents across the Web, reducing the time it takes to create a proposal from weeks to minutes by automatically generating proposals that incorporate information specific to the products being purchased, including marketing literature, spec sheets, and quotes.

17. The application includes an interactive configuration feature that proactively advises users when information is missing from a product configuration, enabling them to "get it right the first time" and eliminate rework delays. It virtually eliminates errors in the ordering process by automating the most critical part of the sales process: generating a correct quote and a valid order.

18. The selling-chain management Web site contains online the entire set of information that is needed by the customer or channel representative in order to provide self-help. This consists of support FAQs, bug-lists, and interactive guidance in selecting software patches, simple interfaces for downloading, extensive documentation, proactive defect alerts, and access to updates and new releases.

19. The application provides an online technical assistance center. If the support information is unable to resolve the issue, an online technical assistance center allows new support cases to be created or previous cases to be opened. The online service improves the support process, speeds resolution of problems, and provides access to support systems and engineers around the clock. This also provides a forum for facilitating building a community among partners and customers via newsgroups as well as a place for customers and partners to provide more structured feedback.

20. The application supports lead generation on the Web. Feedback modules such as simple, one-question sidebars can be automatically placed at appropriate places within documents. The very specific context in which these modules are placed, combined with attractive, professionally designed templates, make them much more effective than simple HTML survey forms that are usually ignored.

21. Automatic partner notification can be initiated when customers or prospects show their interest in the new product or promotion by exploring that section of the Web site in detail. This is an event of great interest to the channel partners who "own" the corresponding territory. The leads module can arrange for automatic notification of this "lead"

event to the partner, based on customization "matching" of information about the browser and information in the Partners catalog. The notification mechanism (e-mail, Web-push, whatever) can be a preconfigured arrangement between the manufacturer and the partner.

22. Event management is supported through Web-based registration and scheduling of seminars, training classes, sales campaigns, and so on.

23. Personalization enables users to choose elements that will appear on their own home page on the site. This allows users to specify the information that they are most interested in seeing.

SUMMARY

An effective selling-chain management application strengthens a company's sales process. It makes it easier for customers and resellers to do business with the company that owns the application. It also reduces errors and cycle times in the order acquisition process.

A selling-chain management application is best implemented on a B2B Web site, where the application can be customized to fit the company's own sales process.

The features of a selling-chain management application can be distilled down to a relatively small list. You can use the list of features presented in this chapter as you build your own selling-chain management application.

Supply-Chain
Management

The key points for this chapter are the following:

- Supply-chain management is necessary to alleviate out-of-stock problems.

- Increasing inventory is a costly and ineffective way to alleviate out-of-stock problems.

- The science of supply-chain management has grown in scope and effectiveness.

- There is a new methodology that effectively delivers the benefits of supply-chain management.

- Supply-chain applications require several features to be effective.

14.1   INTRODUCTION TO SUPPLY-CHAIN MANAGEMENT

In a speech at a White House conference, Federal Reserve Chairman Alan Greenspan spoke of a new economy that has emerged during the past few years that is fundamentally different from the typical postwar business cycle.[1]

This new economy produced a record-length economic expansion, which he credits to the productivity gains that American business experienced during the 1990s. During those years, businesses made significant investments in information systems. According to Mr. Greenspan, these information systems have produced measurable improvements in U.S. business productivity.

---

1. "Technological Innovation and the Economy." Speech by Alan Greenspan at the White House Conference on the New Economy, Washington, D.C., April 5, 2000.
CPFR material used with permission of the Voluntary Interindustry Commerce Standards Association.

These information systems provide managers with timely information about production, the flow of materials, demand, and inventory. With this information, businesses are better able to satisfy their customers while maintaining smaller inventories and using fewer worker hours.

Managers get this type of information from supply-chain management applications. This means that supply-chain management applications are a significant contributor to U.S. business productivity. In addition, when supply-chain management is done right, so that the application includes secure collaboration, it enables businesses to improve their product design process significantly.

14.2   OVERVIEW OF SUPPLY-CHAIN MANAGEMENT

The science of supply-chain management has progressed through several phases of scope and effectiveness. Before exploring the state of the art in supply-chain management, however, it is requisite to explain why supply-chain management is necessary.

14.2.1   THE NEED FOR SUPPLY-CHAIN MANAGEMENT

According to a 1996 study,[2] for every 100 customers who go into a store to buy a specific product, 8 will not be able to purchase the item because it is out of stock.

Eight out of 100 people not finding the product they are looking for might not sound like much of a problem. However, you must realize that when people can't get what they want, they are likely to lose patience with the store and go to another store to do their shopping. A retailer doesn't like it when customers go to a competing store because they may never patronize her store again.

The out-of-stock problem is not limited to retail stores. When any kind of consumer expects to buy a product from any kind of a seller and the seller does not have that product, it is bad for the seller. A stock-out problem in the face of a paying customer is a situation that sellers desperately want to avoid.

The traditional answer to reducing stock-out problems has been to increase inventories. The problem with this, however, is that inventory is expensive. Inventory means capital costs, storage costs, and handling costs, costs that increase as the amount of inventory increases.

In addition to increasing costs, inventory also inhibits the seller's flexibility. If the seller keeps lots of inventory on hand to avoid stock-out problems, he will tend to give those products prominent shelf space (or floor space or screen space) so the products will sell well. This tendency to promote what is in inventory can make it difficult for the seller to react when demand changes to new products that the seller doesn't currently have in inventory.

2. Retailer Operating Data, Prism Partner Store Audits, Coca Cola Retail Council Independent Study, 1996.

In addition to limiting a seller's flexibility to switch to new products when the market demands it, large amounts of inventory can cause the seller to be stuck with obsolete inventory, which can be a huge burden. So maintaining large inventories is a two-edged sword. Inventory can help a seller avoid stock-out problems, but it also can bring high costs for capital, storage, and handling. In addition, there is always the risk that demand will shift and that the products in inventory will become a burden instead of a benefit. The larger the inventory, the bigger the risk.

There are three primary reasons for inventory to exist in the supply chain:

- Demand uncertainty

- Supply uncertainty

- Transportation uncertainty

DEMAND UNCERTAINTY
Demand uncertainty derives from demand variability and businesses' inability to forecast accurately the demand for products. The more demand uncertainty there is, the more inventory the sellers will need on hand to avoid stock-out problems. In other words, sellers need an inventory buffer to deal with uncertain demand, and the larger the degree of demand uncertainty, the larger the inventory buffer must be.

As you are no doubt aware, any product that a consumer buys has made its way through a supply chain of some sort. The product started as raw material sold to a manufacturer. The manufacturer turned that raw material into the parts for the product. Another manufacturer assembled those parts into the finished product. That finished product was sent to a distribution center (DC), where it was warehoused for a time before it was placed in the hands of the seller, who sold it to the consumer. Each of these links in the supply chain must deal with the problem of uncertain demand. Therefore, each link in the supply chain must maintain its own buffer of inventory.

In the case of demand uncertainty, the further away from the consumer an inventory buffer is in the supply-chain chain, the more demand variability that buffer will have to address. Demand uncertainty increases in magnitude at each link as you move upstream in the supply chain.[3]

This has been called the "bullwhip effect." The bullwhip effect means that a small blip in consumer demand can result in huge swings in the demand for parts and raw materials upstream in the supply chain.

These blips in consumer demand can be frequent and are easily created. For instance, a seller doing a promotion of a particular product can cause a blip in consumer demand. A promotion can result in the short term in sales that are several

---

3. Inventory—Traditional vs. CPFR®. Voluntary Interindustry Commerce Standards (VICS) Association, *http://www.cpfr.org/InventoryTraditional.html*. CPFR® is a registered trademark of the Voluntary Interindustry Commerce Standards (VICS) Association.

times the normal demand for a product. It would certainly be possible for the companies that are upstream in the supply chain to misread this one-time promotion as an increase in consumer demand for that product.

Another contributor to blips in demand is the fact that the different groups and companies involved in the supply chain often have conflicting objectives. Retailers look to turn (replace) their inventory as frequently as possible, while manufacturers prefer long, slow lead times for their production runs. A prime example of conflicting objectives in the supply chain is when a sales department pads its forecast to ensure availability of a product. This can cause a blip in demand that can cause the supply chain to be whipped needlessly between extremes.

The bullwhip effect is not necessary, and it is not a characteristic of a healthy and efficient supply chain. Rather, it exists because of a lack of effective management of the supply chain. The idea is to manage the supply chain in order to eliminate the bullwhip effect.

Instead of managing the supply chain effectively, many businesses merely try to manage their inventory costs. They do this by attempting to shift the inventory burden to companies immediately downstream or upstream in the chain. Trading partners may engage in diversion strategies in an effort to coerce one party or the other into incurring the costs of supply-chain inventory. In the short term, this may help the company that is diverting their inventory costs, but these tactics ultimately do not reduce the cost of the finished product. Clearly, the best way to manage inventory is to reduce the need for it by effectively managing the supply chain. That means finding a way to reduce inventory without increasing the risk of stock-out problems.

In addition to demand uncertainty, there are two other contributors to the size of inventory buffers in the supply chain. One of them is the uncertainty of the supply process.

SUPPLY UNCERTAINTY

The problem here is that a supplier might fail to deliver what is ordered at the appropriate time in the appropriate quantity. This requires inventory buffers to be increased as a safety margin in case the supplier is late delivering an order.

TRANSPORTATION UNCERTAINTY

The other contributor to inventory buffers in the supply chain is transportation uncertainty. Carriers, the shipping companies that transport materials, parts, and products throughout the supply chain, have limited capacity. Carriers have only so many trucks, trains, airplanes, and people.

Unfortunately, carriers face demand uncertainty of their own. They typically do not know, until just a few days (or perhaps hours) beforehand, what materials they will be called upon to ship where and in what quantities. Often, the carrier does not have equipment in the right place to handle the demand. This means that sometimes shipments cannot be made on time. This results in companies in the supply chain having to increase their inventory buffers as a safety margin for transportation uncertainty. Transportation uncertainty produces excess inventory and underutilized carrier equipment.

An additional headache is the fact that sellers' and buyers' financial performance is dependent on the treatment of inventory. It is necessary for companies doing financial reporting to account for their inventory. Transportation uncertainty can make this accounting somewhat murky at times.

Transportation uncertainty also results in increased transportation costs because companies might need to use secondary carriers. Companies also may overuse expedited services, which raises transportation costs.

DEALING WITH UNCERTAINTY

Stock-out problems are costly, and companies throughout the supply chain try to avoid them by maintaining inventory buffers. However, inventory brings costly problems. The real solution to stock-out problems is not to increase inventories but to manage the supply chain effectively.

14.2.2 THE PURPOSE OF SUPPLY-CHAIN MANAGEMENT APPLICATIONS

The goal of supply-chain management is to manage the supply chain so that the companies can do the following:

1. Deliver the right products at the right time in the right quantity

2. Improve their product design process

The first objective is accomplished by doing the following:

- Joint business planning among trading partners in the supply chain

- Better forecasting of the demand for raw material, parts, and finished products

- Better forecasting of shipment and arrival times of raw material, parts, and finished products

- Collaboration among trading partners to handle exceptions during the execution of the plans

Each of these activities is important. Joint business planning is important because it creates the framework for effective forecasting. Collaboration during execution is vital because things never go exactly as planned, but forecasting is really the key. Effective forecasting of demand and delivery means the right products delivered at the right time in the right quantity, which means fewer lost sales because of out-of-stock problems. Effective forecasting also means less uncertainty for which excess inventory must be maintained. Accurate forecasting is the key to reducing inventories without increasing the risk of stock-out problems.

The second objective, improving the design process, is accomplished by collaborating on product design with partner companies up and down the supply chain. Collaborative product design enables a company to use all of the intellectual assets in all of the engineering departments throughout the supply chain to do the following:

- Design products that are optimized for manufacture by each supplier in the chain

- Design products that are customer-driven

Collaborative design enables companies to produce goods that customers demand and that can be manufactured readily. It also means fewer engineers flying across the country or around the world for meetings with engineers in suppliers' companies.

Now that you understand the purpose of supply-chain management applications and how these applications should be used, it is time to look at how supply-chain management is currently done in the real world.

14.2.3   CURRENT SUPPLY-CHAIN MANAGEMENT PRACTICES

Supply-chain management practices of companies today fall along a continuum, from companies that are doing little to manage their supply chain to companies that are making a deliberate effort to tame their supply chain and turn it into a competitive advantage.

WORST CASE SUPPLY-CHAIN MANAGEMENT PRACTICES

Aggregate demand across the nation for a product family or for a brand may be easy to estimate, but it can be very difficult to determine the right number of specific products to put in a particular seller's inventory on a particular day. Estimating the right number of specific products to put in a particular inventory on a particular day involves forecasting.

People do forecasting by a lot of guesswork. This guesswork occurs at each link in the supply chain. And this guesswork happens blindly at each link—the forecasts rarely involve any sharing of information or collaboration up and down the supply chain.

As you may have guessed (or experienced), supply chain forecasts done in this manner tend be inaccurate, and inaccurate forecasts mean uncertainty. And as I have said, the traditional remedy is to increase inventories as a buffer against that uncertainty.

Companies' information systems often do not provide the tools needed for effective supply-chain management. The applications used by companies in the supply chain consist of separate legacy applications at the corporate, store, and distribution levels. These legacy applications are primarily host-centric systems that operate on mainframe or mid-range computers. These systems, developed and modified internally over many years or licensed from third parties, represent considerable investments and have been beneficial over the years. But in general, they don't have the flexibility to support diverse and changing operations within a company's business, nor can they respond effectively to changing technologies. Additionally, these applications target only distinct levels of the supply chain and generally have not provided the full benefits of integration, which allows information to be distributed effectively. Despite these limitations, many host-centric systems are still widely deployed due to their strengths in particular segments, as well as to preserve significant hardware and software investments.[4]

The use of stand-alone, legacy information systems and a lack of collaboration between partners in the supply chain (and sometimes between departments within the enterprise) result in inaccurate forecasts, stock-out problems, and the risks that accompany large inventory buffers.

NOT-AS-BAD SUPPLY-CHAIN MANAGEMENT PRACTICES
Forward-thinking companies have advanced beyond these stand-alone, host-centric applications and have implemented enterprisewide applications (such as ERP). These enterprise applications help ensure that all departments in the enterprise talk the same language. They enable "one number planning" to help synchronize all the departments in the enterprise so that they are all working toward the same goal.

However, enterprise applications also tend to be internally focused. They do nothing to synchronize a company's efforts with the efforts of their trading partners up and down the supply chain.

In addition to technology issues, there are people issues that make the supply-chain process operate only inside the enterprise. There can be significant inertia inside companies against intra-enterprise initiatives. It can be difficult to change a corporate culture to one where company employees will work with and trust the employees of the company's trading partners.

In fact, the culture to which everyone is accustomed is one of separate and distinct layers in the supply chain, which is illustrated in Figure 14-1.

Often there is not much collaboration between the businesses up and down the supply chain. There is not much collaboration, but there is a great deal of dependency between the businesses up and down the chain, which is illustrated by the vertical arrows between the layers in Figure 14-1. Competition occurs among the

4. Ravi Kalakota and Marcia Robinson, *e-Business: Roadmap for Success* (Addison-Wesley, 1999), p. 212.

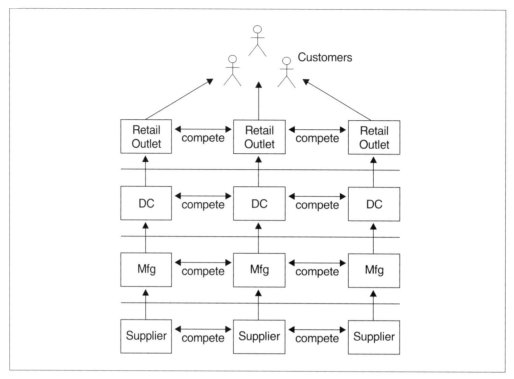

FIGURE 14-1   *Separate Layers in the Supply Chain*

businesses in each layer in the chain, which is illustrated by the horizontal arrows between the columns.

So each company does its utmost by working inside the walls of its enterprise to prosper in its particular role in the supply chain and to compete with other companies that fill similar roles.

Companies that have implemented ERP software find that these enterprise applications do, in fact, help with the forecasting process. A company with enterprise applications will be able to forecast more accurately than a company without them because enterprise applications enable collaboration across departments inside the enterprise. However, to be truly effective, supply-chain management requires collaboration outside the walls of the enterprise.

Aggregate Forecasting and Replenishment   In these worst and not-as-bad cases, companies use, to varying degrees, a supply-chain management process known as Aggregate Forecasting and Replenishment (AFR). The idea with AFR is that each company in the supply chain, with little or no collaboration between partner companies, assembles past sales data and future aggregate forecasts from whatever sources it can. The company then uses that data to produce sales forecasts, which predict demand for products, and order forecasts, which predict when the company will need to process incoming orders. When it comes to execution, each company generates orders expecting 100 percent fulfillment from suppliers; and each company fulfills orders, using whatever inventory it happens to have, and ships materials and products, using whatever capacity its carrier has available.

With AFR, there are lots of demand uncertainty, supply uncertainty, and transportation uncertainty, and there are lots of excess inventory to compensate for all of that uncertainty. The uncertainty exists because of a lack of joint business planning, a lack of accurate forecasting, and a lack of collaboration to make the process run efficiently.

BEST CASE (CURRENT) SUPPLY-CHAIN MANAGEMENT PRACTICES
A relatively small number of companies have extended supply-chain management beyond the walls of their enterprise. These companies have implemented supply-chain processes in cooperation with their trading partners in the supply chain.

Vendor Managed Inventory   Vendor Managed Inventory was developed to alleviate some of the problems with AFR. It involves the vendor or manufacturer keeping track of the inventory at the sellers' locations, which are usually distribution centers or retail outlets.

The vendor or manufacturer monitors inventory levels at the sellers' locations, either by tracking withdrawals from the DC by the sellers or, in some cases, by using the sellers' Point-of-Sale (POS) data. The POS data tends to be more precise than the DC data, but it requires more integration work to be able to use the POS data.

The manufacturer uses this data to keep the sellers' inventories at some agreed-upon level, and the manufacturer does the sales forecasting and order forecasting. The manufacturer puts the order forecasts together in such a way that it is optimized for manufacturing, inventory, and transportation costs.

Though VMI has advantages over AFR, it also has limitations.[5]

- The overall level of collaboration up and down the chain is limited.

- The forecasts are aggregated and typically do not include estimates at the individual product and store level.

- If the manufacturer focuses on POS data instead of warehouse withdrawals at the distribution center, it makes the VMI process more effective. However, manufacturers typically do not use POS data because of the additional integration work that is required.

---

5. Vendor-Managed Inventory Avoids Some of the Problems of AFR. Voluntary Interindustry Commerce Standards (VICS) Association, *http://www.cpfr.org/Vendor-Managed.html*.

- Manufacturers often fail to leverage customer-specific data for production planning effectively. Instead, they continue to make to stock.

- Lack of integration of systems, particularly for store-level VMI, creates operational challenges due to limited visibility into inventory and orders.

Another problem is that retailers have higher expectations of VMI because the pipeline is more visible and the manufacturer has more control. Industry results show, however, that many retailers have been disappointed and have canceled VMI programs. The blame for inadequate performance is frequently equally shared between trading partners. To be most effective, VMI programs depend on strong partnerships with active communication, information sharing, joint problem solving, and commitments to continued development.

Joint Managed Inventory   A small number of companies have moved beyond VMI to Joint Managed Inventory (JMI). JMI focuses on collaboratively planning and executing the supply chain at a much lower level of detail than VMI does.

This allows an increased focus on the consumer and on exploiting opportunities frequently hidden in the aggregated data. JMI uses teams of people working only with key accounts. Frequently, team members are located geographically close to each other, which allows frequent face-to-face meetings. This fosters open communication between functional counterparts, which in turn furthers process customization. The improved understanding of each other's operations and increased interaction that results helps develop trust between the trading partners.

JMI involves a much more intense joint-planning effort and coordination of execution before the process steps begin. The level of customization of the process is driven by the capabilities of each trading partner, with a focus that is much more consumer centric. The JMI approach also increases the integration of planning and execution within each company.

The success of JMI in managing customer-service levels, inventories, and costs has been significant. However, the costs of this process are substantial. Much of the lower-level detail work is done manually or on an adhoc basis. Team members need to filter through great quantities of data to identify opportunities. In addition, the cost of locating JMI teams close together is high. Finally, the tools and processes currently available for interenterprise computing in a real-time environment are limited, and those available are not scaleable. These issues limit the number of trading partner relationships that can be afforded by any company.[6]

---

6. Jointly Managed Inventory Approach Provides a Lower Level of Detail. Voluntary Interindustry Commerce Standards (VICS) Association, *http://www.cpfr.org/JointlyManaged.html*.

The Best of the Best of the Best Done correctly, VMI and JMI can yield significant rewards. However, these processes are expensive and time-consuming to implement, and they are not without limitations.[7]

- Retailers expect 100 percent responsiveness from manufacturers, which is not realistic.

- Identification of supply problems occurs on the retailer's loading dock, which leaves little time to react to shortages.

- Supply planning is not integrated, driving higher inventory levels, lower order fill rates, and increased expedited activity.

- VMI solves some of the problems of AFR, but the level of detail is still high, and collaboration is limited.

- JMI reaches a lower level of detail and is much more consumer centric but is very costly to establish and maintain.

- There are scaleability issues with current VMI and JMI tools.

Fortunately, there is a new supply-chain management process that improves on VMI and JMI. This process delivers the benefits of supply-chain management without the limitations of VMI and the costs of JMI.

14.2.4 NEW PRACTICES IN SUPPLY-CHAIN MANAGEMENT

There is a new supply-chain management process that fully delivers the benefits of supply-chain management. This gives companies a competitive advantage and provides them a tool, in addition to the products that they manufacture or sell, to differentiate themselves from their competition.

Companies that are part of an effective supply chain work as a team up and down the chain. Individually, they are able to prosper over their competitors because they are not plagued by out-of-stock problems, they sell products that are in demand, and they please customers while making more money. They have synergistic relationships with their trading partners, which put them in a position to compete as a team against individual competing companies, as shown in Figure 14-2.

The new supply-chain management process is called Collaborative Planning, Forecasting and Replenishment, or CPFR®[8] for short.

---

7. Current Process State Leaves Room for Improvement. Voluntary Interindustry Commerce Standards (VICS) Association, *http://www.cpfr.org/CurrentProcess2.html*.

8. CPFR® is a registered trademark of the Voluntary Interindustry Commerce Standards (VICS) Association, *http://www.cpfr.org*.

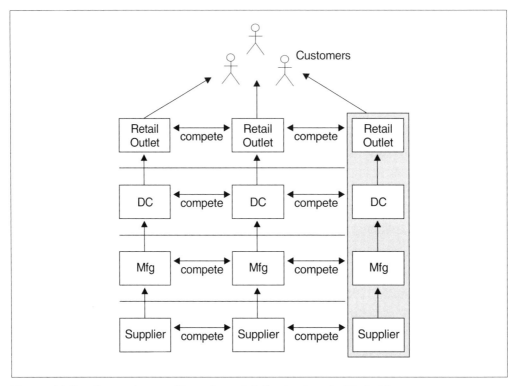

FIGURE 14-2 *Competing as a Team through Effective Supply-Chain Management*

CPFR takes a holistic approach to supply-chain management among a network of trading partners. CPFR builds on the best-in-class practices that have been developed through successful JMI and VMI programs. These are the guiding principles for CPFR:

- The process provides a flexible framework where each trading partner in the supply chain is tasked with the role or roles for which it is best suited.

- Trading partners develop a single shared forecast of consumer demand that drives planning across the supply chain.

- Trading partners use the shared forecast to align their plans, which enables them to remove traditional constraints in the supply process.

FLEXIBLE FRAMEWORK AND THE RIGHT ROLE FOR EACH PARTNER
One key finding that has come out of the VMI and JMI programs is that no single business process fits all trading partners or all situations between trading partners.

Trading partners have different competencies based on their strategies and investments. They also have different sources of information and different views of the marketplace.

CPFR is structured as a set of scenarios or process alternatives for trading partners to use. The scenarios identify the key competencies that the partner companies in the supply chain must address. The trading partners use these key competencies to determine which company should lead which core activities in the process.

A set of trading partners may choose to use more than one scenario in its partnership, depending on the nature of the products, the impacts of promotional or seasonal processes, and the level of importance of the steps to either trading partner.

A SINGLE FORECAST OF CONSUMER DEMAND

Retailers and manufacturers have different perspectives of the marketplace. These differing perspectives, viewed together, can provide valuable insights to the market as a whole. Retailers see and interact with the end consumer in person and infer consumer behavior using POS data. They also see a range of manufacturers, their product offerings, and their plans for marketing those products. Manufacturers see a range of retailers and their merchandising plans. They can also monitor consumer activity, with some delays, by obtaining syndicated sales data.

Given these different perspectives, each of the trading partners can improve its demand-planning capabilities by iteratively exchanging data and business intelligence. By securely sharing the appropriate data, the partners in the supply chain can produce a single, accurate, shared forecast of consumer demand at the points of sale. The trading partners, from manufacturers to retailers, can then use this single shared-demand plan as the foundation for all of their internal planning activities related to each product.

Using a single shared forecast enables the partner companies to forecast to such a level of detail that they can readily discover opportunities in the marketplace. By collaborating with each other, partner companies in the supply chain can exploit these opportunities to grow their revenue and profits.

REMOVAL OF SUPPLY-PROCESS CONSTRAINTS

The value of having a single demand forecast, even if nothing else changes, is better coordination of supply-chain process activities. This coordination would yield significant, but not dramatic, benefits.

Dramatic benefits come from using the demand forecast to lessen the constraints that inhibit supply-process performance. An example of a constraint is manufacturing flexibility. Most manufacturers hold finished goods inventory in sufficient quantities to meet retail demand. Manufacturing capacity is not used because the retailers' normally short order-cycle times are inconsistent with longer manufacturing cycle times.

By extending the retailers' order cycle and thus making it consistent with the manufacturing cycle, production could move to a "make-to-order" process for some products. This removes the need to hold a significant amount of finished goods inventory in the value chain and improves customer service, which produces dramatic benefits.

Another example of constraints that could be addressed involves dynamic interenterprise scheduling to optimize asset utilization across manufacturing, transportation, and distribution centers. CPFR provides the foundation for these and many other breakthrough supply-process improvements.

THE PROCESS

The CPFR process is divided into nine steps:[9]

Step 1. Develop Front-End Agreement: The participating companies identify executive sponsors and establish the guidelines and rules for their collaborative relationship, such as the degree of confidentiality and the processes they will use to resolve disputes. The front-end agreement addresses each party's expectations and the actions and resources necessary for success. The companies also develop a scorecard to track key supply-chain metrics relative to success criteria and establish any financial incentives or penalties.

The output of this step is a published CPFR front-end agreement that gives all partners a blueprint for beginning their collaborative relationship. The document clearly defines the process in practical terms. It also identifies the roles of each trading partner and how the performance of each will be measured. In addition, it spells out the readiness of each organization and the opportunities available to maximize the benefits from the relationship. A sample front-end agreement can be found on the CPFR Web site.

The front-end agreement documents the commitment to pursuing a higher level of performance and willingness to exchange knowledge and share in the risk. It ensures that each company has an adequate commitment to collaboration and that all parties are aligned around common goals. This front-end agreement is typically reviewed on an annual basis.

Step 2. Create Joint Business Plan: The project teams exchange information about their corporate strategies and business plans to develop a joint business plan. The partners first create a partnership strategy and then define category roles, objectives, and tactics. They establish the item profiles, such as order minimums and multiples, lead times, and order intervals. They also share their plans for promotions,

9. The CPFR Process Model. Voluntary Interindustry Commerce Standards (VICS) Association, *http://www.cpfr.org/ProcessModel.html.*

changes in inventory policy, store openings/closings, and product changes for each product category.

The development of a joint business plan improves the overall quality of forecasting by including data from both parties. It also facilitates communication and coordination across the supply chain.

The result of this step is a mutually agreed-upon joint business plan that clearly identifies the roles, strategies, and tactics for the items on which they will collaborate. The joint business plan is the cornerstone of the forecasting process. It is typically revised quarterly or semiannually.

The joint business plan is used to control the day-to-day activities of manufacturing, shipping, and selling products and reduces exceptions and the need for time-consuming collaboration during execution of the plan.

Step 3. Create Sales Forecast: Retailers and suppliers use retailer point of sale (POS) data, causal information, and information on planned promotional events to create a sales forecast that supports the joint business plan. In relationships where a retailer/distributor is one of the parties, this step is carried out by the retailer/distributor. In relationships between manufacturers, the downstream manufacturer is responsible for creating the sales forecast. The sales forecast is initially generated by one party, communicated to the other party, and then used as a baseline for creating the order forecast.

Step 4. Identify Exceptions for Sales Forecast: This step identifies exceptions that occur when partners' plans do not match or when the plans change dramatically. The front-end agreement specifies the exception criteria. The output from this step is a list of exception items. This information is necessary for Step 5.

Step 5. Resolve/Collaborate on Exception Items: The partners resolve sales forecast exceptions by querying shared data, e-mail, telephone conversations, meetings, and so on. The partners adjust the sales forecast to reflect any changes that result.

Parties resolve exceptions through collaborative negotiations and agree upon an adjusted forecast. The increased real-time collaboration enabled by CPFR fosters effective joint decision making between retailers/distributors and manufacturers and increases confidence in the eventual committed order.

Step 6. Create Order Forecast: POS data, causal information, and inventory strategies are combined to generate a specific order forecast that supports the shared sales forecast and the joint business plan. Actual volume numbers are time phased and reflect inventory objectives by product and receiving location. The short-term portion of the forecast is used for order generation, while the longer-term portion is used for planning

The result of Step 6 is a time-phased, netted order forecast. The order forecast allows the manufacturer to allocate production capacity against demand, while minimizing safety stock. It also gives retailers increased confidence that orders will be delivered.

This step establishes a platform for continual improvement among the trading partners. The real-time collaboration reduces the uncertainty between trading partners and leads to consolidated supply-chain inventories. This enables the partner companies to decrease their inventory levels and increase their customer responsiveness.

Step 7. Identify Exceptions for Order Forecast: The parties determine what items fall outside the order forecast constraints. The result is a list of exception items identified from the predetermined criteria established in the front-end agreement. This list of exceptions is used in Step 8.

Step 8. Resolve/Collaborate on Exception Items: Investigate order forecast exceptions through querying of shared data, e-mail, telephone conversations, meetings, and so on and submitting any resulting changes to the order forecast.

The results of this step are the output of the negotiation between retailer and manufacturer and the resolution of item exceptions, which are then submitted as an adjusted forecast. The increased real-time collaboration of CPFR facilitates effective joint decision making and fosters confidence in the order that is eventually committed.

Step 9. Order Generation: This last step marks the transformation of the order forecast into a committed order. Order generation is handled by either the manufacturer or the distributor, depending on competencies, systems, and resources. Regardless of who completes this task, the created order is expected to consume the forecast. The result is a committed order generated directly from the frozen period of the order forecast. An order acknowledgment is sent as a result of the order.

Using CPFR to build a trading partner framework, create a single forecast of consumer demand, and synchronize manufacturer and retailer order cycles creates an interenterprise supply-chain environment that reduces waste and cost while maximizing earnings and customer satisfaction.

CPFR supports marketing, promotion management, manufacturing, transportation, and planning activities. The information shared as part of this process enhances the accuracy of the forecasts and order fulfillment.

CPFR AND COMPLEX PRODUCTS AND RELATIONSHIPS

As you may know, there are many public exchanges on the Web that provide marketplaces for commodities. The goal for public exchanges is to bring buyers and sellers of commodities together and to optimize the processing of transactions. Public exchanges work best in the following situations:

- There is no continuing relationship between the buyer and seller. Their relationship does not outlive the transaction.

- The products are commodities.

- The sole differentiator among products and among sellers is price.

Public exchanges enable buyers and sellers to come together to get the best price on commodity products and to carry out transactions that are simplified through automation. However, hosting an exchange where buyers and sellers can find the best price on commodities and automate their transactions is actually the easy part of B2B.

In contrast to narrow focus of public exchanges, CPFR handles the more prevalent and complex situations under the following conditions:

- There is a ongoing relationship between the buyer and seller.

- The products are complex.

- There are multiple differentiators among products and among sellers.

You could say that CPFR handles the hard part of B2B, which involves managing long-term relationships and complex products.

The requirements for CPFR map nicely to the features of a B2B Web site. As explained in Chapter 12, a B2B Web site provides a forum for secure and targeted collaboration, content, and commerce. A B2B Web site can provide a solid foundation for implementing CPFR.

In addition to providing a platform for CPFR, a B2B Web site can enable the engineers at each of the trading partners in the supply chain to collaborate on product design. The secure workflow, collaboration, and content access that B2B Web sites offer are exactly what design engineers need to work together across enterprise boundaries.

14.3 USERS OF SUPPLY-CHAIN APPLICATIONS

To manage long-term relationships and complex products in a supply chain, several types of users must be involved. According to Syncra Systems, Inc., a supplier of CPFR software, a core assumption of CPFR is that each organization will enter the details of the joint business plans into their online planning systems and then share the results on a regular basis as market conditions change and logistical problems occur. Because each company may manage thousands of products distributed across thousands of locations, it is not feasible for planners to compare these plans manually and determine which changes are significant. Instead, a specialized CPFR system exchanges and compares each value using thresholds that planners have set. If changes in one plan, or differences between them, exceed the threshold, the CPFR system alerts the planner to the problem. Forecast revisions are exchanged on a regular—usually weekly—basis.

The CPFR philosophy is that if plans are "close enough," they probably do not require attention. Even when trading partners have identical objectives, differences in statistical forecasting or constraint-based planning algorithms will produce minor variances in plans. These are not significant relative to statistical deviations in demand, and safety stock will take care of them. CPFR technology is essential to identifying exceptions because of the millions of product/location combinations that are planned and because of the unique product, location, and partner perspectives of each supply-chain participant.

14.3.1 CPFR PROCESS SYNCHRONIZES PLANNING

From a business process standpoint, CPFR defines how retailers and suppliers can synchronize their different planning functions. Retailers are focused on predicting consumer reaction to promotions, competitors, and product category changes, while suppliers usually concentrate on managing the level of inventory at distribution centers. The retailer's objective is to keep products in stock in stores.

The supplier's objective is to create the most efficient production and replenishment process possible. These differences are reflected in each party's sales and order forecasting processes.

SALES (CONSUMER DEMAND) FORECAST COMPARISONS

Retailers produce very detailed sales forecasts, often including weekly or even daily store-level demand per SKU. Suppliers may also gather a great deal of intelligence about what sold from a syndicated data source, typically IRI or Nielsen, but they usually create only market- or account-level forecasts. The CPFR solution aggregates the more detailed sales forecasts from the retailer and compares the total with the supplier's number.

ORDER FORECAST (REPLENISHMENT PLAN) COMPARISONS

Often, retailers do not produce an order forecast at all, but when they do, it may include only base demand. Many handle promotional orders through a totally different process, tools, and personnel. Suppliers, therefore, don't often get an integrated view of the retailer's demand.

A CPFR solution can improve this situation by providing a forum where replenishment order forecasts and promotional orders can be brought together and compared in full. It can also give the retailer better visibility as to how the supplier makes changes to its order forecasts to meet demand.

CPFR SYSTEM DEPLOYMENT

The CPFR solution itself does not have to be deployed at each trading partner. Instead, several companies offer hosting services that run CPFR solutions for a trading community. All each company needs is access to the Internet. Data is uploaded to the hosting service through a secure connection, and then planners access their company's view through a Web browser.[10]

A CPFR solution is typically deployed in a hub-and-spoke configuration. A company that wants to manage its supply chain proactively will purchase and implement a CPFR solution. This company's CPFR application forms a hub in the supply chain, with that company's trading partners acting as clients or spokes of that application.

If any of the company's trading partners have already implemented CPFR applications of their own, it becomes a situation of CPFR hub-to-hub communication. This is perfectly acceptable because CPFR applications are built such that there is no distinction between hubs and spokes in the supply chain.

For example, in the case of large retailers such as Kmart, it might implement a CPFR system to improve its supply chain. Based on their clout in the market, they could be in a position to dictate to their suppliers how the supply process will operate. They would implement the CPFR application and would be a hub. Their suppliers would be spokes and would access Kmart's CPFR application using Web browsers.

By contrast, a large manufacturer such as Procter & Gamble might also implement a CPFR system. Based on its clout in the marketplace, it could perhaps dictate to its retailers how the supply process will operate. It would implement the CPFR application and would be a hub. Its retailers would be spokes and would access Procter & Gamble's CPFR application using Web browsers.

In cases where Procter & Gamble supplies products to Kmart, they would both be hubs within the supply chain. However, because CPFR applications are built to work in a peer-to-peer (or hub-to-hub) model, Procter & Gamble and Kmart could work smoothly together with their CPFR applications.

14.3.2   USER PROFILES

There are three distinct categories of users of supply-chain management applications: planners, managers, and administrators.

- *Planners:* Authenticated Users (see Chapter 5 for a description of Authenticated Users) who are employees of one of the companies in the

---

10. Introduction to Collaborative Planning, Forecasting and Replenishment (CPFR). Syncra Systems, Inc, 2000.

supply-chain relationship. A planner typically is responsible for forecasting particular product or material categories.

- *Managers:* Authenticated Users who are responsible for the supply-chain process at the company that owns the hub of the CPFR system. For instance, a Manager role might be filled by a vice president of merchandising who is tasked with improving the supply chain for his or her company and who has seen to it that the CPFR system was implemented to do so.

- *Administrators:* Authenticated Users who are employees or principals of the company that owns the hub of the CPFR system. They specify which users have the authority to access particular content, collaboration, and commerce within the CPFR system. They also have the authority and the ability to change the structure and organization of the CPFR application.

14.4   FEATURES OF SUPPLY-CHAIN APPLICATIONS

The features discussed here are the base functionality required for typical supply-chain applications. To manage complexity, the capabilities are abstracted to a high enough level to result in a relatively small number of features. This list of features provides the basis for definition, scope management, and project management for building a CPFR supply-chain management application.

1. The CPFR data and functions must be accessible between trading partners, whether they are hubs and spokes, over the Internet.

2. The application must provide high-volume transaction processing to handle large batches of electronic commerce data.

3. The application must have a comparison and exception processing engine that synchronizes multiple information streams from a large number of trading partners.

4. The application must provide planners with rich interactive decision support tools.

5. The application must interface with disparate planning and forecasting applications.

6. The application must handle flexible import and export of sales and order forecasts.

7. The application must import on-hand inventory, POS, and actual order information.

8. The application must import and export spreadsheet formats.

9. The application must interface with major ERP, logistics, resource planning, sales forecasting, and decision support applications.

10. The application must alert users to critical changes in plans, schedules, or events.

11. The application must aggregate information across multiple dimensions of functions, products, partners, locations, and times to accommodate each partner's unique product hierarchy and location hierarchy.

12. The application must generate exceptions at any aggregation level across any dimension.

13. The application must transmit demand and replenishment requirements between partners according to CPFR guidelines.

14. The application must notify users of new promotions, variances in plans, and other exceptions.

15. The application must monitor exceptions graphically by dimensions such as product, location, or time.

16. The application must provide hosting and no-hosting options.

17. The application must exchange plans, forecasts, schedules, and orders between partners using EDI, FTP, e-mail, ANSI X.12, and/or XML.

18. The application must handle exceptions in forecast comparisons, accuracy, differences, and operations.

19. The application must provide graphical comparisons of forecasts with POS information and inventory positions.

20. The application must maintain complete forecast revision histories.

21. The application must define and track critical performance measures by partner, location, or product category.

22. The application must have configurable exception thresholds for each trading partner.

SUMMARY

Effective supply-chain management involves far more than carrying inventory buffers to deal with uncertainty in the supply chain. It requires the use of an advanced methodology such as CPFR.

CPFR, while seemingly costly to implement, offers benefits that far outweigh the costs of implementing it. By implementing CPFR, companies have the opportunity to differentiate themselves from their competition by the quality and effectiveness of their supply chain.

Bibliography

E-BUSINESS

Ravi Kalakota and Marcia Robinson. *e-Business: Roadmap for Success.* Addison-Wesley, 1999.

INTERNET SECURITY

Simson Garfinkel and Gene Spafford. *Web Security and Commerce.* O'Reilly & Associates, Inc., 1997.

Ronald L. Rivest. *Cryptography and Security.* http://theory.lcs.mit.edu/~rivest/crypto-security.html, 2001.

TEAM DYNAMICS AND PROJECT MANAGEMENT

Jessica Burdman. *Collaborative Web Development.* Addison-Wesley, 1999.

Dean Leffingwell and Don Widrig. *Managing Software Requirements.* Addison-Wesley, 2000.

Jim McCarthy. *Dynamics of Software Development.* Microsoft Press, 1995

Steve McConnell. *Rapid Development.* Microsoft Press, 1996

WEB PAGE AND WEB SITE DESIGN

Jennifer Flemming. *Web Navigation.* O'Reilly & Associates, Inc., 1998.

Philip Greenspun. *Philip and Alex's Guide to Web Publishing.* Morgan Kaufmann Publishers, Inc., 1999.

Jakob Nielsen. *Designing Web Usability.* New Riders Publishing, 2000.

SOFTWARE DESIGN AND DEVELOPMENT

Martin Fowler. *Analysis Patterns*. Addison-Wesley, 1997.

Martin Fowler. *Refactoring*. Addison-Wesley, 1999.

John Robbins. *Debugging Applications*. Microsoft Press, 2000.

.NET FRAMEWORK PROGRAMMING

.NET Framework SDK Reference. Microsoft Corporation, 2001.

Jeffrey Richter. *Programming the .NET Framework with* C# training course. Wintellect, 2001

SQL SERVER PROGRAMMING

SQL Server Books Online. Microsoft Corporation, 2001.

Allen G. Taylor. *SQL for Dummies*. 2nd ed. IDG Books Worldwide, Inc., 1997.

APPLICATION INTEGRATION

David S. Linthicum. *B2B Application Integration*. Addison-Wesley, 2001.

Clemens F. Vasters. *BizTalk Server 2000, a Beginner's Guide*. Osborne/McGraw-Hill, 2001.

OBJECT-ORIENTED PROGRAMMING AND RELATIONAL DATABASES

Peter Heinckiens. *Building Scalable Database Applications*. Addison-Wesley, 1998.

Lyn Robison. *Teach Yourself Database Programming with Visual C++ 6 in 21 Days*. Sams Publishing, 1999.

Index

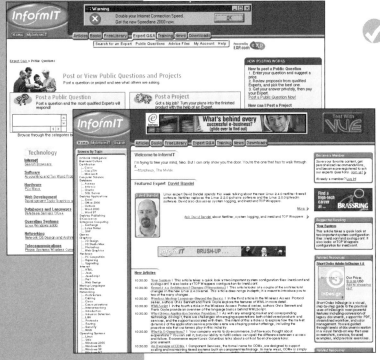